CHRISTIAN SCIENCE AND
THE CATHOLIC FAITH

THE MACMILLAN COMPANY
NEW YORK · BOSTON · CHICAGO · DALLAS
ATLANTA · SAN FRANCISCO

MACMILLAN & CO., LIMITED
LONDON · BOMBAY · CALCUTTA
MELBOURNE

THE MACMILLAN CO. OF CANADA, LTD.
TORONTO

CHRISTIAN SCIENCE AND THE CATHOLIC FAITH

*Including a Brief Account of New
Thought and Other Modern
Mental Healing Movements*

BY

A. M. BELLWALD, S.M., S.T.L.

MARIST COLLEGE, WASHINGTON, D.C.

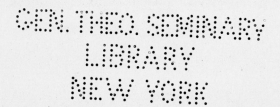
New York
THE MACMILLAN COMPANY
1922

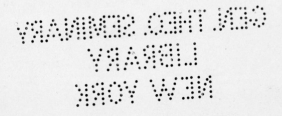

Imprimi potest

    H. DE LA CHAPELLE, S. M.
      Provincialis

Nihil obstat

    CHARLES F. AIKEN, S. T. D.
      Censor deputatus

Imprimatur

    ✝MICHAEL J. CURLEY, D.D.
      Archiepiscopus
        Baltimorensis

Baltimore, Md., March 23, 1922.

PREFACE

Why deal once more with Christian Science? With so many works already on the market, why increase the output by another study on this much debated subject? Christian Science will run its course, as other systems of thought, once much in evidence, have run theirs, and will not be materially influenced by the discussions to which it has given rise. Yet to discuss the subjects of the day is an intellectual need. The process of winnowing out truth from error must go on without interruption, the more so in this case, as Christian Science skims over many subjects of the very highest importance, opening up to controversial minds fair vistas of debatable ground.

But why associate New Thought with its traditional foe? The answer must be sought in the treatise itself, which makes plain that, whatever minor differences there may be between these two organizations, their wider aims and common pursuits unite them in a clearly defined group, and blend together naturally in a common discussion.

Mind healing is not exactly an American invention or monopoly. We shall see that it is practically coeval and coextensive with the human race. Yet in our own days and place it has taken on hues and shapes that differentiate it radically both from its remoter and its nearer ancestors, and it is assuming proportions that may yet put its European prototypes completely in the shade. In its American dress, it has crossed both the Atlantic and the Pacific, and is making a successful bid for world supremacy in its chosen field. Under these circumstances, an inquiry into the origin, the underlying principles, and the methods of these movements must prove of interest, even if, from a religious point of view, they are not of sufficient moment to claim attention.

Such an investigation is no longer a pioneer work. Many Protestant authors have turned their attention to this newer

Protestantism. Not a few scent, in this new gospel of health, danger for what they are pleased to call orthodox Christianity; their works are polemical in character, and, on the whole, of but little intrinsic worth. Others, not particularly interested in the Churches, have been attracted by the psychological problems which the real or pretended successes of these mind-healers have forced on their consideration. These, though pursuing strictly scientific methods of investigation, but too often mar their work by an ill-disguised hostility, or a studied indifference to revealed religion, so that hardly any work of either class could be unreservedly recommended.

From the Catholic viewpoint, few of the publications that have appeared, valuable though they are in their own way, can be said to do justice to the subject. A fairly complete list of these books, pamphlets and articles will be found in the bibliography, page 262. Among these we might single out, as of greater excellence, Father Lambert's *Christian Science before the Bar of Reason*, Fr. Thurston's *Christian Science*, in *Lectures on the History of Religions*, Fr. Searle's work entitled *The Truth about Christian Science*, and especially—in its scientific aspect—Dr. Walsh's various works on psychotherapy. The present essay proposes, besides giving a short historical survey of mental healing, followed by a discussion of the causes that may serve to account for whatever success the movement has achieved, to discuss from the Catholic standpoint more fully than has as yet been done, its philosophical and religious presuppositions, implications and doctrinal statements.

There yet remains for me to fulfill the pleasant duty of thanking all those who have helped me in the preparation of this essay in any way whatever, by counsel, correction, or revision of the manuscript. I desire more particularly to express my sincere thanks to Rev. Charles C. Aiken, D.D., Dean of the Faculty of Sacred Sciences at the Catholic University of America, who suggested this work and who, by advice, encouragement, and kind interest, very materially coöperated in its completion.

CONTENTS

CHAPTER I.

CHAPTER II.

CHAPTER VII.

CHAPTER VIII.

CHAPTER IX.

The real explanation to be sought in the intimate relations between mind and body. The Scholastic philosophy avoids both materialism and excessive idealism. The soul as the *forma substantialis* of the body. The intellectual soul as the principle of all activity in the human compound. Scholasticism vs. Platonism. Distinction of faculties. The imagination as mediating between sense and intellect. The bodily organism is affected by the imagination. The Scholastics were chary about practical application of their theory. Excessive claims for the imagination. A certain influence admitted by all.

CHAPTER X.

Mrs. Eddy's explanations do not explain. Are Christian Science cures natural or supernatural? Christian Science vs. hypnotic cures. Mrs. Eddy's opposition to hypnotism. The effect of waking suggestions and auto-suggestion. Meaning of suggestion and of subconscious mind. Effects of suggestion. Mechanism of mental healing. Respective claims of the intellect and the will. The will according to Mrs. Eddy is essentially evil. The will as a therapeutic agent. Its limits. The will open to suggestion. The intellect, inasmuch as it perceives things as either good or bad. The imagination as a therapeutic agent. Benedict XIV. on the power of the imagination. The heart in mind-healing. Modern mind-cures explained according to these principles. Christian Science causes a real mental revolution in many persons.

CHAPTER XI.

The Spirit of the new movement is towards liberal Christianity. Religion subordinated to the pursuit of health. Christian dogmas rejected or minimized or perverted. The modern mind-movements are ingrafted on historical Christianity. Mrs. Eddy's liberal Chris-

CHAPTER XII.

CHAPTER XIII.

CHAPTER XIV.

CHAPTER XV.

Contents

CHRISTIAN SCIENCE AND THE CATHOLIC FAITH

CHRISTIAN SCIENCE AND THE CATHOLIC FAITH

CHAPTER I

MIND-CURES OF THE PAST AND PRESENT

FROM the world's grayest antiquity down to our own days, man made use of mental powers in the healing of disease. Mental healing has held, and is holding to-day, a well-nigh world-wide sway which links together, in a common practice and belief, reputably the highest with the very lowest types of humanity. To show this relationship between the past and the present, between the practices of civilized nations and those of savages, we must perforce extend the range of our survey and take in subjects which have but a remote connection with the modern mind-movements.

The two main features that characterize these modern healing cults are (1) their preoccupation about health, and (2) the religious element which they contain. Religion differentiates them from scientific psychotherapeutics (mind-healing) and from psycho-analysis (healing by mind analysis), from which the religious element may be conspicuously absent, while preoccupation about health distinguishes them from religions whose principal aim and object is something quite different from mere bodily well-being. This alliance between religion and medicine is at least as old as the oldest written records we possess of man. If Assyria and Babylonia are to us memories with a hazy impression of unimaginable antiquity, we must learn to look upon these nations as young, when we compare them with the Accadians or Sumerians who had occupied their country before them. Mind-healing was in a flourishing condition even at that early date. This we may learn from the Sumerian language

1

which, in the seventh century before Christ, had become a sacred tongue, unintelligible to the masses, yet still in use for religious rites and incantations in the temples. The Sumerian texts, which the last century has unearthed, take us back to the days when Sumerian was as living a tongue as English is to us, and prove beyond doubt that even at that early date the very closest relation existed between religion and healing: the priests were the physicians, and regaining health was, partly at least, a religious exercise; incantations took the place of suggestions, and the expectation of health from the spiritual world advantageously replaced a similar expectation in our own day from mind, be it human or Divine.

The empires of the Medes and the Persians either shared these usages or inherited them at the time when they subdued the earlier kingdoms. Under their scepter, these practices obtained such a vogue that in Roman times, occult arts became all but identified with the Persian priests, or Magi. The very word *magic* is derived from the Persian and remains in our modern tongues as a historical monument, reminding us of the beliefs and practices of those superstitious ages.[1]

But the countries now known as Mesopotamia possessed no monopoly on mental healing. Egypt shared with them the doubtful honor of seeking protection and relief from bodily disease by religious and mental means.

"Diseases and pain," writes Dr. Renouf, "being caused by the intervention of some god, the efficacy of the medicines which are taken is chiefly owing to the prayers or incantations which are said over them. Isis is the great enchantress and she delivers the sick and suffering from the gods and goddesses who afflict them, even as she delivered her son Horus from his wounds received in his battle with Set." [2]

There is a certain charm, as well as intellectual and moral profit, in this work of comparison between the past and the

[1] On this subject may be consulted Lenormant: *Chaldean Magic, Its Origin and Development* (London, 1877); Maspero: *Life in Ancient Egypt and Assyria* (New York, 1892); Morris Jastrow, Jr.: *Aspects of Religious Belief and Practice in Babylonia and Assyria* (New York, 1911).

[2] Renouf: *The Origin and Growth of Religion as Illustrated by the Religion of Ancient Egypt*, Hibbert Lectures for 1879 (New York, 1880), p. 220.

present. Especially at a time when, from every popular source of information, it is unceasingly dinned into the ears of the great public that ours is an age of unlimited progress and immeasurably superior to any that preceded it, it is well to learn humbler sentiments by a backward glance, that reveals, in the remotest past, if not absolutely identical institutions and sentiments,—a thing that no one could reasonably expect,— yet withal recognizable parallels. Not only the modern vogue of mind-healing, but even the underlying sentiments on which the practice is grounded, are a case in point. Of the ancient Egyptians Maspero writes:

"The Egyptians are not yet resigned to think that illness and death are natural and inevitable. They think that life, once commenced, should be indefinitely prolonged; if no accident intervened, what reason could there be for its ceasing? In Egypt, therefore, man does not die, but some one or something assassinates him. The murderer often belongs to our world and can be easily pointed out: another man, an animal, an inanimate object, a stone detached from the mountain, a tree falling upon a traveler and crushing him. Often, though, it belongs to the invisible world and only reveals itself by the malignity of its attacks: it is a god, a spirit, the soul of a dead man that has cunningly entered a living person or that throws itself upon him with irresistible violence. Once in possession of the body, the evil influence breaks the bones, sucks out the marrow, drinks the blood, gnaws the intestines and the heart and devours the flesh. The invalid perishes according to the progress of this destructive work and death speedily ensues unless the evil genius can be driven out before it has committed irreparable damage." [1]

As disease was something mental, so also was its treatment. Maspero continues:

"Whoever treats a sick person has, therefore, two equally important duties to perform. He must first discover the nature of the spirit in possession and, if necessary, its name, and then attack it, drive it out or even destroy it. He can only succeed by powerful magic, so he must be an expert in

[1] Maspero: *Life in Ancient Egypt and Assyria* (New York, 1892), p. 118.

reciting incantations, and skillful in making amulets. He must then use medicine to contend with the disorders which the presence of the strange being has produced in the body; this is done by a finely graduated régime and various remedies. The cure-workers are, therefore, divided into several categories. Some incline towards sorcery and have faith in formulas and talismen only; they think they have done enough if they have driven out the spirit. Others extol the use of drugs. . . . The best doctors carefully avoid binding themselves to either method; they carefully distinguish between those cases in which magic is sovereign and those in which natural methods suffice, whilst their treatment is a mixture of remedies and exorcisms which vary from patient to patient." [1]

If now we pass over from Africa to Europe we meet with similar conditions among the Greeks. Famous in the annals of medicine is the Greek god of the healing art, Æsculapius. If Egypt had its Serapiums or temples dedicated to the god Serapis, where wonderful cures are said to have taken place, Greece numbered among its temples many famous sanctuaries dedicated to Æsculapius, and, preëminent among them, those of Epidauros in Argolis, Greece, and of Ægæ in Cilicia, Asia Minor, where Apollonius of Tyana is credited with having performed some wonderful cures.[2] The sick would resort to these temples, sleep there one or several nights, and not unfrequently recover their health, as it was believed, through remedies indicated in their dreams by the god of health. No one nowadays doubts that the trustful expectation which brought the patients to the temples—an attitude which we now would call auto-suggestion—was a most important factor in their eventual recovery.

The Roman Empire, too, proved a very fertile field for the spread of these beliefs and practices. From everywhere

---

[1] Maspero: *op. cit.*, p. 119. Cf. George Rawlinson: *History of Ancient Egypt* (New York, 1886), Vol. II, p. 269: "Asia poured the fetid stream of her manifold superstitions into Africa, and to the old theology was added a wild and weird demonology which proved wonderfully attractive to the now degenerated Egyptians."

[2] Cf. Farnell, L. R.: *Greek Hero Cults and Ideas of Immortality* (London, 1921).

superstition flocked to Rome, and from Rome, in turn, it radiated in all directions. But a check now begins to make itself felt against all brands of superstition. About this time a fact penetrates into history, small in appearance but mighty in its future possibilities. Boldly it confronts ancient civilization, its corruptions and superstitions, with a new order in which, too, cures play a prominent part. Christianity, slowly but surely, is leavening the ancient mind with new ideas; it sets its miracles against the claims and achievements of the past, and it conquers.

To group together Christian miracles and Pagan marvels with modern mental cures is now looked upon as scientific, as though everything extraordinary must necessarily flow from the same source. At the time, however, when the two civilizations, Pagan and Christian, flourished side by side, people were not caught by superficial resemblances that might exist between the works of God and the works of charlatans. A Simon Magus saw at a glance the differences between his trade and that of the preachers of the Gospel. When, later, a Celsus attempted to do what now modern Christians do without scruple, and, in his attacks on Christianity, sought to identify the miracles of Christ with the performances of Pagan jugglers, he found an Origen who brilliantly refuted the fallacies of his Pagan antagonist.[1] While in the miracles of their Lord the Christians found solid ground for their faith, they either saw in Pagan marvels nothing else but feats of skill or ascribed them to the power of evil spirits.[2] Works must be weighed in the scales

---

[1] Origen: *Against Celsus,* Book I, chap. 6, in *Ante-Nicene Fathers,* Vol. IV, p. 399: "He (Celsus) next proceeds to bring a charge against the Savior Himself, alleging that it was by means of sorcery that He was able to accomplish the wonders which He performed." *Ibid.,* p. 413 (chap. 38). "He desires to throw discredit on them as being done by the help of magic and not by divine power." *Ibid.,* p. 427 (chap. 68): "He immediately compares them to the tricks of jugglers who profess to do more wonderful things and to the feats performed by those who have been taught by Egyptians." The Greek original is to be found in Migne's *Patrologia Graeca,* Vol. XI. The whole treatment of this subject by Origen is well worth perusing.

[2] Tertullian: *Apologeticus adversus Gentes,* chap. 22, says in relation to this: "They (the evil spirits) first harm, then prescribe astonishing remedies, then cease to harm and are believed to have cured. Laedunt enim primo, dehinc remedia praecipiunt ad miracula nova, sive contraria, post quae desinunt laedere, et curasse creduntur."

of a dispassionate judgment; such superficial resemblances as may be established between modern mind-cures and those of Christ do not, on that account, place them in the same rank.

The magical practices of the Pagan world never disappeared entirely. The Church inveighed against them; her ministers warned the faithful against this danger to their faith; even in such intimate matters as that of bodily health, we find St. Augustine giving detailed directions to the Christians; the State undertook to suppress the Pagan cults, but all in vain. When the temples were closed in the cities, the Pagan priests and sorcerers found an asylum in remote country places and continued their practices.[1] When Theodosius II in the first half of the fifth century undertook to clear up also the country places, by destroying the temples and erecting the Cross on their location,[2] the magical practices continued to flourish in secret, adopting gradually certain features borrowed from Christianity, but, on the whole, remaining essentially Pagan.[3]

Among the causes that made people resort to superstitious practices, the desire to secure, protect, and safeguard health must have held a prominent place. It can hardly be doubted that self-deception and self-suggestion played an important part in rendering occult means efficacious and in strengthening by this very success the ancient superstitious beliefs. A good many factors contributed to widen this sway of superstition. There is the question of heredity and tribal solidarity. Clusters of young and impulsive nations, not yet emerged out of barbarism, about this time came to be gathered into the folds of the Church, and, among them, many a deep-seated, long-cherished superstition continued to flourish despite the Church. It might

[1] These districts were called *pagi;* hence about this time the unbelievers came to be called *pagani* or Pagans.

[2] *Corpus Juris Civilis,* Paris, 1628, lib. 25, p. 331: "Cunctaque eorum fana, templa, delubra, si quae etiam nunc restant integra, praecepto magistratuum destrui, collocationeque venerandae religionis Christianae signi expiari praecipimus."

[3] Cf. Maury: *La Magie et l'Astrologie dans l'Antiquité et au Moyen Age* (Paris, 1864), pp. 145 ff. Leuba, in *American Anthropologist,* Vol. XIV (1912), pp. 333 ff., "The Varieties, Classification and Origin of Magic." Saintyves: *La Force Magique* (Paris, 1914). Cf. especially St. Augustine: *De Doctrina Christiana,* lib. I., cap. 23, 29.

change its garment for something more acceptable to Christian minds, but this outward covering could not conceal its Pagan origin. Again, there is the question of ignorance. Not that fabulous absolute darkness which, in certain quarters, has earned for this period the unenviable name of Dark Ages, but that relative ignorance of the laws of nature, which made every disease a mysterious visitation either from on high or from below. It were a vain dream to expect that the learned would rise so high above the common beliefs and fears and hopes of their times as to remain uninfluenced by all their cruder and more immature conceptions. A universal Cartesian doubt was unknown to them. They were men of their own times and of their own stock. Some few might rise head and shoulders above their fellows: an Albert the Great or Roger Bacon might appear who would astonish future ages even more than their contemporaries; [1] yet they remain, in some respects, brilliant exceptions, and in others, children of their own age. [2]

There is a third cause which contributed perhaps as much as the other two combined, if not more, to perpetuate this state of affairs. It was the learned arrogance of the pretended scholars of the day, of the physician who spoke in high-sounding terms and with bold assurance, and of the philosopher who prided himself on knowing all the secrets of the universe. A man like Ibn Sina, better known to the Western World as Avicenna, is a typical representative of this class of men. [3] Considering the extent of the powers which, in his work on the soul, he ascribes

[1] Albert the Great (c. 1206–1280), according to Dr. Kennedy, "expressed contempt for everything that savored of enchantment or the art of magic. 'Non approbo dictum Avicennae et Algazel de fascinatione quia credo quod non nocet fascinatio, nec nocere potest ars magica, nec facit aliquid ex his quae timentur de talibus.'" Cf. *Catholic Encyclopedia,* Vol. I, p. 265.

Roger Bacon (1214-1291), the justly celebrated Franciscan friar, wrote among others a treatise on the nothingness of magic "De Nullitate Magiae." Cf. *Catholic Encyclopedia,* Vol. XIII, p. 112. The article on Roger Bacon is written by the Franciscan, Theophilus Witzel.

[2] Even St. Thomas Aquinas (1225-1274) admitted an indirect influence of the heavenly bodies on the human character (*Summa Theologia,* Pars. I, q. 95, art. 5) and believed in the reality of the evil eye that could physically harm, especially tender children (*ibid.*. q. 117, art. 3, ad 2).

[3] Avicenna (980-1037), an Arabian philosopher and physician exercised great influence over the Christian scholars. Consult *Catholic Encyclopedia,* Vol. II, p. 157, article by Bishop William Turner. Also *Summa Theologia, loc. cit.,* and Delrio, *Disquisitionum Magicarum libri sex* (Mainz, 1624), lib. I, pp. 16 ff.

to the perfect mind, he might well be styled Mrs. Eddy's predecessor and master. Among these powers may be mentioned that of fascination, that of healing at a distance, that of displacing objects, and of producing lightning and rain by sheer power of will. The reasons Avicenna assigns for these beliefs are not unworthy of those of the modern mind-healers. He taught that matter, by nature, obeys spiritual substances rather than other agents, and, consequently, that a strong imagination compels material bodies to conform. His followers, speak of powerful rays that issue from the body of those whom nature has endowed with healing powers, and of bodily humors which the soul can propel far beyond the narrow limits of the body.

Side by side with magical practices there existed all through the Middle Ages a class of mind-cures,—if the appellation may be permitted in this case,—which had nothing to do with occult practices, but relied solely on the protection, intercession and help of God, the angels, and the saints. Even the most staunch believer in the efficacy of prayer for man's bodily, as well as spiritual, welfare will not deny, that, over and above a direct help from heaven, there may exist in prayer a natural virtue, which will benefit sick persons who put their heart and soul into this exercise. On its natural side even prayer may be open to superstitious admixtures, from which it has always been the endeavor of the Church to free it. In vain did the celebrated Jesuit priest Delrio, at the end of the sixteenth century, plead against such an inroad of questionable beliefs and practices. He was answered by a reference to the fact of their success.[1] Soldiers healed their wounds by what was styled St. Anselm's art; in Spain a class of healers practiced with success under the name of "saludadores"; in Italy similar professional healers went by the name of "Gentiles S. Catharinae" or "Gentiles S. Pauli"; in Belgium children born on

---

[1] Delrio: *op. cit.*, p. 24; "Obiiciuntur varia curationum genera mire frequentia." Cf. pp. 24-27. Also Buckley: *Faith-Healing, Christian Science and Kindred Phenomena* (New York, 1892), especially pp. 169-238. Here we might mention the widespread belief in England and France that their kings could cure certain diseases, called on that account king's evil, by their touch or by blessing rings which the patient had to wear.

Good Friday were, by that very fact, believed to be endowed with the gift of healing.

On passing from the civilized to the uncivilized nations to the so-called primitive peoples who, owing to the primitive or low state of their civilization, find themselves on the lowest rung of human culture, we find under other forms the same efforts at mental healing, with the same general belief in the superiority of the spiritual over the material. For what is fetishism but a form of mental culture which, based on superstition, expects protection, preservation, defense, health, fecundity, power, riches, and happiness through the instrumentality of the horn or tooth of an animal, a shell, a stone, or whatever other fetish the savage may believe in? [1] Here we have another important link in the chain of evidence for the universality of mental cures.

We can gather from these considerations that Christian Science does not stand in the world as an isolated event; its pretense to the discovery of a new principle of cure is not borne out by the facts of history. Its claim to be the result of a new revelation has against it, as a *prima facie* objection, an uninterrupted series of facts that bear witness to mental healing throughout all ages. True, there is no identity, properly so-called; yet there is enough similarity to justify its classification with these its antecedents. In the next chapter we shall trace more in detail its historical rise from its immediate forbear, mesmerism.

[1] Cf. Le Roy, Mgr. A.: *La Religion des Primitifs* (Paris, 1911), pp. 270 ff.; also A. Réville: *La Religion des Peuples non civilisés,* Vol. I, p. 81.

CHAPTER II

MODERN MIND-MOVEMENTS

I

DURING the eighteenth century the belief in the prevalence of witchcraft gradually made way for a more natural and cheerful outlook on life.[1] Men ceased to dread the existence everywhere of malign influences, but continued strongly to believe in abnormal curative powers. Even today the names of Paracelsus and Mesmer, to mention only a few among many, are not unknown.[2] While men of lesser note are forgotten, the fame of these is still glimmering sufficiently to show the thread of historic continuity that binds the present to the past. Mesmer is commonly credited with being the father of the modern mind-movements; a hasty sketch of his work and environment must, therefore, find a place here.

In the second half of the eighteenth century an Austrian priest, Gassner by name, won great fame through his remark-

[1] The executions for witchcraft in Salem, Mass., took place from July 19 to September 22, 1692. In 1736 the English statute against witchcraft was repealed, although eight years later (1728) Rhode Island reënacted its laws against witchcraft. The last trial for witchcraft in Germany was in 1749 at Würzburg. In Switzerland, in the Protestant canton Glarus, a girl was executed on this score as late as 1783, and in Southwestern Russia a man was burned as a wizard in 1827. Mrs. Eddy revived substantially the belief in black magic under the new names of mental malpractice or malicious animal magnetism. On this subject consult an article by Father Thurston, S. J., in the *Catholic Encyclopedia,* Vol. XV, p. 674. Also Buckley: *op. cit.,* pp. 205 ff.

[2] Paracelsus (c. 1493-1541) is the reputed founder of the magnetic system of healing. After him Sir Kenelm Digby (1603-1665) achieved fame through his work *On the Cure of Wounds by the Powder of Sympathy* (London, 1658). About the same time Goclenius, a professor of medicine in Marburg published a work entitled *De Unguento Armario* (The Weapon Salve). To this the Jesuit John Robert, who died in 1651, replied with his *Short Anatomy of Goclenius' Treatise on the Magnetic Cure of Wounds.* A controversy resulted in which Van Helmont, one of the most famous physicians and chemists of his day, took part. For curious medical superstitions that could have none but mental effectiveness consult Podmore, *Mesmerism and Christian Science* (Philadelphia, 1909).

able cures. Gassner, like so many others that come to the world with a message of relief, had earlier in his life passed through a long siege of sickness, during which he came to form peculiar views on the nature of many diseases. Convinced that these infirmities were the result, not of natural agencies, but of evil spirits, he resolved to cure them by means of the exorcisms and prayers of the Church. He is commonly considered to be the immediate predecessor of Mesmer. Of these two men and their mutual relations, Podmore says:

"To the most recent of these healers, the Suabian priest J. J. Gassner, Mesmer probably owed many features of his practice. The five or six years ending with 1777—when he was forced, by ecclesiastical interdict and Imperial decree, to quit Ratisbon—were those in which Gassner reached the zenith of his fame. During these years he resided chiefly at Ratisbon; but he traveled about and visited many towns in Bavaria, healing by his word and touch. Mesmer . . . prior to his arrival in Paris in 1778 had for some years journeyed about Europe, amongst other countries in Suabia and Bavaria. If he did not actually meet Gassner—and it is stated that he did—he must have heard of his fame, and been conversant with his methods of operation. A noticeable point in Gassner's treatment was, that, as a preliminary to undertaking a cure, he would cause to be reproduced in the patient the pains and other symptoms of the disease. The exorcism by which he sought to expel the demon (to whose presence in the patient he attributed the disease) generally produced strong convulsions; and the cure commenced only when they were calmed. Again, Gassner constantly chased the pain from one part of the body to another, finally chasing it out, by his command, from the fingers or toes. All these features are characteristic of Mesmer's early treatment, though, as we shall see, they soon disappeared in the practice of his successors." [1]

[1] Podmore: *Mesmerism and Christian Science* (Philadelphia, 1909), p. 27. Cf. Francis J. Schaeffer, in *Catholic Encyclopedia,* art. "Gassner." "Official investigations were made by the ecclesiastical authorities and all were favorable to Gassner except that they recommended more privacy and decorum. . . . He never departed from the Church's teaching or instructions concerning exorcism, and always disclaimed the name of wonder-worker. He was an exemplary priest, full of faith and zeal, and altogether unselfish in his works of mercy."

Francis Anthony Mesmer (c. 1734-1815) is the real founder of the modern mind-movements. He is the link between the old and the new, between medieval magic and modern mind-healing. His doctoral dissertation, entitled *On the Influence of the Planets on the Human Body*, fitly illustrates the medieval bend of his mind. Only a century earlier, he might have been a famous astrologer; but at the end of the eighteenth century, with the world boasting of its enlightenment and scientific proficiency, he quite naturally exchanged the somewhat stale explanation of stellar influence for the newer, and perhaps truer, concept of human magnetism.

Mesmer was a Viennese physician; but in reality his history begins with his arrival at Paris, in February, 1778. It is there that he achieved his success; thence his disciples departed, to become in other lands the enthusiastic apostles of his discoveries; there he established his famous "baquet," the supposedly magnetized vat, which became the instrument of his success.

"In a room dimly lighted and hung with mirrors, his patients were seated around a circular vat of considerable size, covered with a lid and containing various chemicals. A long cord connected the patients with one another, while in the lid of the tub were several holes, through each of which passed an iron rod bent in such a way that its points could be applied to any part of a patient's body. The patients were requested not to speak, the only sounds in the room being strains of soft music. When expectancy was at its flood, Mesmer would enter, clad in the robe of a magician and carrying an iron wand. At one patient he would gaze intently, another he would stroke gently with his wand. Soon some would burst into laughter, others into tears, while still others would fall into convulsions, finally passing into a lethargic state, out of which it is claimed they emerged cured or on the high road to a cure." [1]

Mesmer's philosophical views were a peculiar amalgamation of science and superstition, of shrewd calculations and plain guesswork. There existed—so he taught—a universal fluid,

[1] Bruce: *The Riddle of Personality* (New York, 1917), p. 17. Cf. Podmore, *op. cit.*, p. 6 ff.

subject to unknown mechanical laws, but akin to magnetism and to the electric current, and binding together in a common cause the celestial, terrestrial, and living bodies. The human body, in particular, did not remain outside its sphere of influence, but was in itself a living magnet, endowed with negative and positive poles, and subject, like other magnets, to influences both celestial and terrestrial. Hence the name of animal magnetism. This mysterious entity, like electricity, was scarcely subject to the restrictions of space; mirrors reflected and increased it, sound spread and amplified it. It was especially efficacious in nervous diseases, but even in other cases it was highly beneficial. If any magnetic treatment proved successful, it was entirely due to the presence, in man, of this animal magnetism.

Mesmer's successes won for him the active support of Charles Deslon, the Regent of the faculty of Medicine in Paris University and physician to the Comte d'Artois. Another distinguished disciple was the Marquis de Puységur who became the founder of the "Harmonie," one of the most celebrated magnetic societies. Having paid his hundred "louis d'or" to learn Mesmer's secret, he returned to his patrimony to practice the new art at his leisure. His experiments brought to light a number of curious facts which are now well known to every hypnotist, such as somnambulism, clairvoyance, and telepathy. He abandoned Mesmer's "baquet" and obtained like successes by means of a "magnetized" tree. "The tree," he wrote to his brother, "is the best baquet possible; every leaf radiates health and all who come experience its salutary influence." [1]

In the course of time Puységur profoundly modified Mesmer's theory of a universal magnetic fluid. In an address delivered at Strassburg in 1785 he assured his audience that "the whole secret of animal magnetism lay in these two words: '*Croyez et veuillez*,' believe and will." "Animal magnetism," he declared, "does not consist in the action of one body upon another, but in the action of the thought upon the vital principles of the body." [2]

[1] Cf. Podmore: *op. cit.*, pp. 63, 76-77.
[2] Cf. Surbled, in *Catholic Encyclopedia*, Vol. VII, pp. 605 ff., article "Hypnotism."

These principles received a more systematic and complete development from the Indo-Portuguese priest Faria, of whom Dr. Surbled writes in the *Catholic Encyclopedia:*

"The abbé Faria was the first to effect a breach in the theory of the magnetic fluid, to place in relief the importance of suggestion and to demonstrate the existence of auto-suggestion; he also established the truth, that the nervous sleep belongs only to the natural order. From his earliest magnetizing séances in 1814 he boldly developed his doctrine. Nothing comes from the magnetizer, everything comes from the subject and takes place in his imagination. Magnetism is only a form of sleep. Although of the moral order, the magnetic action is often aided by physical or rather by physiological means: fixedness of look and cerebral fatigue. Herein the abbé Faria showed himself a true pioneer, too little appreciated by his contemporaries, and even by posterity. He was the creator of hypnotism; most of the pretended discoveries of the scientist of today are really his. We need not recall here that he practiced suggestion in the waking state and post-hypnotic suggestion." [1]

After the storms of the French Revolution had somewhat subsided, interest in animal magnetism was revived. In Russia an imperial commission had reported in its favor as early as 1815. In 1821 the Academy of Berlin proposed a prize for the best essay on this subject. England was overrun by a band of traveling mesmerists. In 1831 a commission of the French *Académie des Sciences* declared this mysterious magnetic power of importance for physiology and therapeutics. [2] The physician Alexandre Bertrand, who in his youth had come under Faria's influence, now welded together Mesmer's theories with those of Faria, by granting a large influence to the imagination, without, on the other hand, denying the existence of a magnetic fluid. [3]

[1] Surbled, in *Catholic Encyclopedia,* Vol. VII, p. 604-605; Janet, Pierre: *Les médications psychologiques,* Vol. I, pp. 143 ff.

[2] In Mesmer's time a similar commission, of which Benjamin Franklin and Lavoisier were members, had pronounced against the reality of Mesmer's magnetic fluid and against attributing any scientific value to his theories. On this later occasion the Academy paid no attention to the recommendations of the commission, and its report remained unprinted.

[3] Cf. Surbled: *op. cit.,* p. 605. Concerning Bertrand's views Dr. Surbled remarks: "We are inclined to think that his view of the matter was a just

It does not fall within the scope of this inquiry to trace in detail the vicissitudes of mesmerism. Only a bare mention can be accorded to a man whose pioneer work in these lines has won for him universal recognition. Dr. Braid, the Manchester surgeon, more open-minded than most of his colleagues, satisfied himself of the reality of the mesmeric phenomena, and as a result of his own researches embraced and developed the views of Faria and Bertrand. He insisted that mental cures were the work of the patient's imagination under the directing influence of a hypnotic suggestion.[1]

Meanwhile mesmerism has crossed the Atlantic. There is a magnetic society in New Orleans as early as 1833. Three years later the French lecturer Charles Poyen tours the New England states in behalf of mesmerism and arouses general interest either in its favor or against it. The subject is taken up by a Dr. Collyer who, in 1838, lectures in Belfast, Maine, the home of the future "Dr." Quimby. Here in America, mesmerism splits into its component parts, or rather, develops into hypnotism, spiritism, and mental healing properly so-called.[2] Only the latter phase concerns us.

The man who became instrumental in this transformation of mesmerism into the modern mind-movements, was one of humble origin, an eccentric, who was always ready to champion new ideas, and always willing to question existing beliefs and institutions. A kind-hearted man, nevertheless, he was, and his great success was not a little due to his winning ways, to his sympathetic personality.[3] Phineas Parkhurst Quimby

one, and apt to lead up to the definite solution." On the other hand, the praises which Podmore (*op. cit.*, p. 92) withholds from Faria to bestow them on Bertrand are really due the former. Faria's views, however, are not original with him, but represent in a recognizable manner the teaching of the Scholastics, and of Pope Benedict XIV.

[1] Dr. Braid substituted the name of neuro-hypnotism, later on simplified into hypnotism, for the older names of animal magnetism and mesmerism.

[2] Spiritism is commonly dated from the mysterious so-called Hydesville or Rochester rappings which occurred in 1848. Simultaneously with it, the mind-cure movements developed.

[3] Consult Dresser, Horatio W.: *A History of the New Thought Movement* (New York, 1919); *idem, The Spirit of the New Thought* (New York, 1917); *idem, Handbook of the New Thought* (New York, 1917). Milmine, *Life of Mary Baker G. Eddy and History of Christian Science* first published serially in *McClure's Magazine*, 1907-1908, revised and published in book form, New York, 1909.

(1803-1866) had acquired the reputation of being a skillful clockmaker, when, about 1838, the lectures of Poyen and Collyer converted him into an ardent mesmerist. He gave up his trade, chose as his partner a young man named Burkmar, over whom he exerted a most wonderful control, and began to give public exhibitions along the traditional lines.

But Quimby's keen, though wholly untutored, mind was not long satisfied with the theories he had at first accepted. He became convinced that Burkmar's supposedly objective diagnosis of various ailments did but reproduce the opinions either of the patient or of some others actually present at the time of this diagnosis, and that Burkmar's astonishing results in the healing art were due, not to the remedies he prescribed, but solely to the blind faith of the patient. An all too bold generalization next led him to hold, not only that of itself no physical remedy was efficacious, but even that disease itself was nothing but a belief.

This simplified mesmerism wonderfully. The gist of Quimby's teaching, still maintained both in Christian Science and in New Thought,[1] can be thus summarized: "Disease is belief, and so is its cure. If you believe that you are sick, change this into the opposite belief, and you are well." With this principle to guide him, Quimby, in 1859, opened an office in Portland, Maine. His name and fame spread far and wide, and clients came flocking to him in ever increasing number. It was not until his own health broke down that he closed his office. This was in the summer of 1865. Quimby died early the following year (January 16) at his residence in Belfast, Maine, aged sixty-four.[2]

"Quimbyism" did not die with its founder. Rev. Warren

---

[1] The expression *New Thought* has been used in England to express an entirely different system of thought. It is in its American meaning that the expression is to be understood throughout this work.

[2] Quimby's education was of the scantiest. The son of a blacksmith, he had but a very brief period of schooling. This accounts for the fact that he was little of a reader and less of a writer. As a thinker he does not rank high, though we may allow him the honor of being an original and independent thinker. He left in manuscript ten volumes of his original thoughts. Mr. George A. Quimby, in whose possession his father's notes are, persistently refused permission to publish them during Mrs. Eddy's lifetime. They have been recently (1921) edited by Dr. Horatio W. Dresser.

Felt Evans, at one time a Methodist minister, but, at the time when he placed himself under Quimby's treatment, a follower of Swedenborg, was the first to give it wider currency by means of the press. Quimby, always anxious to explain his theories to those willing to learn, was pleased to find in this clergyman an interested and intelligent disciple. At the time when Evans' first production in the interest of the new science appeared (in 1869), Quimby himself had been dead for three years, and Mrs. Eddy, the founder of Christian Science, was working with might and main at a production which, eventually, was to eclipse the fame of all similar productions, but which was not to appear in print for another six years. This field, then, was far from being preëmpted; Evans was sowing in a virgin soil and reaped not an inconsiderable following. Even now his influence persists among the adherents of the New Thought movement.[1]

II

Mr. Evans, however, soon met with this rival, whose future success no human being would have ventured to predict at that time. Mary Baker, the now famous Mrs. Mary Baker G. Eddy, self-styled discoverer and founder of Christian Science, was born on a farm at Bow, New Hampshire, on July 16, 1821.[2] Her earlier life, owing to her delicate constitution and nervous temperament, was marred by long periods of illness. When twenty-two years old, she married George Washington Glover, a

[1] The chief works of Mr. Evans are *The Mental Cure* (Boston, 1869) and *The Divine Law of Cure* (Boston, 1881). Mr. Evans bolsters Quimby's theories with numerous citations from the idealistic philosophers, both ancient and modern, mentioning among others Anaxagoras, Pythagoras, Plato, Schelling, Fichte, and Hegel. His star witness, however, is Bishop Berkeley's *Treatise Concerning the Principles of Human Knowledge*. Evans finally established a mind-cure sanatorium in Salisbury, Massachusetts, where he died in 1889.

[2] The most trustworthy life of Mrs. Eddy is Miss Milmine's *Life of Mary Baker G. Eddy and History of Christian Science* (New York, 1909). Entirely untrustworthy are Mrs. Eddy's *Retrospection and Introspection* (Boston, 1899), and Miss Sibyl Wilbur's *Life of Mary Baker Eddy* (Boston, 1907). Other works that may be recommended are Peabody, Frederick W.: *The Religio-Medical Masquerade*, a complete exposure of Christian Science (New York, 1910 and 1915) and Mark Twain's humorous, though at the same time quite serious, essays entitled *Christian Science* (New York, 1907).

friend of the family and a bricklayer by trade.   Mr. Glover took his young bride to South Carolina, but within six months he died, leaving his widow almost destitute among strangers (1844).   The Freemasons gave Mr. Glover a decent burial and conveyed his widow back to her father's house in Tilton, New Hampshire, where her only child was born.   She named him after his deceased father, George Washington Glover.

In 1853, after ten years of widowhood, marred by almost continuous ill-health, Mrs. Glover became the wife of an itinerant dentist named Daniel Patterson.   The state of her health continued most unsatisfactory.   It was as Mrs. Patterson that she visited on two occasions (1862 and 1864) Dr. Quimby, whose influence over her mental and physical life had such far-reaching results.   Not long after the second visit, in 1866, Mr. Patterson declared common life with his wife unbearable, made provision for her support and abandoned her.[1]   Now began a most distressful period in Mrs. Eddy's life, the memory of which she would have liked to blot out.   Abandoned by all, even by her nearest kin, she had to obtrude herself on strangers, who soon tired of her and forced her to look for another hospitable roof.   A change only came when, in 1870, she entered into partnership with Richard Kennedy, a young Irish lad, who did the practical work of healing while Mrs. Glover (for she had resumed this name) devoted her energies to teaching and writing.   Her so-called textbook *Science and Health* did not appear until the year 1875, Mrs. Glover at that time being fifty-four years old.   In 1877 she married a man of her own choice, Asa Gilbert Eddy, whose name she was to make famous. Her husband died only five years after, in 1882.   From that date till her death in 1910, Calvin A. Frye became her closest associate in her ever-widening affairs, her man of all works, as Mrs. Eddy called him, her "steward, bookkeeper, secretary, and footman," as others have described him, so important in Mrs. Eddy's household that for some time all Mrs. Eddy's

---

[1] "In 1873 Mrs. Patterson applied for and obtained a divorce on the ground of desertion.   The doctor did not contest the suit.   His end was melancholy.   Evidently his experiences preyed upon his mind; he wandered aimlessly around for many years, and eventually lived the life of a hermit near Saco, Maine.   There he died in 1896."   Milmine: *op. cit.,* in *McClure's Magazine,* Vol. XXVIII, p. 241.

personal property was listed in his name.[1]   In 1888, however, a rival to Mrs. Eddy's favor was introduced into her household in the person of Dr. Ebenezer Johnson Foster, a man then forty-one years old, whom in that year Mrs. Eddy legally adopted as her foster son.   Her own son, meanwhile, was living in the West, estranged from his mother, who had never cared for him, but had allowed him to be adopted by a neighboring woman and to accompany her westward.   Dr. Foster-Eddy himself was practically, though not legally, disowned, in 1897, when his foster mother exiled him from her presence.[2]

Among the works which Mrs. Eddy undertook and carried to a successful issue at an age when most people feel that their life's work is almost done, we may enumerate the following:

In 1875 Mrs. Eddy published the first edition of *Science and Health,* a book which she kept on revising and practically rewriting many times over, up to near the end of her life.   In the same year, being then fifty-four years old, she founded the first Christian Science organization.

In 1878 she preached regularly in a Baptist church.

In 1879 she founded the Church of Christ, Scientist, and had herself ordained the first pastor.

In 1881 when sixty years old, she founded the Massachusetts Metaphysical College, of which she was the principal and, for most of the time, the entire faculty.   She closed the College in 1889.

In 1883 she founded and edited the *Christian Science Journal,* a monthly publication in the interest of Christian Science.

In 1884 she taught a class in Chicago and in 1888 she attended the Chicago convention, where she achieved a most remarkable personal triumph.

[1] "From the day Calvin Frye entered the service of Mrs. Eddy, he lived in literal accordance with the suggestion of that passage in *Science and Health* (ed. 1906, p. 31), where Mrs. Eddy reminds us that Jesus acknowledged no family ties. . . . When his father died, Calvin went down to Lawrence to attend the funeral.   On the way to the cemetery he stopped the carriage and boarded a street car in order to catch the next train back to Boston.   By the time his sister Lydia died, Calvin had become so completely absorbed in his new life and duties that he did not acknowledge the notification of her death, did not go to her funeral, and did not respond to a request for a small amount of money to help defray the burial expenses." Milmine: *op. cit.,* in *McClure's Magazine,* 1907, p. 575.

[2] Dr. Foster, a homeopathic physician before becoming a follower of Mrs. Eddy, was adopted shortly after a visit to Mrs. Eddy by her son, Mr. Glover.

In 1889 she dissolved and reorganized her Church in Boston.

In 1890 she founded the *Christian Science Quarterly*.

In 1894 The Mother Church was erected and dedicated in her honor.[1]

In 1895 she inaugurated the Concord Pilgrimages (1895-1904) when great crowds of Christian Scientists flocked to Concord to get a look at their beloved Leader. In the same year she published the *Church Manual*.

In 1896 she published *Miscellaneous Writings* (1883-1896) and, in 1899, *Retrospection and Introspection*.

In 1898 she taught her last class and founded the *Christian Science Sentinel*, a weekly publication.

In 1906 the immense annex to the Mother Church in Boston was dedicated.

In 1908 at the age of eighty-seven, she founded the daily *Christian Science Monitor*.[2]

This eventful career was brought to a close on December 3, 1910, when Mrs. Eddy died of pneumonia at the age of eighty-nine. The announcement of Mrs. Eddy's death was made simultaneously the following day, which was Sunday, by Judge Clifford P. Smith, first reader of the Mother Church, and by Alfred Farlow, of the publication committee, in a statement to the press. Few of the congregation at the morning service knew that their leader and teacher had passed away. The service was as usual and the two readers, Judge Smith and Mrs. Leland T. Powers, read the sermon of the day *God, the only Cause and Creator*, with voices that were without emotion or had any suggestion of sadness. The service in every Christian Science Church is the same and closes with a hymn, the reading of *the scientific statement of Being*, and the benediction. The routine was strictly followed on this day until just before pronouncing the benediction. Judge Smith broke through the usual formula with the following announcement:

[1] An inscription over the front entrance reads: "The First Church of Christ, Scientist, erected Anno Domini 1894. A testimonial to our beloved teacher, the Rev. Mary Baker G. Eddy, discoverer and founder of Christian Science; author of *Science and Health with Key to the Scriptures;* president of the Massachusetts Metaphysical College, and the first pastor of this denomination."

[2] For further details in Mrs. Eddy's life consult Chapter XV, and for a complete list of her works with succinct description of contents, the Bibliography.

"I shall now read part of a letter, written by our revered leader and reprinted on p. 135 of *Miscellaneous Writings:*

" 'MY BELOVED STUDENTS: You may be looking to see me in my accustomed place with you, but this you must no longer expect. When I retired from the field of labor, it was a departure socially, publicly, and finally, from the routine of such material modes as society, and our societies demand. Rumors are rumors—nothing more. I am still with you on the field of battle, taking forward marches, broader and higher views, and with the hope that you will follow. . . .

" 'All our thoughts should be given to the absolute demonstration of Christian Science. You can well afford to give me up, since you have in my last revised edition of *Science and Health* your teacher and guide.' [1]

"Although these lines," said Judge Smith, "were written years ago, they are true today and will continue to be true. But it becomes my duty to announce that Mrs. Eddy passed from our sight last night at quarter before eleven o'clock, at her home on Chestnut Hill."

Only those who sat through the service with the knowledge of the event of thirteen hours before, heard the benediction. The greater part of the congregation tried to realize what had happened and left their seats in a sort of dazed silence. Here and there was a little gathering and a few interchanges of sentiment, but there were no words of sorrow, and although many a tear was shed, no one would acknowledge a loss of any sort, and the great organ pealed its recessional as joyously and triumphantly as ever.[2]

III

Mrs. Eddy's unusually and unexpectedly long life was marked in its latter half by a feverish activity and by marvelous business aptitudes; throughout, it was a career replete with

---

[1] These words were written by Mrs. Eddy to be read at the meeting of the Massachusetts Metaphysical College Association, June 3, 1891.

[2] This account is taken substantially from the *Boston Evening Transcript* of December 5, 1910. It is here reproduced at length, because it gives a correct account of the Christian Science church services, and of the personal attitude assumed by many Christian Scientists.

the most varied fortunes, lending itself well to the legendary embellishments with which Mrs. Eddy's followers, encouraged by her own example, have surrounded it.[1] Of her life it can truly be said that fact is stranger than fiction.   How this woman, whose life for forty years, with but short intermissions, was a long succession of ailments that seemed to bring her more than once to death's door, came before the world with the claim of having been cured without doctor or drug; how she passed the rest of her life, for nearly half a century, denying the reality of sin, sickness, death, and of matter itself; how she, an illiterate woman, who at the age of forty neither wrote nor spoke correct English, became the author of a book which is put by many on a level with the Sacred Scriptures themselves; how, in spite of the fact that she repeatedly denied the existence of the supernatural, she persuaded hundreds of thousands that hers was a new and final revelation; how, though penniless at the age of fifty and living on the charity of others, she amassed before her death a fortune of considerably more than two million dollars; how, after questioning the usefulness of church organizations and forcing her followers to give up their church membership, this remarkable woman founded a new Church with affiliations in every important center of the United States and in almost every country of the world; how this was accomplished when she had reached the ripe old age of nearly three score and ten; how she surrounded herself with a loyal band of men and women, ever ready to carry out her every wish, no matter how great the sacrifices involved: all this is a story too long to be told in these pages, for details of which her biographies must be consulted.

It had been predicted that the death of Mrs. Eddy would spell the end of Christian Science. Time has given the lie to this prophecy. Legal contentions there are not a few;[2] but despite these, if signs can be trusted, the religion is prosperous. It may be that Mrs. Eddy, by leaving the bulk of her fortune

---

[1] For proof of this assertion, cf. Miss Sibyl Wilbur: *Life of Mary Baker Eddy* (Boston, 1913).

[2] Consult chapt. XV for details.

to her Church, materially strengthened its foundations;[1] at the same time it is evident that her doctrines have such a hold on the imagination of her adherents that the Church is in no immediate danger of collapse.

The progress of Christian Science is indicated by the following figures. In 1879 about a score of persons under the presidency of Mrs. Eddy met together to found a religious organization to be known as the Church of Christ (Scientist). The charter members numbered but twenty-six. About ten years later (1890), this organization reported 221 churches with a membership of 8724; sixteen years later (1906) the United States Religious Census Report gave it a total membership of 82,332 with 16,116 children in their Sunday schools, almost ten times as many as sixteen years before. Since then no official census has been taken, as Mrs. Eddy has ordered that "Christian Scientists shall not report for publication the number of the members of the Mother Church nor that of the branch churches."[2] Dr. Snowden, however, on the basis of the lists of organizations regularly published in the *Christian Science Journal*, has reckoned that in December, 1919, there was a total of 1702 organizations, of which 1504 were in the United States, and 198 in foreign countries. These organizations are divided as follows:

	Churches	Societies	Total
United States	840	664	1504
Other Countries	122	76	198
Total	962	730	1702

[1] Mrs. Eddy's will and two codicils provided for all but about $250,000 of her estate, conservatively valued at $2,250,000, going to the Christian Science Church. Each one of the four children of Mr. Glover was to receive $10,000. Mr. Frye was bequeathed $20,000 with the right to reside at 385 Commonwealth Avenue as long as he lived; also $500 worth of Mrs. Eddy's personal belongings. One hundred thousand dollars was to be set aside for the teaching of indigent practitioners.

[2] *Church Manual* (89th ed.), Art. VIII, sect. 28: It is believed that the slackening rate of increase induced Mrs. Eddy to put this prohibition on her statute book. Cf. Carroll: *The Religious Forces of the United States* (revised 1896), pp. 96-98. At that time the association owned only seven church edifices.

In June, 1907, the Mother Church, according to the last report of the secretary, had 43,876 members. It must, however, be noted that owing to the peculiar organization of the Christian Science Church, by far the larger number of these belonged at the same time to some branch church. Figuring on an average membership of 100 for every church and of 25 for every society, we get a total of about 114,700 Christian Scientists at the end of 1919. As this number does not include the children, who are not enrolled as members, this figure must be doubled or tripled to obtain an idea of the number of people who come under Christian Science influences.[1]

Even though this falls far short of the millions which some people believe they number, and still far shorter of the estimate Mr. Clements ventured to make some years back,[2] yet, for a society that in its original form is hardly more than fifty years old, and in its reorganized form not much more than thirty, the numerical strength is quite remarkable.

No less significant is the social standing of the average Christian Scientist. Whether it be that its appeal does not interest the lower classes, or that Christian Science is too expensive a luxury to indulge in, the fact is that the Christian Science congregations are largely composed of the well-to-do, with a fair sprinkling of educated men among them. Here it may be a lawyer, or a judge, who makes himself the apostle of the new Creed and the defender of its founder; there a physician or a clergyman gives up his profession to throw in his lot with the Christian Scientists.[3] On January 5 and 6, 1915, United States Senator Works in a lengthy, well-documented speech took up the defense of Christian Science before his colleagues in the Senate.[4] As far back as 1898 the Earl of Dunmore, a

---

[1] Snowden: *The Truth about Christian Science* (Philadelphia, 1920), p. 221. Cf. *Official U. S. Religious Census* for 1916, Vol. I, p. 11. Wilder D. Quint in *New England Magazine*, 1909: *The Growth of Christian Science*, p. 317.

[2] Mark Twain, *op. cit.*, p. 72: "It is a reasonably safe guess that in America in 1920 there will be ten million Christian Scientists, and three millions in Great Britain; that in America in 1920 the Christian Scientists will be a political force, in 1930 politically formidable, and in 1940 the governing power in the Republic—to remain that, permanently."

[3] Cf. Milmine: *op. cit.*, pp. 209 ff.

[4] Cf. *Congressional Record*, Vol. 52, Part I, pp. 1021-1057.

peer of the Scottish realm, came with his wife to Boston to study Christian Science and both were received by Mrs. Eddy, who at that time resided at Concord, New Hampshire. Lady Dunmore was also present at the June Communion of the following year. On this occasion her son, Lord Fincastle, is said to have come from India to join his mother in this service and to have returned immediately. Her daughter also came to America to attend the annual communion.[1]

Mrs. Eddy's success is thus explained by Miss Milmine:

"Mrs. Eddy's philosophy makes a double appeal to human nature, offering food both to our inherent craving for the mystical and to our desire to do well in a worldly way and teaching that these extremes are not incompatible in *Science*. Indeed, as one of the inducements offered to purchasers of the first edition of *Science and Health*, Mrs. Glover advertised it as a book that 'affords opportunity to acquire a profession by which you can accumulate a fortune,' and in the book itself she said that 'men of business have said this science was of great advantage from a secular point of view.' And in later and more prosperous days Mrs. Eddy has written in satisfied retrospect: 'In the early history of Christian Science among my thousands of students few were wealthy. Now, Christian Scientists are not indigent; and their comfortable fortunes are acquired by healing mankind morally, physically, and spiritually.'

"Whatever may be the Christian Science theories regarding the nothingness of other forms of matter, the various forms of currency continue to appear very real to the spiritualized vision of its followers. Mrs. Eddy insists that her healers shall be well paid. She says, 'Christian Science demonstrates that the patient who pays what he is able to pay, is more apt to recover than he who withholds a slight equivalent for health.'

"Worldly prosperity, indeed, plays an important part in the Christian Science religion today. Poverty is believed to be an error, like sin, sickness, and death; and Christian Scientists aim to make what they call their *financial demon-*

---

[1] Cf. Milmine: *op. cit.*, p. 448. The annual communion service which formed an event in the earlier days of the Mother Church was later suppressed by Mrs. Eddy.

stration early in their experience.   A poor Christian Scientist is as much of an anomaly as a sick Christian Scientist." [1]

What a contrast between this new religion which pretends to be Christian and that of the Son of Man who had not whereon to lay His head!

IV

When Mrs. Eddy, assuming the tone of an inspired prophet, deliberately ignored and slurred Dr. Quimby, she roused the dormant energies of Quimby's admirers and friends.   Unwittingly she became instrumental in gathering together into a movement what, without this incentive, would probably never have got beyond the stage of half-hearted and desultory attempts at healing in imitation of Quimby.   The latter found valiant defenders in Mr. and Mrs. Julius A. Dresser, who, in the early sixties, had both been his patients.   Mr. Dresser had worked under Quimby; it had been his duty to explain the first principles of the new science to new comers and to usher them into the "Doctor's" presence.   In this capacity he had made the acquaintance of Mrs. Patterson, the future founder of Christian Science.   When Quimby died, Mrs. Patterson earnestly entreated Mr. Dresser to continue Dr. Quimby's practice. Had he done so, Christian Science might never have been born. But Mr. Dresser's health was impaired; he and his wife both dreaded the publicity connected with such an undertaking; they had decided to try a change of climate and started for the West.   Their departure left the field clear, and Mrs. Patterson hastened to occupy it.

When Mr. Dresser returned from the West, he was surprised to learn of the growing fame and of the extravagant claims of his former friend, who had reassumed the name of her first husband.   He now no longer hesitated: he took up mental healing as a means of livelihood and defended the title of his friend and benefactor Quimby to the honor of having invented this new system of healing.   Mrs. Glover retorted, and thus was launched that famous Quimby controversy, out of which Mrs. Eddy emerged so ingloriously, and the details of which

[1] Milmine: *op. cit.,* p. 209.   Except when otherwise stated, the book, and not the magazine articles, are quoted.

may be read in Miss Milmine's *Life,* in Horatio W. Dresser's *History,* and in Peabody's *Masquerade.*

Mr. Dresser's championing of Dr. Quimby's claims bore fruit in opening the eyes of some who had been misled by Mrs. Eddy's assumption of superior knowledge. It cannot be said that, at that early date, anything like a concentrated opposition took shape; nevertheless, forces that would have spent themselves, if left alone, began to gravitate around this semblance of an organized opposition. Many practitioners who might have religiously adhered to a divinely appointed guide, now boldly struck out for themselves on independent lines and created in various sections of the country various centers of mental healing. These are the raw material which in the course of time congregated into what is now known as the New Thought movement. Of this stage of development Dr. Horatio W. Dresser writes:

"Passing by the beginnings of Christian Science (1875-1882) we come to a time when the idealistic interpretation of Quimby's theory, set on foot by the writings of Mr. Evans and Mrs. Eddy, had gained sufficient hold in Boston, so that readers and former students began to branch out for themselves. The *Mind-Cure* or *Boston Craze,* as it was first called, gradually spread to other cities, assuming new forms with each new leader. Thus a former student of Christian Science established the new movement in Hartford, Connecticut, and from that center teachers went to New York, where a variation of the Mind-Cure became known as metaphysical healing. Gradually the movement spread to western cities, where it became known under yet other names, such as Practical Christianity in Kansas City, and Divine Science in San Francisco and Denver.

"After 1890 a new school of writers appeared, among them Henry Wood and R. W. Trine, who gave a larger meaning to the original term and endeavored to make of the *Thought* a comprehensive theory for the whole of life. A Church was established in Boston as early as 1886, and since that time many Sunday meetings have flourished for brief periods. Magazines also began to appear early and active propagandism began. A general convention was also held

during that period, although it was many years before a
national convention was undertaken. The first Metaphysical
Club was organized in 1895. It was followed by similar clubs,
centers and circles in various parts of the country. Pres-
ently the diversity of books and magazines became such that it
was difficult even for close students of the movement to keep
the run of them. Out of this diversity has come the New
Thought as known today." [1]

We must briefly pass in review this ever widening circle of
mental cults, In 1894 Mrs. Van-Anderson organized the
Church of the Higher Life in Boston. The same year Miss
Sarah J. Farmer established the Greenacre Conferences, a summer camp which, though not exclusively devoted to New
Thought, was largely instrumental in bringing persons of the
same mind together, and continued to do so, until Miss Farmer
espoused Bahaism and other vagaries not directly connected
with New Thought. The same year also was organized at
Boston the *Procopeia,* the first New Thought Society which,
however, was short-lived and eventually merged into the *Metaphysical Club* organized about the same time. Of this club Mr.
Dresser says:

"This was the first permanent New Thought club and it
set the standard for such societies elsewhere. It was the first
mental-healing society to put its special interests on a large
basis with a view to reaching the world. It was the beginning
of the activities which grew in the course of time into a world-
wide movement. It led the way for the establishment of centers, circles, or other organizations with the same general
interests in view, whatever the names attached to them. The
fact that it came into existence was a sign that the mental-
healing movement had passed out of its preliminary or ex-
perimental stage and was assuming the general characteristics which it was to continue to possess. . . . Other attempts were made to develop a national movement. But it
was the movement which began in Boston that eventually
succeeded. Out of it grew the effort to form a permanent
international organization." [2]

[1] Dresser: *Handbook of the New Thought* (New York, 1917), p. 33 ff.
[2] Dresser's *History,* p. 183.

The first New Thought Convention, using that name, was held in Boston in 1899. Previous to this, Divine Science, that modified Christian Science, which had taken such firm roots in the Far West, had held annual conventions from 1894 to 1899 (with the exception of the year 1898) in San Francisco (1894, 1899), Chicago (1895), Kansas City (1896), and St. Louis (1897), which cities are still strong centers of the movement. In 1899, Boston, the home of Christian Science, began also to lead in New Thought. Up to then, the various independent organizations, scattered throughout the length and breadth of the land, almost invariably owed their existence directly or indirectly to Mrs. Eddy. Chicago had long since its contingent of mind-healers: there Mrs. Ursula Gestefeld drew upon herself the wrath of the Boston autocrat by publishing an explanation of *Science and Health;* there also appeared in 1891 Miss Yarnall's *Practical Healing for Mind and Body*, and Anna W. Mills' *Practical Metaphysics for Healing and Self-Culture.* In San Francisco Mrs. Hopkins had taught in 1887 a class of 250 people and had laid the foundation for the establishment of Christian Science Homes, now called Homes of Truth, in San Francisco, Los Angeles, San Diego, Oakland, San José, Sacramento, Berkeley and Sierra Madre in California, also at Victoria, British Columbia, and Walla Walla in Washington State. In Denver, Colorado, the psycho-therapeutic movement which is now in a flourishing condition there, was inaugurated and fostered by the pioneer work and teaching of Melinda E. Cramer, the author of *Divine Science and Healing*, 1907, and ably seconded by Fannie B. James, the author of *Truth and Health*, a book "lovingly dedicated to the World." Here also the Colorado College of Divine Science was incorporated in 1898. "Satisfactory work in all the courses (primary, training, theological and normal, each one covering a period of from two to four weeks) entitles the student to the College diploma, and this signifies that he is a fully equipped healer, minister and teacher." [1]

---

[1] Cf. James: *Truth and Health. Science of the Perfect Mind and the Law of its Demonstration*—New Light upon Old Truths. The Textbook of the Colorado College of Divine Science (3d ed., Denver, Colo., 1905), p. 368. Gestefeld: *A Statement of Christian Science* (Chicago, 1888).

In St. Louis the movement assumed the name of Practical Christianity, inaugurated a German branch and, since 1893, published a German periodical, entitled *Das Wort*. Cleveland saw the founding, by the Rev. J. F. C. Grumbine, of the *Order of the White Rose* and also of the College of Divine Science and Realization. In Philadelphia, Pennsylvania; Washington, D. C., and other places the movement also soon obtained a sure footing. Mr. Sabin was a pioneer in *Reformed Christian Science* in Washington, D. C., and Mr. Mason in Brooklyn, New York.[1] Thus the way was prepared for the attempt to group these several bodies under one general organization.

The first New Thought convention properly so-called gave birth to the International Metaphysical League; this was transformed in 1905 into the World New Thought Federation, and, in 1908, into the National New Thought Alliance, which, in name, if not yet in fact, became in 1914 again international. Since this its final reorganization, so-called international congresses have been held in San Francisco, St. Louis, Boston, Kansas City, and in Washington, D. C., which has now become the headquarters for the movement.

The League, Federation, or Alliance has no easy time trying to keep so many divergent elements harmoniously united in the one association. However, the work of organization seems to be now fairly under way and to work satisfactorily. New Thought never excited quite the same amount of opposition as Christian Science, because it does not claim so much for itself as its rival. It is likely that its growth will continue unchecked for many years to come. Being less compact, it is more elastic and also more elusive than Christian Science. Criticism will, therefore, naturally center on the latter, and touch the former indirectly.

A word or two on kindred subjects and studies will help to give to this essay its proper orientation. There is nowadays no dearth of literature on these topics.

"In recent years," writes Dr. William Sadler, "we have been literally deluged with literature on suggestion, mental healing, hypnotism, psychotherapy, psychic fads, and various

[1] Dresser's *History*, pp. 232-253, 196 ff.

healing 'isms,' not to mention New Thought, Christian Science, and other systems of religious healing. It would seem as if doctor, preacher and layman were now vying with one another in an effort to atone for their past indifference to, and neglect of, the important subjects mental healing and moral therapeutics." [1]

It is perhaps too much to say that the mind of the scientific world has completely reversed itself on the score of magnetic or hypnotic healing; it has at least divested itself of that supreme contempt with which it used to treat these matters. Hypnotic facts have acquired rights of citizenship in scientific circles. Credit for this changed attitude is due in no small measure to the investigations of two rival camps, the Paris and the Nancy school of hypnotism with their respective leaders Charcot and Bernheim. As their conclusions will have no small bearing on our subject, it may be as well to indicate here in a general way that the Paris school has conceded fully and explicitly that the Nancy school has found the proper explanation for the common phenomena which they both investigated.

Charcot, the head of the Paris school, had looked upon hypnosis as a pathological state, and upon hypnotic influence as a real transference of vital powers from the operator to the subject. Bernheim, the founder of the Nancy school, on the contrary, proved successfully that hypnosis was not a pathological condition, and that the real cause of its phenomena was not a sort of electric current of vital powers passing from operator to subject, but was due to the power of suggestion, which would direct the subject's subliminal mind to perform unconsciously certain definite acts. [2]

It is from this latter hypothesis that the two quasi-scientific mental cures, inaugurated by Dubois and Freud, start. Dr. Paul Dubois of Bern, Switzerland, who has been trained in the Nancy school, discards hypnotism altogether and confines himself to the treatment by suggestion in the waking state. His plan consists in reëducating intellectually and morally nervous

---

[1] Sadler: *The Physiology of Faith and Fear* (Chicago, 1912), Preface, p. vii.

[2] Cf. Bernheim: *La Suggestion* (Nancy, 1884); Pierre Janet: *Les Médications Psychologiques* (Paris, 1919), Vol. I, pp. 159-166.

patients that are brought to him. There is little essential difference between his practice and that of our mind-healers,
though there is no parity whatever between his theories and
theirs.[1] The same thing may be said concerning the much-
talked-about psycho-analytical method of the recently defunct
Viennese professor Freud. This latter insisted especially on
the danger of suppressed emotions and disagreeable reminiscences to the health of the individual. Freud has pushed his
system to extremes by finding for all such suppressed fears
and hidden impulses a sexual basis. This, however, need not be
considered essential to his system.[2]

Mental or faith-healing, since its apparent success in Christian Science, strongly appeals to certain Protestant communi-
ties. The question has been seriously asked whether Protestantism must adopt Christian Science or at least Christian Science
healing.[3] Some churches have not waited for this question to
be broached. Mr. J. M. Hickson, a lay member of the Church
of England, has for years held healing services in England,
claiming that the gift of healing is essential to the Christian
Church. Before the Pan-Anglican Congress in 1908 he stated
"that we should always keep clearly before us the fact that
there is only One Healer, the Lord Jesus Christ Himself, who is
the Truth, the Way and the Life of spiritual healing"; that
"because Christ is the Healer, there is no limitation to His
work, except that of man's receptiveness, and that His healing
is not only for the body, but also for the mind and spirit." [4]
Mr. Hickson has lately toured the United States, drawing
everywhere large crowds to his healing services. His example
was immediately followed by a host of other advocates of
divine healing.

[1] Dubois: *The Influence of the Mind over the Body,* translated by L. B.
Gallatin from 5th French edition (New York, 1906); *The Psychic Treatment of Nervous Disorders,* translated by Jelliffe and White (New York,
1906).

[2] Cf. Wolfram: *Gegen Psycho-Analyse* (Leipzig, 1918); Jones, J.: *Psycho-Analysis* (1915); Maeder in *L'Année Psychologique,* Vol. XVIII (1912),
"Sur le Mouvement Psycho-Analytique."

[3] Hegeman, in *North American Review,* December, 1913, p. 823, and July,
1914, p. 122.

[4] *Report,* Vol. III, sect. B., p. 20. Cf. Paget: *Faith and Works of Christian Science* (New York, 1909), pp. 187 ff.

Even more important than the work of Mr. Hickson in England is that inaugurated in 1906, by Dr. Elwood Worcester in the Emmanuel Church, Boston, Massachusetts. It differs from other movements in this, that it limits itself to nervous diseases and requires the coöperation of the physicians. The authors of this innovation insist that their movement "bears no relation to Christian Science, either by way of protest or of imitation." "We have taken our stand," they declare, "fairly and squarely on the religion of Christ, as that religion is revealed in the New Testament, and as it is interpreted by modern scholarship, and we have combined with us the power of genuine science." [1] In spite of these emphatic statements, few, I think, would deny that the Emmanuel, and similar, movements owe indirectly their existence to the success and the danger of Christian Science.

This rapid survey shows only imperfectly the importance which attaches nowadays to the modern mind-movements, in general, and to Christian Science, in particular. Ridicule has been tried and has been found wanting. In spite of sarcasm and invective, Christian Science has steadily grown. Nor must we neglect its rival movements which become daily of greater importance. Men of note, like the late Professor William James or the late Hugo Münsterberg, both of Harvard University, or like James H. Leuba of Bryn Mawr College, who have investigated these movements, do not speak slightingly of them. Hardly any subject is more frequently alluded to in our days in public speech or print. In 1906 Mgr. Benson in a conference on Christian Science could still give the following advice:

"You will forgive me perhaps, if I end with two or three recommendations to any who have to deal with persons suffering from this distressing form of thought. First, I am sure that we must keep our tempers, and secondly, our sense of humor. If it is true that Protestantism rises in any degree from the absence of this latter virtue, I am certain that Christian Science, its latest development, rises almost entirely from it. I do not say that no 'scientist' possesses a grain

---

[1] Cf. Worcester-McComb-Coriat: *Religion and Medicine* (New York, 1908), p. 13; also Worcester-McComb: *The Christian Religion as a Healing Power* (New York, 1909).

of humor, but that such is bound to keep it in a locked cupboard when he treats of his religion.   Let us therefore bring to bear this genial solvent of laughter and see whether Christian Science is as impervious to it as to so many other facts of the world in which we live." [1]

After all that precedes, it must be apparent that ridicule can no longer be the main weapon that we must wield against this new philosophy and new religion.   It becomes necessary that we should try to see it as the Christian Scientist sees it, and to discover in it that grain of truth which renders it acceptable to so many.   At the same time we must keep in view the danger against revealed religion which all modern mind-movements contain, at least implicitly.

[1] Benson, R. H.: *A Book of Essays;* essay on "Christian Science," p. 17.

CHAPTER III

CHRISTIAN SCIENCE, alone among all modern mind-cults, lays claim to an extraordinary, not to say supernatural, origin. It assumes the mask of a new religious revelation; it claims to be the revival of original Christianity, the result of a divine inspiration. This claim has probably been the most powerful contributing cause to its success. Had Mrs. Eddy been content with an appeal to experience and science, she would have remained the butt of a good-natured and fun-loving public; but when she began to speak as one having authority, she gathered around herself a handful of followers who rapidly increased in number. Thus was laid the foundation of that organization whose rapid progress and widespread ramifications astonish us today.

Nothing seems to be quite as easy as to launch a new religion. Garb any idea, be it ever so fantastic, in the mantle of religion and it is assured of a following. Men may revile religion, even resent its intrusion, and chafe under its restraints, but quite indifferent to it they seldom are. Deep down in their hearts, often unacknowledged, and oftener unappreciated, there slumbers that mysterious impulse to worship which craves to be satisfied. At the same time the average man is very human: actual needs and wants take up by far the largest share of his thoughts and aspirations. To possess and enjoy the good things of life, to increase his worldly prestige and influence, to get beyond the range of want, this, it would almost seem, is the sole goal of his desires. It is only religion that imposes restraints on these his material pursuits. St. Paul's classical description of the interior struggle between sin and the soul, with the latter often worsted in the conflict, remains universally true. Now if, by any possibility, the interests of religion can be made to square with those of nature, if the wide gulf which

35

is commonly supposed to exist between religion and world-liness can be shown to be nothing but an illusion, and if to be religious-minded means to be worldly-prosperous, this reconciliation of the two men in us must greatly attract such as formerly groaned under their incompatibility. Mrs. Eddy's religion offers such a combination.

Mrs. Eddy may never have analyzed the elements of her success. She cannot have foreseen and foreordained all that she accomplished. To let now the light of later developments play on the origin of her institutions and to explain this origin in the light of subsequent history is to misread the trend of events. Mrs. Eddy had no wide visions, no definite and pre-arranged plan. If she succeeded, it was not that she unflinch-ingly pursued a set goal, to be reached through a series of important steps, but because, her vision being limited, she bent her heart and soul on an immediate goal, which, when reached, served as a stepping stone to further projects. Oftentimes she would follow rather than lead; she would swim with the current; she would adapt herself to that daily conflict which was so characteristic of her active life. When necessary, she would retrace her steps, and, when a new opportunity opened, she would advance with renewed zest. The precise form that Christian Science has taken was largely determined by circumstances.

But back of all her scheming lay the fundamental conceit that she, Mrs. Eddy, had rediscovered primitive Christianity; that hers was a mission parallel to that of Christ and of the prophets of old; that her message contained a new, a most perfect revelation graciously granted by God to the people of the present age.

"In the year 1866," she writes, "I discovered the Christ Science, or divine laws of Life, and named it Christian Science. God had been graciously fitting me during many years for the reception of a final revelation of the absolute divine Principle of scientific being and healing. This apodictical Principle points to the revelation of Immanuel, 'God with us,' the sovereign ever-presence delivering the children of men from every ill that flesh is heir to." [1]

[1] Eddy: *Science and Health* (351 ed.), p. 107.

Christian Science is deeply rooted in Mrs. Eddy's personal experiences. Her own personality occupies in her work almost as great a prominence as that of Christ in the establishment of Christianity. Mrs. Eddy copied well, and if at times she overshot the mark, she always had enough practical sense to explain away, before it could do any lasting harm, whatever was too offensive to her friendly critics. Mrs. Eddy, of set purpose, surrounded her life with a supernatural sheen. Under her pen the most trivial circumstances took on a brilliant hue. New incidents were invented to increase the glory of "the discoverer and founder of Christian Science." Every precaution was taken that her name should not be forgotten, or obscured. This process of self-glorification, which went on merrily whenever feasible, took an upward jump with the founding of the *Journal of Christian Science* in 1883, and reached a climax, in 1889, with the publication of that fairy-tale autobiography, entitled *Retrospection and Introspection*, and of that presumptuous production, in 1893, known as *Christ and Christmas*, at which even Christian Scientists were scandalized to such a degree that Mrs. Eddy temporarily suppressed it.[1]

To come to some detailed illustrations of these statements, let us begin at the beginning and learn something of Mrs. Eddy's entrance into this world. In the days of her destitution, before success had smiled on her, Mrs. Eddy related how she had been born into the world an unwelcome child, and how every man's hand had been against her. But the wheel of fortune turned, and with it also the version of her birth. Now the legend went that Mrs. Baker, her mother, had "felt as if all the vital forces of the world had united in her, and she knew that she was to bring forth a prodigy." [2]

[1] "In 1893 Mrs. Eddy published *Christ and Christmas,* an illustrated poem, which she afterwards temporarily suppressed, because the pictures were displeasing to many people. One picture represents Jesus Christ standing beside a big, black, upholstered coffin, raising to life an emaciated woman. Another represents a woman, strangely like Mrs. Eddy's authorized photographs in appearance, standing at a bedside and raising a prostrate form while a great star burns above her head. In another, Christ is represented as hand in hand with a woman who bears a tablet, inscribed Christian Science. Mrs. Eddy wrote the text of this grim gift-book, and a fly-leaf accredits the pictures to Mary Baker G. Eddy and James F. Gilman, artists." Milmine: *op. cit.,* p. 418.

[2] *Ibid.,* p. 415.

Mary Baker, the future Mrs. Eddy, is pictured by eye-witnesses as a neurotic child, endowed with an ugly, selfish, domineering and unmanageable temper, yet capable of the most winning ways and manners. Constitutionally and temperamentally unfit for any protracted work, seeing that she was subject to frequent fainting spells that threatened her life more than once, she attended school rarely and received but the scantiest common school education. This little creditable fact is thus transformed into something quite different by Mrs. Eddy who writes late in life:

"My father was taught to believe that my brain was too large for my body and so kept me much out of school, but I gained book knowledge with far less labor than is usually requisite. At ten years of age I was as familiar with Lindley Murray's *Grammar* as with the *Westminster Catechism;* and the latter I had to repeat every Sunday. My favorite studies were Natural Philosophy, Logic, and Moral Science. From my brother Albert I received lessons in the ancient tongues, Hebrew, Greek, and Latin."

Fortunately for this precocious child, who might later on have been called upon to give proof of this vast activity and learning, all her knowledge suddenly vanished.

"After my discovery of Christian Science, most of the knowledge I had gleaned from schoolbooks vanished like a dream. *Learning was so illumined that grammar was eclipsed.* Etymology was divine history, voicing the idea of God in man's origin and signification. Syntax was spiritual order and unity. Prosody, the song of angels, and no earthly or inglorious theme." [1]

With a similar disregard of truth Mrs. Eddy writes of her earliest religious experiences:

"From my very childhood I was impelled by a hunger and thirst after divine things—a desire for something higher and

[1] Cf. Milmine: *op. cit.,* p. 18. "Mrs. Eddy's schoolmates are not able to reconcile her story with their own recollections. They declare frankly that they do not believe Albert Baker taught her Hebrew, Greek, and Latin. He entered college, when Mary was nine, and left home when she was thirteen. . . . They insist that Mary's education was finished when she reached long division in the district school."

better than matter, and apart from it—to seek diligently for the knowledge of God as the one great and ever-present relief from human woe. The first spontaneous motion of Truth and Love acting through Christian Science on my roused consciousness banished at once and forever the fundamental error of faith in things material; for this trust is the unseen sin, the unknown foe, the heart's untamed desire which breaketh the divine commandments." [1]

Quite different is the picture drawn for us by Miss Milmine.

"It was an age," she writes, "when languishing manners were fashionable. As a little girl even, Mary Baker adopted and exaggerated that pose. Her behavior was mincing and artificial, and by contrast it stood out in that rather rough and primitive community. Strong in the memory of the old inhabitants is her appearance at Church. She hardly ever entered until the rest of the congregation were seated. Then she tripped in, dressed a little conspicuously, but always in taste—a picture of fashionable beauty which made strangers and visitors stare. These baits lured the village boys; and at church festivals all the young farmers were at her feet." [2]

True to her purpose of giving to her life the appearance of a special divine protection, Mrs. Eddy relates two other incidents, calculated to remind us of the Biblical accounts of Samuel's vocation, on the one hand, and of the twelve-year-old child Jesus, on the other. Like the little Samuel, she frequently heard (so Mrs. Eddy tells us) a voice distinctly calling her. Her mother, at last, instructed her to reply in the words of Samuel, "Speak, Lord, for thy servant heareth." "When the call came again," Mrs. Eddy continued, "I did answer in the words of Samuel; but never again to the material senses was that mysterious call repeated." [3]

So again like the child Jesus who, at the age of twelve, sat among the doctors "hearing them and asking them questions," Mary Baker, at the age of twelve, when (according to her own account) she was admitted to the Tilton Congregation Church, had her dispute, and this with her pastor, "an old-school ex-

[1] *Retrospection*, p. 37.
[2] Milmine, *op. cit., McClure's Magazine*, Vol. XXVIII. (January, 1907), p. 235.
[3] *Retrospection*, p. 10.

pounder of the strictest Presbyterian doctrines," who was "apparently as eager to have unbelievers in these dogmas lost, as he was to have elect believers converted." The subject of the discussion was that abstruse doctrine of "Unconditional Election or Predestination" which has tried the intellectual acumen of more than one staid and learned divine. "So perturbed was I," Mrs. Eddy tells us, "by the thoughts aroused by this erroneous doctrine that the family doctor was summoned and pronounced me stricken with fever." Mary's mother wisely induced her to pray, whereupon "a soft glow of ineffable joy came over her," and "the horrible decree of Predestination" forever lost its hold on her. But she still had to stand the test of a rigid examination prior to her admission into the Church and, of course, spoke so earnestly "that even the oldest Church members wept," and even the good clergyman's heart melted, and he received her into their communion, and her protest with her.[1]

These narratives must be read in the light of the following facts: (1) Mary Baker was seventeen, not twelve, years old when she joined the Church at Tilton, as the authentic records of the Church show; (2) the unsupported claim of hearing voices and of disputing the official Calvinistic teaching of his pastor on exactly the same doctrine at exactly the same age was made shortly before Mrs. Eddy wrote by one of her contemporaries, a spiritist and a quack, the notorious Andrew Jackson Davis, the supposed author of *The Magic Staff* (1826-1910).[2]

Mrs. Eddy by thus ennobling her childhood tried to render more credible her claim of a divine origin for her textbook. These embellishments of her earlier life, however, were an afterthought. So little certain was Mrs. Eddy as to the date when this revelation was vouchsafed her, that she has given at various times various dates. If the year 1866 finally triumphed it was because it had over others certain advantages which rendered it more suitable both for defense and offense. For Quimby was dead at that time, and her fall on a slippery

[1] Eddy; *Retrospection*, pp. 12-15.
[2] Cf. Podmore: *op. cit.*, p. 221.

sidewalk afforded a spectacular setting for this occasion. Unfortunately for Mrs. Eddy, it was impossible to expunge her earlier printed statements which give the same honor to three other years, 1844, 1853, and 1864 respectively.

In the first edition of *Science and Health* (1875) this discovery is placed in the year 1864: "We made our first discovery that Science mentally applied would heal the sick in 1864 and since then have tested it on ourselves and hundreds of others and never found it to fail to prove the statement herein made of it." Eight years later she said in a letter to the *Boston Post:* "We made our first experiments in mental healing about 1853 when we were convinced that mind had a science which, if understood, would heal all disease." Finally, in 1887 she wrote in the *Christian Science Journal:* "As long ago as 1844 I was convinced that mortal mind produced all disease, and that the various medical systems were in no proper sense scientific. In 1862 when I first visited Mr. Quimby, I was proclaiming to druggists, spiritualists and mesmerists that science must govern all healing." [1]

From 1866 on, the history of this "revelation" and "discovery" is easy to follow. Mr. Quimby had died early in that year (January 16). Two weeks later occurred, at Lynn, Massachusetts, that fall from which Mrs. Eddy dates her discovery. On that occasion, to quote her own words, she suffered "an injury that neither medicine nor surgery could reach." Her "immediate recovery" from the effects of that injury was "the falling apple" that led her "to the discovery how to be well herself, and how to make others so." [2] Mrs. Eddy's narrative places this accident, in itself real and serious enough, in a false light. She did not recover immediately, but was under the physician's care from February 1 to February 13. Nor did the doctor pronounce her case hopeless, as is witnessed to by the following affidavit, based on his written notes:

"When I left her (Mrs. Patterson) on the thirteenth of February, she seemed to have recovered from the disturbance caused by the accident, and to be practically in her normal

[1] Milmine: *op. cit.,* p. 77.
[2] *Retrospection,* p. 28.

condition. I did not at any time declare, or believe, that there was no hope for Mrs. Patterson's recovery, or that she was in a critical condition, and did not at any time say, or believe, that she had but three, or any other limited, number of days to live. Mrs. Patterson did not suggest, or say, or pretend, or in any way whatever, intimate, that, on the third or any other day of her said illness, she had miraculously recovered or been healed, or that, discovering or perceiving the truth of the power employed by Christ to heal the sick, she had, by it, been restored to health." [1]

Two weeks after the accident Mrs. Eddy herself wrote to her friend Mr. J. A. Dresser:

"Two weeks ago I fell on the sidewalk and struck my back on the ice and was taken up for dead, came to consciousness amid a storm of vapors from cologne, chloroform, ether, camphor, etc., but to find myself the helpless cripple I was before I saw Dr. Quimby. The physician attending said I had taken the last step I ever should, but in two days I got out of my bed *alone* and *will* walk; but yet I confess I am frightened, and out of that nervous heat my friends are forming, spite of me, the terrible spinal affection from which I have suffered so long and hopelessly. . . . Now, can't *you* help me? I believe you can. I write this with this feeling: I think that I could help another in my condition if they had not placed their intelligence in matter. This I have not done, and yet I am slowly failing. Won't you write me if you will undertake for me if I can get to you?" [2]

At the time this letter was written, Mrs. Patterson still was leaning for relief on Mr. Julius Dresser as the probable successor of Dr. Quimby. Her hopes lay in Quimby's system. Just to induce Mr. Dresser not to abandon her in her distress, she suggests: "I think that I could help another in my condition, if they had not placed their intelligence in matter." There is in all this no sign of a new discovery, still less any indication of a new revelation. None the less, it is quite prob-

[1] Cf. Milmine: *op.cit.,* p. 87.
[2] *Ibid.,* p. 85. It must be remembered that at this time Quimby was dead, and Mrs. Eddy looked upon Mr. Dresser as his logical successor.

able that, during the course of this year, Mrs. Eddy acquires a certain independence of action, forced upon her by the utter wretchedness of her life.   Her father is dead; her husband deserts her; her sister, Mrs. Tilton, who has frequently nursed her with a mother's care, closes forever her door against her. Her lot is thrown in with comparative strangers, on whose charitableness she largely depends, and, as her only assets, she possesses what she knows of Dr. Quimby's art of healing.[1]

And during all these years (1866-1870), the memory of which Mrs. Eddy in the days of her prosperity wished to see blotted out, she never attributed the invention of the new way of healing to herself.   Quimby remained the source of her inspiration as well as the topic of her conversation. She taught from his manuscript and she practiced his method wherever she went.   Ten times during these few years Mrs. Eddy changed her residence. She resided successively at Lynn, Swampscott, East Stoughton, Taunton, Amesbury, Stoughton, and again at Amesbury. From her first residence she was evicted, ostensibly because she could not pay the rental of $1.50 a week, but in reality because her presence was no longer wanted. She stopped but a short time at the next two places; at her fourth change of residence she met with a kindly reception from the gentle spiritualist Mrs. Wheeler, but this kindness she repaid before long with the most insulting and abusive language and conduct.[1]

Her next home she left to join the Crafts at East Stoughton for the purpose of teaching Mr. Crafts, a shoe worker, the

---

[1] "In the fall of 1865 Mark Baker, Mrs. Patterson's father, died, and about the same time her sister, Mrs. Tilton, closed her door forever against Mrs. Patterson. Her only child, George Glover, at that time a young man, she had sent away in his childhood.   Mrs. Patterson was, therefore, for the first time in her life, practically alone in the world, and largely dependent upon herself for support. Untrained in any kind of paid work, she fell back upon the favors of her friends or chance acquaintances, living precariously upon their bounty, and obliged to go from house to house, as one family after another wearied of her." Milmine: *op. cit.*, p. 108.

[1] Cf. Milmine, *op. cit.*, pp. 108-131. "Mrs. Patterson was soon after this requested to leave the Wheeler house and did so. Mrs. Wheeler received nothing in payment for Mrs. Patterson's board. When Mrs. Wheeler asked Mrs. Patterson for a settlement, Mrs. Patterson replied to the effect that she had 'treated' a wounded finger for Mr. Wheeler and that this service was equivalent to what she had received from Mr. and Mrs. Wheeler in board, lodging, etc." (p. 110).

science of mental healing. It was not long before she tried to induce Mr. Crafts to obtain a divorce from his wife, and, as this attempt failed, she had, of course, to leave. From her next home she had literally to be ejected, as she refused to comply with the command to go.[1] After that she enjoyed the hospitality of the Wentworths in Stoughton for about two years. As in the case of Mr. Crafts, so here she would have liked to break up the family circle, this time by inducing Mrs. Wentworth to leave husband and family in order to practice with her "the Quimby treatment." Ordered to leave, she chose for her departure a day when everybody was absent, and when the members of the family returned they were shocked to find the contents of the room she had occupied maliciously damaged.[2]

It is to this period of strife and stress that dates the very natural origin of the book which has been accepted with so much reverence by an overcredulous multitude. Up to then, Mrs. Eddy had used in her teaching and practice only the copy she had made from Quimby's Manuscript. In Stoughton Mrs. Eddy wrote a preface to it, signed Mary M. Glover, and introduced in it slight changes with a few additions. This preface was later on incorporated in the text, and the original title page reading *Extracts from P. P. Quimby's Writings* was omitted. Thus transformed, the manuscript was named *The Science of Man, or, The Principle which Controls Matter.* This production was copyright in 1872, but was not published until 1876, under the title *The Science of Man, by Which the Sick are Healed, Embracing Questions and Answers in Moral Science arranged for the Learner by Mrs. Mary Baker Glover.* Grad-

[1] Milmine, *op. cit.,* p. 117. Mary Ellis Bartlett testified: "My father commanded Mrs. Glover to leave, and when she steadfastly refused to go, he had her trunk dragged from her room and set it outside the door, and when she was outside, he closed the door and locked it. I have often heard my father describe this event in detail, and I have heard him say that he had never expected in his whole life to be obliged to put a woman into the street."

[2] *Ibid.,* p. 124. "We found every breadth of matting slashed up through the middle apparently with some sharp instrument. We also found the feather bed all cut to pieces. We opened the door of a closet. On the floor was a pile of newspapers almost entirely consumed. On top of these papers was a shovelful of dead coals. These had evidently been left by the last occupant. The only reasons that they had not set the house on fire evidently were because the closet door had been shut, and the air of the closet was so dead." (Affidavit by H. T. Wentworth.)

ually two other treatises were written, entitled respectively *Scientific Treatise on Mortality as taught by Mrs. M. B. Glover* and *Soul's Inquiries of Man.* "At first, however, Mrs. Glover gave Quimby credit for the authorship of the three manuscripts, even for the two which seem to have been partly her own composition."[1] An important change was introduced in the spring of 1872 when as a result of her break with Richard Kennedy, she discontinued manipulation, which Quimby, without putting any stock in it, had tolerated. She ever afterwards denounced it as the sign and badge of mesmerism. *Science and Health* itself came from the press in 1876. The history of this book includes, therefore,

"1. The writing of a signed preface and the amending of the original Quimby manuscript.

"2. The incorporating of this preface in the text.

"3. The composition of a second manuscript, partly her own, from which she was able to teach successfully.

"4. The discontinuation of *manipulation* in treatment.

"5. The belief, fostered by her students, that her interpretation of the Quimby manuscript was far beyond the manuscript itself in scope and understanding.

"6. The writing of the book *Science and Health*, begun in the later sixties and finished in 1875, in which Mrs. Glover undoubtedly added much extraneous matter to Quimbyism and developed self-confidence by presenting ideas of her own."[2]

This book, which Mrs. Eddy in her autobiography styles *The Precious Volume,* was, therefore, in the making from the year 1866, when Mrs. Eddy claims the great discovery to have taken place, till 1875, when the book was published at the expense of two students who were found willing to advance the money for its publication.[3] During all these years Mrs. Eddy was continually engaged in writing and rewriting what she

---

[1] Milmine: *op. cit.,* p. 163.

[2] *Ibid.,* p. 166.

[3] "Mr. Barry and Miss Newhall lost over fifteen hundred dollars on the edition, and Mr. Spofford paid out five hundred dollars of his own money for advertising and personal expenses, besides giving his time for several months. Mrs. Eddy made no effort to reimburse them." Milmine, in *McClure's Magazine,* Vol. XXIX, p. 342.

sometimes called her Bible, and yet, "even after her eight years' struggle with her copy, the book as printed in 1875 is hardly more than a tangle of words and theories, faulty in grammar and construction, and singularly vague and contradictory in its statements." [1]   It contained eight chapters which in the course of its many revisions increased to eighteen. To show the metamorphosis which this singular book "of revelations" underwent, I here reproduce in parallel columns the table of contents of the first and of a later edition, the numbers in brackets being inserted to facilitate comparison.

First Edition	*Later Editions*
1. Natural Science (6)	1. Prayer (5)
2. Imposition and Demonstration (4 and 5)	2. Atonement and Eucharist (5)
3. Spirit and Matter (10)	3. Marriage (6)
4. Creation (9)	4. Christian Science and Spiritualism
5. Prayer and Atonement (1 and 2)	5. Animal Magnetism
6. Marriage (3)	6. Science, Theology, Medicine (1)
7. Physiology (7)	7. Physiology (7)
8. Healing the Sick (12)	8. Footsteps of Truth
	9. Creation (4)
	10. Science of Being (3)
	11. Some Objections Answered
	12. Christian Science Practice (8)
	13. Teaching Christian Science
	14. Recapitulation
	KEY TO THE SCRIPTURES
	15. Genesis
	16. The Apocalypse
	17. Glossary
	18. Fruitage

If we are asked what the relations are between Mrs. Eddy' "textbook" and Quimby's essays, we can state in fairness tha

[1] Milmine: *op. cit.*, p. 178.

Mrs. Eddy's work is her own, though its basic ideas, its inspiration and some of its phrases are undoubtedly borrowed from Quimby. What the famous Quimby controversy has brought to light is not that there is nothing original in Mrs. Eddy's work, but that there is nothing essentially new in her system, nothing that might be called her discovery (except perhaps her concept of malicious animal magnetism), nothing that could justify Mrs. Eddy's claim to be a divinely inspired teacher for the present age. In Miss Milmine's words:

"The basic ideas of the book and much of the terminology were, of course, borrowed from the Quimby papers which Mrs. Glover had carried reverently about with her since 1864, and from which she had taught his doctrines. But in the elaboration and amplification of the Quimby theory, Mrs. Glover introduced some totally new propositions and many an ingenious argument." [1]

If, then, Mrs. Eddy has been a loser through this controversy, it is not so much because of what she borrowed from Quimby, but because of her unwillingness to admit her obligation to him, an unwillingness which had its roots in her pretensions to a divine revelation.

The first edition, despite the untiring efforts of Mrs. Eddy and one of her students, Mr. Spofford, to make it known, was far from creating a widespread interest and from being a financial success.

"Mrs. Glover and Mr. Spofford advertised the book by means of handbills and through the newspapers, printing testimonials of the wonderful cures made by the application of the Science, and urging all to buy the book which would tell them all about it. Copies were sent to the leading New England newspapers for review, accompanied by a request to the editors to print nothing about the book, if a favorable notice could not be given. This request was respected by some of the papers, but others criticized the book severely, or referred to it flippantly. Copies were also sent to the University of Heidelberg, to Thomas Carlyle, and to several noted

[1] Milmine: *op. cit.*, p. 178. Cf. on the Quimby controversy, pp. 71-104, 162 ff. Dresser's *History*, pp. 97-125.

theologians and literary men.   But the book made no stir, and, outside of the little band of devoted Christian Scientists, its advent was unobserved." [1]

Other ways and means to bring it before the public had to be devised.   Mr. Spofford was induced to give up his practice and devote all his time to further the sale of the book, paying out of his own pocket for advertising and personal expenses five hundred dollars which were never reimbursed.   Meanwhile Mrs. Eddy was scheming to extend her influence.   In a letter dated April, 1877, she urged her partner "to try to get students into the field as practitioners," and thus, she continued, "healing will sell the book and introduce the Science more than aught but *my* lecturing can do.   Send the name of any you can get to study for the purpose of practicing, and in six months or thereabouts we will have them in the field helping you." [2]

In July, 1877, Mr. Spofford closed out the first edition and paid over the money which he received to George H. Barry and Elizabeth M. Newhall, who had furnished the money to publish it.   But long before this Mrs. Eddy had busied herself with the preparation of a second edition.   She became enraged at Mr. Spofford for not turning the receipts over to herself, classed him with the mesmerists and had him expelled in January, 1878.[3]   She went further.

"The second edition which Mr. Spofford had labored upon and helped to prepare, was hastily revised and converted into a running attack upon him, hurried to press, labeled Volume II, and sent panting after *Science and Health*, which was not labeled Volume I, and which had already been in the world three years.   This odd little brown book, with the ark and troubled waters on the cover, is made up of a few chapters snatched from the 1875 edition, interlarded with vigorous rhetoric such as the following apostrophe to Spofford:

"'Behold! thou criminal mental marauder, that would

[1] Milmine: *op. cit.,* p. 177.
[2] *Ibid.,* p. 216.
[3] *Ibid.,* p. 233.   Mr. Spofford received the following notice: "Dr. D. H. Spofford of Newburyport has been expelled from the Association of Christian Scientists for immorality and as unworthy to be a member." Immorality meant disloyalty to Mrs. Eddy.

blot out the sunshine of earth, that would sever friends, destroy virtue, put out Truth, and murder in secret the innocent, befouling the track with the trophies of thy guilt,—I say, Behold the "cloud no bigger than a man's hand" already rising in the horizon of Truth, to pour down upon thy guilty head the hailstones of doom.' " [1]

In all this there is little enough that savors of the supernatural, but even as a natural means for securing health but little confidence can be placed in this discovery, seeing that the discoverer, at the very time when she offered health to others, was herself suffering intensely from ill-health. The following letter, written about this time to her ephemeral friend Spofford, whom she still called familiarly Harry (Harrison), is typical of her perturbed state of mind.

"BOSTON, April 14, 1877.

"DEAR STUDENT: This hour of my departure I pick up from the carpet a piece of paper write you a line to say I *am* at length driven into the wilderness. *Everything* needs me in science, my doors are thronged, the book lies waiting, but those who *call on me mentally* in suffering are in belief killing me! *Stopping my work* that none but me can do in their supreme selfishness; how unlike the example I have left them! Tell this to Miss Brown, Mr. McLauthlen, Mrs. Atkinson, and Miss Norman but do not let them know they *can call* on me thus if they are doing this ignorantly and if they do it consciously tell *McLauthlen* and *them all* it would be no greater crime for them to come directly and thrust a dagger into my heart they are just as surely in belief killing me and committing murder.

"The sin lies at their door and for them to meet its penalty *sometime*. *You can teach* them better, see you do this.

"O! Harry, the book must stop. I can do no more now if ever. They lay on me suffering inconceivable.

"If the students will continue to think of me and call on me, I shall *at last* defend myself and this will be to cut them off from me utterly in a spiritual sense by a bridge they cannot pass over and the effect of this on them they will then learn.

[1] Milmine: *op. cit.*, p. 225.

"I will let you hear from me as soon as I can bear this on account of my health; and will return to prosecute my work on the Book as soon as I can safely. I am going far away and shall remain until you will do your part and give me some better prospect.

"Ever *truly,*

"MARY." [1]

We have seen how by an irony of fate this second edition of which Mrs. Eddy here speaks so feelingly to Mr. Spofford eventually was turned into a personal attack on the same Mr. Spofford on whom at this time Mrs. Eddy leaned so heavily. The second, as well as the first, edition is now tabooed and as far as possible suppressed. Two other editions followed and then Mrs. Eddy decided to have her fifth edition revised by one who had been a Unitarian minister, but had retired from the ministry and devoted himself to writing and editing. After examining the manuscript, Mr. Wiggin told Mrs. Eddy "that he could do nothing by merely correcting her manuscript; that to improve it he would have largely to rewrite it. To his surprise, she willingly consented to this. During the autumn of 1885 Mr. Wiggin occupied himself with this task, which Mrs. Eddy carefully supervised to see that he did not in the least modify her views and that her favorite phrases were allowed to stand." [2]

Mr. Wiggin rendered other services to Mrs. Eddy. Though he never was a Christian Scientist, he did for four years editorial work for the *Journal of Christian Science,* and did his best "to keep Mrs. Eddy from making herself ridiculous," as he himself often said. Mrs. Eddy appreciated his services and sometimes she would slyly remark: "Mr. Wiggin, do you know, I sometimes believe God speaks to me through you." On one occasion Mr. Wiggin became even co-author of *Science and Health:* he persuaded his literary client to omit a portion of the chapter on Malicious Animal Magnetism, because he considered it libelous, and in order not to have to renumber the

---

[1] Milmine: *op. cit.,* p. 214, italics are Mrs. Eddy's. The original punctuation has been preserved.

[2] *Ibid.,* p. 328.

pages, she inserted at Mr. Wiggin's suggestion a sermon he had written for her, cutting it down to the required size. "The chapter was called 'Wayside Hints (Supplementary), and Mrs. Eddy put her seal upon it by inserting under the subject of squareness a tribute to her deceased husband: 'We need good square men everywhere. Such a man was my late husband, Dr. Asa G. Eddy.' " [1]

"Many a time," writes Mr. Peabody, "have I heard Mr. Wiggin say with a chuckle of amusement that it was a source of much mirth to him to hear from time to time Mrs. Eddy's devotees exclaim, with pious earnestness, that the chapter he had written at so much per word was the very most divinely-inspired portion of the divine volume." [2]

Since Mr. Wiggin was so closely associated with Mrs. Eddy and knew her so intimately, it will be interesting to read part of his criticism on Christian Science, written by him about this time to an old college friend and reproduced in part by Miss Milmine. I shall select chiefly that section which applies directly to Mrs. Eddy and her textbook.

"As for the High Priestess of it (of Christian Science)," he wrote, ". . . she is—well, I could *tell* you, but not write. An awfully (I use the word advisedly) smart woman, acute, shrewd, but not well-read, nor in any way learned. What she has, as documents clearly show, she got from P. P. Quimby of Portland, Maine, whom she eulogized after death as the great leader and her special teacher. . . . She tried to answer the charge of the adoption of Quimby's ideas, and called me in to counsel her about it; but her only answer (in print) was that, if she said such things twenty years ago, she must have been under the influence of *animal magnetism*, which is *her* devil. Much more could I say if you were here. . . .

"Only experience can teach these fanatics (the Christian Scientists), i. e., the real believers, not the charlatans who go into it for money. . . . As for the book, if you have any edition since December, 1885, it had my supervision. Though now she is getting out an entirely new edition, with which I

---

[1] Milmine: *op. cit.*, p. 335.
[2] Peabody: *op. cit.*, p. 68.

have nothing to do, and occasionlly she has made changes, whereof I did not know. The chapter B—— told you of is rather fanciful, though, to use Mrs. Eddy's language in her last note, 'her friends think it a gem.' It is the one called 'Wayside Hints,' and was added after the work was not only in type, but cast, because she wished to take out some twenty pages of diatribe on her dissenters. . . . I do not think it will greatly edify you, the chapter. As for clearness, many Christian Science people thought her early editions much better, because they sounded more *like* Mrs. Eddy. The truth is, she does not care to have her paragraphs clear, and delights in so expressing herself that her words may have various readings and meanings. Really that is one of the tricks of the trade. You know sibyls have always been thus oracular, to 'keep the word of promise to the ear and break it to the hope.'

"Quimby had definite ideas, but Mrs. Eddy has not understood them. . . .

"When I first knew Christian Science, I wrote a defensive pamphlet called 'Christian Science and the Bible' (though I did not believe the doctrine). . . . I found fair game in the assaults of orthodoxy upon Mrs. Eddy, and support in the supernaturalism of the Bible; but I did not pretend to give an exposition of Christian Science, and I did not know the old lady as well as I do now.

"No, Swedenborg and all other such writers, are sealed books to her. She cannot understand such utterances, and never could, but dollars and cents she understands thoroughly.

"Her influence is wonderful. . . ." [1]

The space devoted here to the composition and make-up of *Science and Health* is not excessive considering the importance of the "textbook" for every Christian Scientist. Mrs. Eddy needed a divine book to attain her end and she created one. On other points she might recede; on this one she must remain firm. For this purpose she placed herself—by innuendo at least—on a level with Christ. She saw herself in the woman of the Apocalypse (chapter 12), clothed with the sun, the

---

[1] Milmine: *op. cit.,* pp. 337-339.

moon under her feet, and upon her head a crown of twelve stars. She writes, apocalyptically enough:

"The twelfth chapter of the Apocalypse . . . has a special suggestiveness in connection with this nineteenth century. In the opening of the sixth seal, typical of six thousand years since Adam, the distinctive feature has special reference to the present age. . . . The woman in the Apocalypse is the vignette which illustrates as man the spiritual idea of God, and God and man as the divine Principle and divine idea. . . . As Elias represents the fatherhood of God through Jesus, so the Revelator completes this figure with woman as the spiritual idea or type of God's motherhood." [1]

Mrs. Eddy went so far as to place her "precious volume" above the Bible. "Even the Scriptures," she declares, "gave no direct interpretation of the Scientific basis for demonstrating the spiritual Principle of healing, until our Heavenly Father saw fit, through the Key to the Scriptures in *Science and Health*, to unlock this 'mystery of godliness.'" [2]

Mrs. Eddy was evidently doing her very best to secure for her book, the fruit of her tireless industry, the object of her greatest affections, that honor, veneration and implicit belief which Protestantism was wont to bestow on the Bible, and on the Bible alone. She took, at the same time, all necessary precautions that the mother should not be forgotten in the growing fame of the child. The *Church Manual*, first issued in 1895, as it regulates all the details of Christian Science church life, became the most efficient instrument for this purpose. Whenever any new emergency arose, a new by-law was added, to which all Christian Scientists at once religiously bowed. For by this time Mrs. Eddy had trained her vine so as to be responsive to the slightest touch of her hand. A set of by-laws, bearing on the Textbook, serve the purpose, not only of enhancing the prestige of the book and proclaiming the fame of its author, but also of securing for it a ready sale. For these

---

[1] *Science and Health*, pp. 559-562.

[2] *Retrospection*, p. 47. Cf. *Christian Science Journal*, November, 1885. "What a triumphant career is this for a woman! Can it be anything less than the tabernacle of God with men, the fulfillment of the vision of the lonely seer on the Isle of Patmos, the wonder in heaven delivering the child which shall rule all nations?"

reasons some of the by-laws form an interesting study. One
secures Mrs. Eddy's honor by imposing on every member the
bounden duty not to quote from her works without mentioning
her name:

> "*Art.* XV, *sect.* 1: To pour into the ear of listeners the
> sacred revelations of Christian Science indiscriminately, or
> without characterizing their origin, and thus distinguishing
> them from the writings of authors who think at random on
> this subject, is to lose some weight in the scale of right think-
> ing. Therefore it is the duty of every member of this Church,
> when publicly reading or quoting from the books or poems
> of our Pastor Emeritus, first to announce the name of the
> author. Members shall also instruct their pupils to adopt
> the aforenamed method for the benefit of our Cause."

Another by-law copes with the danger that might arise to
the Cause from the too great prominence which some preachers
were quickly acquiring. To obviate such a calamity, a
ukase went out in 1895 which demanded of all pastors to step
down from their pulpits and to make room for the one, only and
perpetual preacher and pastor, the Textbook:[1]

> "*Art.* XIV, *sect.* 1: I, Mary Baker Eddy, ordain the Bible
> and *Science and Health with Key to the Scriptures*, Pastor
> over The Mother Church,—the First Church of Christ, Scien-
> tist, in Boston, Massachusetts . . . they will continue to
> preach for this Church and the world."

This leaves the Christian Science services without preachers
and without sermons. Instead, two readers are appointed to
hold office for the term of three years. Originally, the First
Reader, the one higher in dignity and drawing a larger salary,
was to read from the Bible, and the Second Reader, from
Science and Health; but Mrs. Eddy soon reversed this order,
and now the First Reader reads the so-called "correlative"

---

[1] In *Miscellaneous Writings* (p. 382) Mrs. Eddy makes this ludicrous
pronouncement even more general, saying: "In 1895 I ordained that the
Bible and *Science and Health with Key to the Scriptures,* the Christian
Science textbook, be the pastor, on this planet, of all the churches of the
Christian Science denomination. . . . Whenever and wherever a church
of Christian Science is established, its pastor is the Bible and my book."

passages from the Textbook. This reading is called the Lesson-Sermon, which, since 1897, the First Reader always introduces with the following explanatory note:

"FRIENDS: The Bible and the Christian Science Textbook are our only preachers. We shall now read Scriptural texts, and their correlative passages from our denominational textbook—these comprise our sermon. The canonical writings together with the word of our textbook, corroborating and explaining the Bible texts in their spiritual import and application to all ages, past, present and future, constitute a sermon, undivorced from truth, uncontaminated and unfettered by human hypotheses, and divinely authorized.

"The afternoon (or evening) service is a repetition of the morning service." [1]

To guard against the danger that a Reader might circumvent the law abolishing preaching by adding explanations to his reading, the Readers are warned against such an abuse of power.

"*Art.* III, *sect.* 6: They (namely the Readers) shall make no remarks explanatory of the LESSON-SERMON at any time, but they shall read all notices and remarks that may be printed in the *Christian Science Quarterly.* This By-Law applies to Readers in all the branch churches." [2]

If Mrs. Eddy, by effectually crushing all individuality out of Christian Science, raised herself to a position of authority to which very few mortals ever aspired, she did not on that account lose sight of the mere material advantages which accrued to her from this monopoly. She had advertised the first edition of *Science and Health* as a book "that affords an opportunity to acquire a profession by which you can accumulate a fortune." [3] Consistently with this creed, she took extraordinary pains to make her fortune out of her book. A few facts will make this clear. Her book was *hers*, and no one was entitled to

---

[1] Consult any number of *Christian Science Quarterly.*
[2] Branch churches are all called Christian Science churches with the one exception of *The Mother Church,* the First Church of Christ, Scientist, in Boston, Mass.
[3] Cf. Milmine: *op. cit.,* in *McClure's Magazine,* Vol. XXXI, p. 186.

derive any benefit from it except he was willing and able to own his own copy.

"*Art.* VIII, *sect.* 9: No member shall use written formulas, nor permit his patients or pupils to use them as auxiliaries to teaching Christian Science, or for healing the sick. Whatever is requisite for either, is contained in the books of the Discoverer and Founder of Christian Science. Sometimes she may strengthen the faith by a written text as no one else can.

"*Sect.* 10: A member of this Church shall not publish profuse quotations from Mary Baker Eddy's copyrighted works without her permission and shall not plagiarize her writings. This By-Law not only calls more serious attention to the Commandment of the Decalogue, but tends to prevent Christian Science from being *adulterated*."

Yet lest there should remain any doubt about her wishes in this so important matter, she published in *Science and Health* a statement which leaves nothing to be desired in point of clearness. She says:

"A Christian Scientist requires my work *Science and Health* for his text-book, and so do all his students and patients. Why? *First:* Because it is the voice of Truth to this age, and contains the whole of Christian Science, or the Science of healing through Mind. *Second:* Because it was the first published book containing a statement of Christian Science; because it gave the first rules for demonstrating this Science, and registered the revealed Truth, uncontaminated by human hypotheses. Other works which have borrowed from this book without giving it credit, have adulterated the Science. *Third:* Because this book has done more for teacher and student, for healer and patient, than has been accomplished by other books." [1]

In order to multiply its sale, Mrs. Eddy multiplied its editions and expected that at least every practitioner should

---

[1] *Science and Health,* p. 456. Malevolent critics have added a fourth and more cogent reason than any of the others: it is this that every volume sold brought in the sum of three dollars, the greater part of which was pure profit for Mrs. Eddy. It is through the sale of this book chiefly that she amassed a fortune of several millions.

use always the latest edition, however trivial might be the
changes she had introduced. The extremes to which she went
in this direction can be gauged from a notice that appeared in
the *Journal* as late as February, 1908, Mrs. Eddy then being
nearly eighty-seven years old. Here is its exact reproduction.

Take Notice

I request Christian Scientists universally to read the
paragraph beginning at line thirty of page 442 in the edition
of *Science and Health* which will be issued February 29. I
consider the information there given to be of *great importance* at this stage of the workings of animal magnetism, and
it will *greatly aid* the students in their individual experiences.

MARY BAKER G. EDDY.

The edition sold fast on the strength of this notice; but
the information of *great importance* which Christian Scientists
thus acquired, filled just two lines inserted in a blank space
at the end of a chapter and necessitated the change of no other
plate of a single page in the book. It would have occupied
considerably less space than the notice recommending its per-
usal and reads as follows: "Christian Scientists, be a law to
yourselves, that mental malpractice can harm you neither when
asleep nor when awake." [1]

As there will be no other occasion to come back on this
subject, the following proofs, among others, of Mrs. Eddy's
commercialism may find a place here. In March, 1897, she
forbade all her followers to teach any student for one year,
commencing on March 14, 1897, the motive for this sweeping
prohibition being the publication of her new work *Miscellaneous
Writings*.

"*Miscellaneous Writings*," she there announced, "is calculated to prepare the minds of all true thinkers to understand the Christian Science textbook more correctly than a
student can. The Bible, *Science and Health with Key to the
Scriptures*, and my other published works are the only proper
instructors for this hour. It shall be the duty of all Christian Scientists to circulate and to sell as many of the books

[1] Cf. Peabody: *op. cit.*, p. 138.

as they can. If a member of The First Church of Christ, Scientist, shall fail to obey this injunction, it will render him liable to lose his membership in this Church."

MARY BAKER G. EDDY.

The following notice needs no comment:

Christian Science Spoons.—On each of these most beautiful spoons is a motto in bas-relief that every person on earth needs to hold in thought. Mother [1] requests that Christian Scientists shall not ask to be informed what this motto is, but each Scientist shall purchase at least one spoon, and those who can afford it, one dozen spoons, that their families may read this motto at every meal, and their guests be made partakers of its simple truth.

MARY BAKER G. EDDY.[2]

The price of these spoons was three dollars for the plain silver one, and five dollars apiece for those with gold plated bowls.

We have exposed abundantly Mrs. Eddy's assumption of superior knowledge, practical infallibility and divine authority for her alleged revelation. It matters little that for Mrs. Eddy everything is supremely natural,[3] and that, consequently, the word revelation can have no intelligible meaning for her, other than that of a dawning of new ideas with no supernatural origin and no supernatural guarantee. That the word revelation did not have for Mrs. Eddy the meaning which Christians attach to it never entered into the minds of her credulous followers. They took her words as they sounded and looked upon her as an inspired prophet. This belief profoundly influenced their thoughts and lives, and, as a fundamental part of their new-found faith, is undoubtedly an important factor in their cures.

We must, however, absolutely reject Mrs. Eddy's claims to a divine revelation. Her conflicting statements about the date of this revelation, Quimby's manuscript as the source of her

---

[1] Mrs. Eddy had reserved the endearing title Mother for herself, until Mr. Clemens' attacks induced her to exchange it for that of Leader. Cf. Mark Twain: *Christian Science* (New York, 1907), pp. 331 ff.

[2] Peabody: *op. cit.*, pp. 143 ff., 134 ff.

[3] "Now as then his mighty works are not supernatural, but supremely natural." *Science and Health*, Preface XI.

inspiration, her commercialism, the changes constantly introduced in her work, all tell against her. Mr. Peabody reaches this conclusion.

"When the most corrupt tree in the orchard brings forth the sweetest and most beautiful fruit of all, it will be believed that Mary Baker Eddy *can* be the channel through which God has revealed Himself to mankind, and it will not be believed until then. . . . I am of those who believe that there can be no religion but a religion based on revelation. Either God reveals Himself to us, or He remains unknown and unknowable. . . . This great truth has been and is the common belief of mankind, and every unprincipled person who has appealed to human credulity along religious lines, knowing mankind so to believe, has faked a revelation from God. Mrs. Eddy has put herself in a class by herself by the boldness, the irreverence, the recklessness, the blasphemy of her pretended intimacy with God." [1]

[1] Peabody: *op. cit.*, p. 56.

CHAPTER IV

METAPHYSICAL BASIS

"It is difficult to give a condensed summary of the contents of *Science and Health* because of the lack of order and system in its arrangement and in its ideas. The chapters themselves have several times been shifted around in a different order, and they might be shuffled again without any loss of logic. The very titles of the chapters sometimes have little aptness as designations of their contents. The order of the paragraphs in the chapters also follows no inherent plan and progress and frequently baffles the reader to find and follow any thread of connection. There are only a few fundamental ideas in the book, and these are endlessly iterated and reiterated until one's sense of interest and attention is dulled into drowsiness: reading the book is like listening to a player on a violin who keeps sawing on one string and making few variations on that. One really has to maintain a firm grip on his attention to keep from falling into a stupor while perusing these monotonous pages." [1]

This estimate of Dr. Snowden's is well deserved. It is the general complaint of all who had to study Mrs. Eddy's textbook.

"For," says Mark Twain, "of all the strange and frantic and incomprehensible and uninterpretable books which the imagination of man has created, surely this one is the prize sample. It is written with a limitless confidence and complacency, and with a dash and stir and earnestness which often compel the effects of eloquence, even when the words do not seem to have any traceable meaning." [2]

Mrs. Eddy admits the indictment, but places the blame on "the inadequacy of material terms" for metaphysical state-

[1] Snowden: *The Truth about Christian Science,* p. 102.
[2] Mark Twain: *Christian Science* (New York, 1907), p. 29.

60

ments and the consequent difficulty of so expressing metaphysical ideas as to make them comprehensible to any reader
who has not personally *demonstrated* Christian Science. "The
great difficulty is to give the right impression when translating
material terms back into the original spiritual tongue." [1]

The real reasons for Mrs. Eddy's difficulties are not the
inadequacy of the English language, but are in the first place
the author's lack of logical thinking and of any mental training
in philosophical reasoning, and, secondly, her custom of putting
strange, unconventional and fanciful meanings on the most
ordinary words, thus intentionally introducing a source of
confusion and obscurity of thought where clearness of expression is above all desired. Her *Key to the Scripture*, representing as it does her spiritual interpretation of the sacred text,
is nothing but just such a jumble of words. To give a few
examples, Issachar, Jacob's son, is defined as *corporeal belief;*
Jacob himself as *a corporeal mortal embracing duplicity, re-
pentance, sensualism*, and yet—*mirabile dictu*—representing at
the same time *Inspiration and the Revelation of Science* (Christian Science of course); Jerusalem becomes *mortal belief and
knowledge, obtained from the five corporeal senses;* Jesus is
the highest human corporeal concept of the divine idea; Joseph
is, like Jacob, *a corporeal mortal, but with a higher sense of
Truth, rebuking mortal belief or error;* Judah is, like Issachar,
only more so *a corporeal material belief progressing and disappearing*, while at the same time it is *the spiritual understanding
of God and man appearing*.[2]

Not only is this freedom with human speech employed for
the spiritual interpretation of the *Scripture*, but it runs all
through her work. "After the author's sacred discovery," she
herself says, "she affixed the name *Science* to Christianity; the
name *error* to corporeal sense, and the name *substance* to
Mind." [3]   In *Retrospection and Introspection* Mrs. Eddy
makes a similar avowal and is to all appearances quite satisfied
with her achievement.

---

[1] *Science and Health*, p. 115.
[2] *Ibid., Glossary*, p. 589.
[3] *Ibid.*, p. 483.

"The Bible was my textbook. It answered my question as to how I was healed; but the Scriptures had to me *a new meaning, a new tongue*. Their spiritual significance appeared; and I apprehended for the first time, in their spiritual meaning Jesus' teaching and demonstration, and the Principle and rule of spiritual Science and Metaphysical Healing,—in a word, Christian Science.

"I named it *Christian*, because it is compassionate, helpful and spiritual. God I called *Immortal Mind*. That which sins, suffers and dies I named *mortal mind*. The physical senses, or sensuous nature, I called *error* and *shadow*. Soul I denominated *Substance*, because soul alone is truly substantial. God I characterized as individual entity, but His corporeality I denied. The Real I claimed as eternal; and its antipodes, or the temporal, I described as unreal. Spirit I called the *reality*; and matter, the *unreality*." [1]

Here then we have a key to Mrs. Eddy's writings which will prove much more serviceable than her so-called key to the Scripture ever will be. Why she should not call God, the physical senses, the soul, matter and the other things by their rightful names is inexplicable except on the ground that she wished to mystify her students by unintelligible jargon. That she, Mrs. Eddy, the founder of a new religion and of a new Church, called the senses an error and a shadow, and called spirit the reality, and matter the unreality, neither added to, nor detracted from, the received connotation of these words. With as much reason she might call a horse a house, and a house a horse, and nobody would know the drift of her conversation, but forsooth, the privileges of the *revelator* and the prophet of a new religion would be safe. For Mrs. Eddy *the real* means the eternal, *the unreal* means matter, that which sins, suffers and dies, is called *mortal mind*: such are a few of the choice flowers taken from Mrs. Eddy's vocabulary; not as though there was anything in these terms that made them synonymous, but Mrs. Eddy without proof or reason just chose to *call, name, denominate or characterize* them so, no doubt because she thus rendered herself less intelligible, more mystifying. After these

[1] *Retrospection*, p. 29-30.

preliminaries we may set ourselves to the task of explaining the principles that underlie Christian Science and New Thought.

I. THE UNIVERSAL MIND

A chasm, wide and deep, must at the very beginning be drawn between *Mind* and *mind*. With a capital, Mind is God, the real; with a small initial, mind is mortal mind, error, illusion, the unreal.

Mind (with a capital M) is defined in the Glossary as "The only I, or Us"; again as "the only Spirit, as Soul, as divine Principle, and Substance, as Life, Truth and Love." Again it is defined as "the one God," as the "Deity which outlines, but is not outlined." It is expressly stated that it is not that which is *in* man (small m), but that it is the divine Principle (or God) of whom Man (with a capital M) is the full and perfect expression.[1]

Here we possess a wealth of synonyms which, on the whole, advance us but little. So we try again.

God is the great I AM. He is all-knowing, all-acting, all-wise, all-loving and eternal. He is Principle, Mind, Soul and Spirit. He is Truth and Love. He is all substance. He is Intelligence. God is Life, and Life is the divine Mind, and the divine Mind is eternal; Life, therefore, cannot be limited: it has neither beginning nor end. God is Soul or spirit. Consequently "there is no finite soul or spirit." These terms mean "the only mind and cannot be rendered in the plural." All these terms are consequently absolutely synonymous. "They refer to one absolute God and nothing else." There is not more than one Principle. "Principle is divine, one Life, one Truth, one Love, and this is God omnipotent." "Mind is all and matter is naught is the leading factor in Mind-Science," for "Christian Science reveals incontrovertibly that Mind is All-in-all, that the only realities are the divine Mind and idea."[2]

Here we may be permitted to stop for a few considerations. Mrs. Eddy's concept of God, despite her protests, is pantheistical. In the beginning she objected to calling God a person,

[1] *Science and Health,* p. 591. Cf. pp. 468-469, 587.
[2] *Ibid.,* p. 109.

precisely because, not knowing the import of the word, she imagined it destroyed her pantheistical conception of God. Later on she wrote:

"As the words *person* and *personal* are commonly and ignorantly employed, they often lead, when applied to Deity, to confused and erroneous conceptions of divinity, and its distinction from humanity. If the term personality, as applied to God, means infinite personality, then God *is* infinite *Person*, —in this sense, but not in the lower sense. An infinite Mind and a finite form do not, cannot coalesce." [1]

The expression *Principle*, so dear to Mrs. Eddy, leaves the reader or hearer cold and indifferent. That God should be called Soul is unjustifiable, except on the pantheistic principle that he is the world-soul; or on the scientistic principle that there is no other soul, no other spirit, no created soul and no created spirit. "The term *souls* or *spirits* is as improper as the term *gods*," says Mrs. Eddy. [2]

Is this Pantheism? By no means, retorts Mrs. Eddy. And to prove it, she publishes a small pamphlet of fifteen pages, retailing at twenty-five cents a copy, entitled *Christian Science vs. Pantheism*. There is, however, a hitch in her demonstration, and it lies in the fact that as many other words, so also the word Pantheism receives from the Founder of Christian Science a scientistic twist which takes it out of the common man's vocabulary and gives it a new meaning altogether. "Pantheism," Mrs. Eddy says, "may be defined as a belief in the intelligence of matter." [3] It surely *may be* so defined; Christian Science also may be so defined; no dictionary, however, would agree with this definition. Any dictionary would have told Mrs. Eddy that Pantheism is "the doctrine that the universe is God," or "the system of theology in which it is maintained that the universe is the supreme God." And this is exactly what Mrs. Eddy maintains. A pantheistical conception of the universe,

---

[1] *Science and Health,* p. 116.
[2] *Ibid.,* p. 466. Eddy: *No and Yes* (Boston, 1917), p. 20. "When the term divine Principle is used to signify Deity, it may seem distant or cold until better apprehended. This Principle is Mind, substance.—Life, Truth Love. When understood, Principle is found to be the only term that fully conveys the ideas of God,—one Mind, a perfect Man, and divine Science."
[3] *Ibid.,* p. 129.

undoubtedly, underlies her whole teaching, call it an idealistic Pantheism, if you wish, but Pantheism, just the same. This places Christian Science outside the sphere of genuine Christianity and accounts for the great difference between Mrs. Eddy's conception of God and our own. Our God is Mind and Free Will; hers is only Mind, without any freedom of activity. How this works out in practice remains to be seen.

II. THE UNREALITY OF MATTER

Nothing in Mrs. Eddy's system seems to be more certain than that matter has no existence; but, on the other hand, nothing seems to be more plain than that it has. Is this merely a delusion of *mortal mind?* Is it that Mrs. Eddy did not see the contradiction in her system or is it merely a question of words, a *logomachia*, introduced to baffle and impress those who take Mrs. Eddy seriously? This we have to find out.

The following extract contains in a way Mrs. Eddy's profession of faith in the unreality of matter.

"I, therefore," she says, "plant myself unreservedly on the teachings of Jesus, of his apostles, of the prophets, and on the testimony of the Science of Mind. Other foundations there are none. All other systems—systems based wholly or partly on knowledge gained through the material senses— are reeds shaken by the winds, not houses built on the rock.

"The theories I combat are these: (1) That all is matter; (2) that matter originates in Mind, and is as real as Mind, possessing intelligence and life.

"The first theory, that matter is everything, is quite as reasonable as the second, that Mind and matter coexist and coöperate. One only of the following statements can be true: (1) that everything is matter; (2) that everything is Mind. Which one is it?" [1]

Repeatedly Mrs. Eddy argues, almost pleads with, her readers that God, being Spirit, could not possibly create anything material. Instinctively she felt that by this statement she was taking issue with all theistic philosophers. In the absence of any rational argument she resorts to the practice of impress-

[1] *Science and Health,* pp. 269-270.

ing by the frequency of repetition. On the ground, apparently, that you have only to assert long enough and loud enough, to have almost anything accepted, she again and again dins into the ear of her hearers the same old statement of the unreality, the non-existence, the non-actuality, even the impossibility of matter.

If we should object that if there is anything certain, it is the existence of matter, that we may doubt about its nature, its constituent parts, its final analysis and its origin, but not about its existence of which our senses give us direct evidence, Mrs. Eddy would promptly reply: How can you rely on your senses? Have they not been proved over and over again untrustworthy? If senses play you false when they display before your eyes the mirage of a beautiful, but non-existent landscape, how can you trust them when they impress you with something that cannot possibly exist? Matter cannot exist because it is unreality; the very senses that we suppose give testimony of its existence, are themselves an illusion of the mind: they are no more real than the rest of the material errors.

With the reality and trustworthiness of the senses denied, there is, of course, no possibility of arguing in a rational manner. The only hope of convincing the opponent of his error is to show that neither he nor any one else has ever consistently maintained, throughout, this pretense of a thoroughgoing idealism. Take as an instance the following passages picked at random: On page 277 Mrs. Eddy writes:

"Natural history presents vegetable and animals as preserving their original species,—like producing like. A mineral is not produced by a vegetable, nor the man by the brute. In reproduction, throughout the entire round of nature, the order of genus and species is preserved."

And again on page 211:

"Nerves are not the source of pain nor pleasure. We suffer or enjoy in our dreams, but this pain or pleasure is not communicated through a nerve. A tooth extracted sometimes aches again in belief, and the pain seems to be again in its old place. A limb amputated has continued, in belief, to pain the owner. If the sensation of pain in the limb can return and be prolonged, why could not the limb reappear?"

Surely these passages do not sound like denying the reality of the material world. Even when she is arguing against the reality of matter, as she is in these cases, she is forced to take for granted many things that could not be so but for the existence of matter. The very words she uses—nerves, tooth, limb, vegetable, animal, mineral—are meaningless, if matter is unreal in the full sense of this word. But Mrs. Eddy is not thus easily silenced. She always left a loophole open through which she could retreat when circumstances required. Her final plea, applicable in all emergencies, was that her words did not represent her meaning:

"If our words fail to express our deeds, God will redeem that weakness, and out of the mouth of babes he will perfect praise. . . . The opponents of Christian Science must be charitable, if they would be Christian. If the letter of Christian Science appears inconsistent, they should gain its spiritual meaning, and then the ambiguity will vanish. . . .[1] In Christian Science there are no discords, because its logic is as harmonious as the reasoning of an accurately stated syllogism, or of a properly computed sum in arithmetic." [2]

What, then, is this spiritual meaning Mrs. Eddy boasts of? She tells us that matter is not real, but also that "the real I claimed as eternal, and its antipodes, or the temporal, I *described* as unreal. *Spirit I called the reality, and matter the unreality.*" [3] If we take our clew from these words, we come to the conclusion that, after all, if the expression may be permitted, there is question only of "naming" the child: Spirit *I called* the reality, and matter, the unreality. We should much prefer to speak of the eternal as the eternal, and of the real as the real, and to abide by the meaning our dictionaries predicate of the words. "Real" means anything that is not merely fictitious or imaginary; but if we could take it in the sense of eternal, we would, of course, all agree that God alone is real.

[1] *Science and Health*, p. 354.
[2] *Ibid.*, p. 129.
[3] *Retrospection*, p. 30.

Yet, even now we have not caught the full meaning of Mrs. Eddy's assertion that God is real and the material world unreal. This means not merely that God is eternal and matter is not, but that matter has no existence, I do not say independently of God, what we all would admit, but outside of Mind. Mrs. Eddy is an idealist for whom all realities are ideas. In vain do her Protestant critics labor to prove that she cannot be considered a representative of any of the idealistic schools of philosophy, be it that of Plato, of Fichte, of Schelling, of Hegel, or particularly of Berkeley. Though all these systems undoubtedly differ widely from each other in detail, yet they have this in common among themselves and with Mrs. Eddy and the followers of the New Thought movement, that their world is one of ideas.

There can be no question about this relationship. It cannot, indeed, be proved that Mrs. Eddy directly drew from any of these sources. In fact, the contrary seems to be more likely. It may, nevertheless, be stated with confidence that she came indirectly under their influence. About that time Ralph Waldo Emerson (1803-1882) was making Concord, Massachusetts, the Mecca whither flocked many of the staunchest supporters of a mystical, idealistical and pantheistical naturalism. These formed between themselves a close group of transcendentalists, whose influence made itself widely felt through their literary activities, whether in the writing of books or in the editing of magazines or in the publishing of newspaper articles. From 1840 to 1844 Emerson and Margaret Fuller, "the most intellectual woman of her time in America," published the *Dial*, a quarterly magazine, devoted to the Transcendentalist movement.

A woman of Mrs. Eddy's character, so fond of novelties and of the public gaze, could not but feel the reverberation, so to say, of these bold innovations. The very foundations on which her system rests are to a great extent the conclusions that these philosophers reached. In fact, the chief difference between them lies in this that Mrs. Eddy was not a philosopher at all, but accepted without criticism as the foundation of her practical and religious system of thought the conclusions they tried to establish on rational grounds. Mrs. Eddy's arbitrary method of giving new meanings to old terms renders her perhaps a degree more obscure and unintelligible than the philosophers, but, on the whole, it is condemnation enough to say that with them all she completely discounts the testimony of the senses, thus opening the way to an arbitrary subjectivism.

The necessities of her position as an inspired messenger of God forced Mrs. Eddy to disclaim any connection with contemporary idealism. The New Thought writers, on the other hand, from W. F. Evans downward, gladly admit this kinship on their behalf. They almost look upon Emerson as a prophet of their own. His essay on *Brahma or the Over-Soul* might well be cited in New Thought literature as an introduction to the whole movement. In charming language Emerson extols what Mrs. Eddy tries laboriously to preach in uncouth accents. To show how deeply the modern mind-movements have drunk from the waters of New England Transcendentalism, the following lengthy extracts from Emerson's *Over-Soul* will here be given without comment.

"Man is a stream whose source is hidden. . . . Always our being is descending into us from we know not whence. The most exact calculator has no prescience that somewhat incalculable may not balk the very next moment. I am constrained every moment to acknowledge a higher origin for events than the will I call mine. . . . As with events, so it is with thoughts. When I watch that flowing river which, out of regions I see not, pours for a season its streams into me,—I see that I am a pensioner—not a cause, but a surprised spectator of this ethereal water; that I desire and look up, and put myself in the attitude of reception, but from some alien energy the visions come." [1]

"We live in succession, in division, in parts, in particles. Meantime within man is the soul of the whole; the wise silence; the universal beauty to which every part and particle is equally related; the eternal ONE. And this deep power in which we exist and whose beatitude is all accessible to us, is not only self-sufficing and perfect in every hour, but *the act of seeing and the thing seen, the seer and the spectacle,*

[1] Emerson's *Essays*, First Series (Chicago), p. 254.

the subject and the object are one. We see the world piece by piece, as the sun, the moon, the animal, the tree; but the whole of which these are the shining parts, is the soul." [1]

"A wise old proverb says, 'God comes to us without bell': that is, as there is no screen or ceiling between our heads and the infinite heavens, *so is there no bar or wall in the soul where man, the effect, ceases, and God, the cause, begins.* The walls are taken away. We lie open on one side to the deeps of spiritual nature, to all the attributes of God. . . . The soul circumscribeth all things. As I have said *it contradicts all experience. . . . Some thoughts always find us young and keep us so. . . .* The soul looketh steadily forward, creating a world always before her, and leaving worlds always behind her. She has no dates, nor rites, nor persons, nor specialties, nor men. The soul knows only the soul. All else is idle weeds for her wearing." [2]

"Ineffable is the union of man and God in every act of the soul. The simplest person, who in his integrity worships God, becomes God; yet forever and ever the influx of this better and universal self is new and unsearchable. . . . When we have broken our god of tradition and ceased from our god of rhetoric, then may God fire the heart with his presence. It is the doubling of the heart itself, nay, the infinite enlargement of the heart with a power of growth to a new infinity on every side." [3]

We are now enabled to give a more connected account of Christian Science philosophy. Its often repeated statements that matter is nothing, is unreal, unactual, even non-existent, could be paralleled by an equally formidable array of testimonies to the effect that matter, though by no means real in the Eddian sense of the word, is quite real in its ordinary sense. Occasionally Mrs. Eddy herself forgets the rôle she is playing and applies the word *real* to such unrealities as sin, sickness and death. "Sin, sickness and death," she says, "are the vague *realities* of human conclusions. To material sense the unreal is the real until this sense is corrected by Christian Science." [4]

[1] Emerson: *op. cit.,* p. 255.
[2] *Ibid.,* p. 257-260.
[3] *Ibid.,* p. 277.
[4] *Science and Health,* p. 297.

Mrs. Eddy's ideal world—and this applies with equal force to New Thought—in spite of all assertions to the contrary, is not a world of fancy and fiction. It is a world in which "things are thoughts, and thoughts are things." Thus understood, this ideal world is not without grandeur: taken in the abstract, it is rather an improvement on some other idealistic conceptions of the world. For the Mind that thinks such splendid thoughts as the world, nature, the universe, man himself included, is, after all, the Divine Mind. That this truth is indissolubly linked with the grossest errors, accompanied with a denial of the trustworthiness of the senses and the materiality of matter; that, at least implicitly, it holds these thoughts to be the necessary operations of the divine Mind; that it explicitly denies secondary causes and secondary causality, these are so many flaws, very serious in themselves, and sufficient to wreck the whole system; yet they do not detract from that grand and true conception of God as the author of all that is. Herein lies one of the reasons why so many intelligent men, in spite of all the shortcomings of this new religion, and in spite of all opposition to it, still continue to proclaim themselves convinced and loyal Christian Scientists.

Others are attracted by the mystical element which pervades its teaching. Taken in its pragmatical sense as a value judgment, the unreality of matter, that means its fleetiness, its unstable and transitory character, its lack of intrinsic and permanent value, strongly appealed to many a Catholic saint to whom the visible world became more and more unreal as he grew more and more in the love of God. Yet what a difference in attitude between these men who forsook the world to serve God, and Mrs. Eddy who claimed to serve God and who denied the reality of matter, the more surely to acquire the material goods and comforts of this world! There is no better criterion of sincerity of belief than practice.

Before proceeding to another subject, let us briefly sum up the false conclusions to which Mrs. Eddy's false premises have led her. These are as follows: Since God alone is real, the world, plants, animals, man are one and all His ideas. These individualized ideas have no real activity of their own, but their whole seeming activity is *directly* from God.[1]   God's ideas are as necessary as Himself.   This identification is so complete that Mrs. Eddy finds herself compelled to speak of man, not only as immortal, but as eternal; of his birth and death as unreal, as mere phenomena and illusions; of his waxing old as a fiction; of his body and senses as errors; of his needs and wants as mere beliefs.   It is to these beliefs that we must now turn our attention.

[1] It may not be out of place to recall here that Malebranche (1638-1715) and other Catholic philosophers have held similar views.

CHAPTER V

IF Mrs. Eddy's metaphysics are difficult, her psychology is impossible. It is only by willfully closing her eyes to evidence that stares her everywhere in the face, that she can propound the views that underlie all her teaching. If we believe, with Mrs. Eddy, that there is only one Mind, how account for the fact of the many contradictory ideas that are current? If with her we deny the existence of matter, how can we account even for the mere concept of matter in general and of numberless material objects? If all things that in our foolish ignorance we held to be real, are in fact unreal, how can we account for the belief in their reality? For surely, if matter is an unreality, then, of all mysteries the belief in matter is the most mysterious. The common sense of mankind will rightly consider these questions an acid test which will prove or disprove Mrs. Eddy's system. If she cannot satisfy us on the origin and nature of this universal belief in matter, her metaphysics must go to pieces on this rock of truth.

Mrs. Eddy distinguishes, obscurely enough, between three sorts of mental acts which she christens belief, faith and understanding. A knowledge of these is, to say the least, as necessary for a proper evaluation of Christian Science as is the doctrine concerning the All-ness of God. The fact that this inquiry will lead into subtle, and perhaps unintelligible distinctions, into a region where Mrs. Eddy's own mind is bemuddled, must not stop us from attempting it. The fundamental discrimination between these three concepts in Mrs. Eddy's mind is this, that understanding or science is the highest possible knowledge, the only one that has a right to live, while faith is an intermediary state of mind, hard to describe as it seems to partake of both belief and understanding, and belief

73

is always an error.   We shall begin our investigation with the latter.

I.   BELIEF

Mrs. Eddy, despite a wealth of synonyms that she employs, nowhere clearly defines what she means by belief.   And how could she, seeing that belief is something negative, an error, an illusion, an unreality, a nothing?   Scholastics used to distinguish between the mere absence of things (*absentia rei*) and the *absentia* or *privatio rei debitae*, the absence of things that should be present, that means defects.   For Mrs. Eddy belief is essentially a defect which somehow exists somewhere.   It is not, as one might be inclined to infer, a merely subjective disposition —though it is essentially this; it is not a mere discrepancy between subjective mind and objective reality—though it is also this; but it is in some way objective, creating for itself in some mysterious manner a whole world of evil, which, nevertheless, has no existence outside this realm of belief.

For Mrs. Eddy every belief is error.   The word has an absolutely odious significance and can no longer be employed to express intellectual conviction, or intellectual surmise; it must be used only to express that which is not so in reality. Now, as according to Mrs. Eddy the whole material world is not so, the whole world is the object, yea, the creation of belief.   Among this stock of false beliefs that exist somehow in the world, we may mention the belief in matter, or the materiality of the universe; the belief in the laws of nature; the belief in the existence of our own bodies; the belief in the trustworthiness, nay, the existence of our senses; the belief in the reality of sickness; the belief in the reality of sin; the belief in the reality of death; the belief in the necessity of drugs and the necessity of hygiene; the belief in the reality of evil and misery of all kinds, of poverty and pain, of poison and destructive physical powers; the belief even in the existence and separate powers of created minds; the belief also in the necessity of food and drink for the sustenance of life; the belief of men being born in time, growing up as children, increasing in size with age, declining with the advancing years and finally, being subject to the inevitable decree of death: all these beliefs are so many falsehoods and errors of *mortal mind*, of which the Christian Scientist must rid himself.

Another group of beliefs, much less extensive, but hardly less comprehensive and sweeping than the former, springs from the first one of Mrs. Eddy's great metaphysical principles, namely that God is All-in-all. This group of errors is characterized especially by the belief in the existence of minds many, and souls many, with faculties and powers of their own, this, in Mrs. Eddy's philosophy, a most pernicious heresy, derogating greatly from the supreme and absolute oneness of divine Mind.

A third group of erroneous beliefs seems to have its origin in that unaccountably strange experience that bodies which have no real existence, nevertheless, are diseased or disabled, and make man feel rather uncomfortable at times. Little "camels" these, which a good Christian Scientist is expected to swallow without wincing!

For all these false beliefs are easily dismissed by the supreme and overpowering conviction that God, being Good and Mind, is All-in-all; that consequently there can be no matter; there can be no individual created mind, and, seeing that God is supremely good, there can be no evil. There can be no sickness, for a variety of reasons: on the one hand, the goodness of God cannot create what is evil; but sickness is evil; consequently, there cannot be any sickness; in the second place, sickness is a bodily state; but there is no human body that could be sick and mind cannot be sick, consequently there is no sickness. Similarly, there is no sin, since God, Who is All-in-all and the author of all things, cannot sin; there is no death, since death is something evil, and, besides, life cannot die; there is no need of food or drink or raiment, since these are for the benefit of a body that has no real existence. This is the lesson that we have to learn before we can share in the inestimable blessings of Christian Science.

Such is that logic of a Christian Scientist of which Mrs. Eddy boasts that it is "as harmonious as the reasoning of an accurately stated syllogism or of a properly computed sum in arithmetic." [1] Granting the premises, the process of reasoning is, indeed, logical enough. But there is in logic something else besides mere reasoning. It teaches certain lines of argument which will help the sincere inquirer to detect error and reach the truth. One of these arguments is called *reductio ad absurdum*. If by logically following your premises you reach conclusions that are manifestly absurd, it is time to face about and examine anew your premises, for undoubtedly there is some hidden error lurking in them. If ever, this is a case where the *reductio ad absurdum* finds its fullest exemplification.

II.   MORTAL MIND

Mrs. Eddy herself felt the incongruity of allowing these false beliefs to hang, as it were, in the air. As they are false, they cannot possibly be in the Mind of God; and as in reality, so Mrs. Eddy teaches, there are no created minds, these beliefs must be acts without an actor, deeds without any one to do them. To overcome this anomaly, Mrs. Eddy introduces a *deum ex machina*, the so-called mortal mind, whose nature and origin no person on earth, not even Mrs. Eddy herself, could explain.

Mrs. Eddy calls this term *mortal mind* "a solecism in language," and admits that it "involves an improper use of the word *mind*." [2] You may, if you prefer, choose other names and call it, for instance, hypnotism or animal magnetism; for Mrs. Eddy is no puritan on close and exact definitions. In fact, the vaguer they are, the better they suit: you will get along much better by not being too precise. "As used in Christian Science," Mrs. Eddy tells us, "animal magnetism or hypnotism is the specific term for error, or *mortal mind*. It is the false belief that mind is in matter, and both evil and good; that evil is as real as goodness and more powerful. This belief has not one quality of Truth or good." [3]

At best, therefore, this term mortal mind is a concession to common usage. For, we are told, "usage classes both evil

---

[1] *Science and Health*, p. 129.
[2] *Ibid.*, p. 114.
[3] *Ibid.*, p. 103.

and good together as *mind*; therefore, to be understood, the author calls sick and sinful humanity *mortal mind*, meaning by this term the flesh, opposed to Spirit, the human mind, and evil, in contradistinction to the divine Mind, or Truth and good." [1] Not only does Mrs. Eddy concede that mortal mind is a "spiritually unscientific definition."—she should rather say a conglomeration of contradictories—but she finally grants that "this so-called mind is a myth." [2] "Indeed," Mrs. Eddy says, "if a better word or phrase could be suggested, it would be used; but in expressing the new tongue, we must sometimes recur to the old and imperfect, and the new wine of the Spirit has to be poured into the old bottles of the letter." [3]

So much for the term itself; but how about its meaning? From the citations just made we learn that it is "sick and sinful humanity," "the flesh," "the human mind" and "evil." These are intelligible concepts, even if we might justifiably quarrel about the juxtaposition of the flesh, the human mind and evil as synonymous expressions. These, I say, are intelligible concepts, as long as we take these words in their ordinary meaning; but in Mrs. Eddy's theories all these things are unrealities, not only in the sense that they are opposed to the Supreme Reality of God, but even in the sense that they can have no existence whatever. For God being the only Reality, the Cause of all things, and supremely good, there can be no place anywhere for such concepts as those just described. Hence Mrs. Eddy's *"harmonious logic,"* again, is not at fault when she tells us at last that "as Mind is immortal, the phrase *mortal mind* implies something untrue and, therefore, unreal; and as the phrase is used in teaching Christian Science, it is meant to denote something which has no real existence." [4]

As mortal mind is not mind at all,[5] and as it cannot be matter long since ruled out of court, but as it must be something—else why should Mrs. Eddy labor so hard to make plain what it means—we reach at last the sublime conclusion that it

[1] *Science and Health*, p. 114.
[2] *Ibid.*, p. 152.
[3] *Ibid.*, p. 114.
[4] *Ibid.*, p. 114.
[5] "What is termed mortal mind, or carnal mind—erring, sinning and dependent on matter for manifestation and life—is not Mind." *Ibid.*, p. 311.

is "something which has no real existence," that means, something which is nothing, and nothing which is something.

In other words, Mrs. Eddy is unable to get out of the entanglements into which her system has led her!

III.   THE WORKS OF MORTAL MIND, SO-CALLED

And yet, how infinitely powerful is this nothing which is something! In the first place—*mirabile dictu*—though itself "is based on the evidence of physical senses which makes minds many," yet in turn all the bodily organisms, and therefore all the physical senses, are created by it: "My discovery that erring, mortal, misnamed *mind* produces all the organisms of the mortal body, set my thoughts to work in new channels and led up to my demonstration of the proposition that Mind is all, and matter is naught, as the leading factor in Mind-science." [1] This in spite of the fact that all causation is reserved to the one primal cause, God: "There is but one primal cause. Therefore there can be no effect from any other cause; and there can be no reality in aught which proceeds not from this great and only cause. Sin, sickness, disease, and death belong not to the Science of Being. They are the errors which presuppose the absence of Truth." [2] Consequently, "matter which takes divine power into its own hands and claims to be a creator, *is a fiction*, in which paganism is so sanctioned by society that mankind has caught its moral contagion." [3]

This fiction of a mortal mind, strange as it may sound, is a "Pandora box from which many evils have gone forth, especially despair." From it proceed all diseases, all accidents, all sins, all vices, all mental anxieties, death, aging, weariness and worry. In spite of its unreality, there proceeds from it also that *Red Dragon*, called *Malicious Animal Magnetism*, to which, owing to its prominence in *Scientism*, we have to consecrate a special chapter. Stranger still, from it also proceeds a certain intangible, mystical something which creates an unhealthy atmosphere, against which even Christian Science is frequently powerless. For

[1] *Science and Health*, pp. 108 and 114.
[2] *Ibid.*, p. 207.
[3] *Ibid.*, p. 171.

"the universal belief in *physics* weighs against the high and mighty truths of Christian *metaphysics*. This erroneous general belief—which sustains medicine and produces all medical results—works against Christian Science; and the percentage of power on the side of this Science (that is, Christian Science) must mightily outweigh the power of popular belief, *in order to heal a single case of disease.*" [1]

Here is how Mrs. Eddy explains this strange power of mortal mind:

"Disease arises, like other mental conditions, from association. Since it is a law of mortal mind that certain diseases should be regarded as contagious, this law obtains credit through association,—calling up the fear that creates the image of disease, and its consequent manifestation in the body." [2]

From this it follows that a mother's fears may be her child's disease. The mere thought of sickness may produce it, not merely in the one that harbors this dangerous thought, but in others who are innocent of it:

"If a child is exposed to contagion or infection, the mother is frightened and says, 'My child will be sick.' The law of mortal mind, and her own fears govern her child more than the child's mind governs itself, and produce the very results which might have been prevented through the opposite understanding." [2]

Such is the strange influence of this fiction of a mind that has no real existence.

IV. MORTAL MIND, MIND-CURES AND MEDICINE

To us it seems that we are dangerously near treading on the forbidden ground of the reality of human minds, and dangerously near the theories of mind-healers and thought-curists, whose theories and practices Mrs. Eddy so unsparingly chastizes. To all appearances Mrs. Eddy's *mortal mind* and the *human mind* of other psychotherapists are identical, endowed

[1] *Science and Health*, p. 155.
[2] *Ibid.*, p. 154.

with exactly the same properties and powers, only that—to emphasize this difference once more—*mortal mind* is overburdened with an indefinite number of very erroneous and mischievous beliefs, which *human mind* will look upon as very close approximations to such truths as are within its reach.

As if to confirm this suspicion, Mrs. Eddy refrains from denying all sphere of influence to mortal mind, not only for evil, what we should expect in her system, but even for good. Any good results that drugs may secure, are not to be looked upon as effects of the drug, but of mortal mind and its false belief in their efficacy. An enlightening paragraph of *Science and Health* bears precisely on this point:

"Before this book was published," writes Mrs. Eddy, "other books were in circulation which discussed *mental medicine* and *mind-cure*, operating through the power of the earth's magnetic currents to regulate life and health. Such theories and systems of so-called mind-cures which have sprung up since are as material as the prevailing systems of medicine. *They have their birth in mortal mind* which puts forth a human conception in the name of Science, to match the divine Science of immortal Mind, even as the necromancers of Egypt strove to emulate the wonders wrought by Moses. Such theories have no relationship with Christian Science which rests on the conception of God as all Life, substance and intelligence, and excludes the human mind as a spiritual factor in the healing work. . . . Erroneous mental practice may seem for a time to benefit the sick. but the recovery is not permanent. This is because erroneous methods act on and through the material stratum of the human mind, called brain, which is but a mortal consolidation of material mentality and its suppositional activities. A patient under the influence of mortal mind is healed only by removing the influence on him of this mind, by emptying his thought of the false stimulus and reaction of will-power and filling it with the divine energies of Truth." [1]

Again Mrs. Eddy says:

"Human belief is an autocrat, though not deserving its power. It says to mortals, 'You are wretched' and they be-

[1] *Science and Health,* pp. 185-186.

come so; and nothing can change this state until the belief changes. Human belief says, 'You are happy' and mortals are so; and no circumstances can alter the situation until the belief on this subject changes." [1]

But if mortal mind, mortal belief can relieve suffering, why not be satisfied with this? Why is it necessary to embrace the Christian Science Creed and code of laws? Would it not be just as well to let human mind perform the cure without having recourse to the transcendent help of the eternal Mind? These questions a true Christian Scientist will answer with an emphatic no. For faith-cures are no real cures, but mere make-shifts; they are more than useless; for while they do not cure permanently, they but fasten error on the human mind, and it is in any case better to be suffering until divine Science establishes the Truth than to be perfectly well, and yet hold the erroneous belief that matter is able to suffer. Such is the drift of Mrs. Eddy's teaching; such, the faith of a Christian Scientist. Mrs. Eddy says on this point:

"The medicine of Science is divine Mind, and dishonesty, sensuality, falsehood, revenge, malice are animal propensities and by no means the mental qualities which heal the sick. The hypnotizer employs one error to destroy another. If he heals sickness through a belief, and a belief originally caused the sickness, it is a case of the greater error overcoming the lesser. This greater error thereafter occupies the ground, leaving the case worse than before it was grasped by the stronger error." [2]

And on the contrary:

"Science not only reveals the origin of all disease as wholly mental, but it also declares that all disease is cured by divine Mind. There can be no healing except by this Mind, however much we trust a drug or any other means toward which human faith or endeavor is directed. It is mortal mind, not matter, which brings to the sick whatever good they may seem to receive from drugs. But the sick are never really healed, except by means of the divine power.

[1] *Science and Health*, pp. 296-297.
[2] *Ibid.*, p. 104.

It is only the action of Truth, Life, and Love that can give harmony." [1]

Hence the final conclusion that "Whatever teaches men to have other laws, and acknowledge other power than the divine Mind, is anti-Christian. The good that a poisonous drug seems to do is evil, for it robs man of reliance upon God, omnipotent Mind, and according to belief poisons the human system." Hence also "discomfort under error is preferable to comfort. In no instance is the effect of animal magnetism, recently called hypnotism, other than the effect of illusion. Any seeming benefit derived therefrom is proportional only to one's faith in esoteric magic." [2]

The reader must have noticed the keen anxiety of Mrs. Eddy to draw a clear distinction between her own system of healing and that of others. This attitude of mind, unfortunately for her, is not proper to her; it is characteristic of mind-healers generally, and is evidently an essential part of the trade. Each one has the only genuine brand of mind-healing, leaving all the others out in the cold as mere quacks and charlatans. Mrs. Eddy calls hers divine Science, makes it a real religious creed and stigmatizes all the other systems as essentially wrong and harmful. Yet, as we shall see, the difference is chiefly in the name; the methods and means employed are largely identical; and the effects in one case are no more striking than in the others. Hers is the same position as that taken by a famous mind-healer with whom Mr. Buckley relates the following personal experience:

"There is an old proverb," he says, "that 'when rogues fall out, honest men get their dues.' It also is true that when quacks fall to discrediting each other, principles may be discovered.

"In 1865 there came to Detroit, Michigan, a pupil of Dr. Newton, Bryant by name, who performed cures as successfully as Newton himself. In company with Dr. J. P. Scott, a Presbyterian minister there, I visited Dr. Bryant and saw him operate upon a score or more of patients (one of whom had been supposed to be doomed to a speedy death with ovar-

[1] *Science and Health*, p. 169.
[2] *Ibid.*, p. 101.

ian tumor; Dr. Bryant removed the tumor, after which she lived some months—and died of debility). To comprehend his method fully, I was operated on for dyspepsia.

"About a year later, returning from New Orleans to Memphis, Tennessee, I found on board the steamer Dr. Newton, who had just come from Havana. He told me that in one day eight hundred persons had applied to him in that city. . . . For several hours a day during four days I conversed with him concerning his career and principles. My conviction is that he believed in himself, and also that he would use any means to accomplish his ends. He would glide from fanaticism into hypocrisy, then into fanaticism, and from that into common sense with the rapidity of thought. . . . When I mentioned having seen 'Dr.' Bryant, Dr. Newton instantly denounced him as an 'unmitigated fraud who had no genuine healing power.' He claimed that he had cured Bryant of a malignant disease with which he found him suffering in a hospital; that Bryant had acted as his amanuensis for some time, and then left him, and had since been acting in opposition to him. Knowing that the manipulations by Bryant had been followed by some wonderful results in Detroit, I said to Dr. Newton:

" 'If Bryant be an unmitigated fraud, how do you account for his cures?' 'Oh,' said the doctor, 'they are caused by the faith of the people and the concentration of their minds upon his operations, with the expectation of being cured. Now (said he) none would go to see Bryant unless they had some faith that he might cure them, and when he begins his operations with great positiveness of manner, and they see the crutches he has, and hear the people testify that they have been cured, it produces a tremendous influence upon them; and then he gets them started in the way of exercising, and they do a good many things they thought they could not do; their appetites and spirits revive, and if toning them up can possibly reduce the diseased tendency, many of them will get well.'

"Said I, 'Doctor, pardon me, is not that a correct account of the manner in which you perform your wonderful works?' 'Oh, no,' said he, 'the difference between a genuine healer and a quack like Bryant is as wide as the poles.' " [1]

[1] Buckley: *Faith-Healing, Christian Science and Kindred Phenomena* (New York, 1892), pp. 33-35.

How very much like the attitude Mrs. Eddy took towards all other systems of healing. There can positively be but one brand of mind-healing, and that the brand each one practices in opposition to every one else. But enough of mortal belief; we shall now proceed to discuss Mrs. Eddy's concept of *faith* and *understanding,* as distinguished from mere belief.

V.   FAITH AND UNDERSTANDING

Mrs. Eddy gives us a summary description of the transformation of mortal mind into full understanding, a transformation which she misnames *Scientific translation of mortal mind.* It contains three stages or degrees and leads from *depravity* through the disappearance of false beliefs into full understanding. The first stage is called physical, the second moral and the last spiritual. Here is the exact reproduction of this so-called scientific description:

SCIENTIFIC TRANSLATION OF MORTAL MIND
First degree: Depravity
Physical. Evil beliefs, passions and appetites, fear, depraved will, pride, envy, deceit, hatred, revenge, sin, sickness, disease, death. (All this in the margin is styled *Unreality.*)
Second Degree: Evil beliefs disappearing
Moral. Humanity, honesty, affection, compassion, hope, faith, meekness, temperance. (The marginal gloss calls these *transitional qualities.* As mortal mind is evil, it may be asked whether these transitional qualities also must be considered evil. No direct answer is given.)
Third Degree: Understanding
Spiritual. Wisdom, purity, spiritual understanding, spiritual power, love, health, holiness. (The marginal gloss reads *Reality.* The explanation that follows says: "In the third degree mortal mind disappears; and man as God's image appears." [1]

The second degree is identical with what Mrs. Eddy in other places calls *faith.* As a curative factor, faith stands a degree higher than belief. Of course, the words are often taken to be synonymous, but, in fact, the word faith is of wider im-

[1] *Science and Health,* p. 115.

port. It may mean belief; it may mean trustfulness; it may mean trustworthiness. If it means mere belief, it is, in Mrs. Eddy's words, "as a pendulum swinging between nothing and something, having no fixity"; if it means trustfulness, it signifies that he who has faith entrusts his welfare to others, a condition which Mrs. Eddy characterizes as "the helplessness of a blind faith"; but if it is the highest kind of faith, a faith which should not be called faith, but understanding, it is that disposition which "understands divine Love and how to work out one's own salvation with fear and trembling." [1] In its specific sense as intermediary between belief and understanding, faith is thus described:

"Faith is higher and more spiritual than belief. It is a chrysalis state of human thought, wherein spiritual evidence, contradicting the testimony of material senses, begins to appear, and Truth, the ever-present, is becoming understood. Human thoughts have their degrees of comparison. Some thoughts are better than others. A belief in Truth is better than a belief in error, but no human opinions are founded on the divine rock. They can be shaken; and until belief becomes faith, and faith becomes spiritual understanding, human thought has little relation to the actual or divine.

"A belief fulfills its own illusive conditions. Sickness, sin and death are the vague realities of human conclusions. Life, Truth and Love are the realities of divine Science, which dawn in faith, and glow full-orbed in spiritual understanding. As a cloud hides the sun it cannot extinguish, so false belief silences for a while the voice of immutable harmony; but it cannot destroy Science armed with faith, hope and fruition." [2]

From this it appears that *understanding* is the goal of a *Scientist's* fervent aspirations. It is the promised land of plenty, the Paradise of spiritual pleasures, the haven of health and happiness. Hence its supreme importance.

"It is essential to understand, instead of believe, what relates most nearly to the happiness of being. To seek Truth through belief in a human doctrine is not to understand the

[1] *Science and Health*, p. 23.
[2] *Ibid.*, pp. 297-298.

infinite. We must not seek the immutable and immortal through the finite, mutable, and mortal, and so depend upon belief instead of *demonstration;* for this is fatal to a knowledge of Science. The understanding of Truth gives real faith in it, and is better than all burnt-offerings." [1]

I am not aware that Mrs. Eddy gives anywhere a clearer definition of what she means by science or understanding. At first sight it might appear to be an exceedingly simple matter: nothing but a firm conviction that God, All-in-all, is good, and that, consequently, evil in its triple variety of sin, sickness and death—others add poverty to this trinity—is unreal and in a manner non-existent. Yet, this simplicity is more apparent than real; for understanding has a negative, as well as a positive function: it must destroy as well as build up. Its gigantic task consists in destroying all error, that means all belief: for "belief and understanding never mingle. The latter destroys the former." Consequently, "when we fully understand our relation to God, we can have no other mind but His,—no other Love, wisdom or Truth, no other sense of Life, *and no consciousness of the existence of matter*, or error." [2]

At this juncture Mrs. Eddy draws from her lively imagination a pen picture of what this future struggle between understanding and belief, or mortal mind, will be. A battle royal must be waged both in every individual and in the world at large, and this battle will be pathetically terrific. In the individual the process is one of *mental fermentation* during which old ideas must gradually give way to the new:

"Mortal mind will vanish in a moral chemicalization. This mental fermentation has begun, and will continue until all errors of belief yield to understanding. Belief is changeable, but spiritual understanding is changeless. As this consummation draws nearer, he who has shaped his course in accordance with divine Science will endure unto the end. As material knowledge diminishes and spiritual understanding increases, real objects will be apprehended mentally instead of materially." [3]

[1] *Science and Health,* p. 286.
[2] *Ibid.,* pp. 205, 276.
[3] *Ibid.,* p. 96.

This personal, individual conflict will increase a million fold in the struggle for the emancipation of the whole race from the strangle-hold of belief.

"This material world is even now becoming the arena for conflicting forces. On one side there will be discord and dismay; on the other there will be Science and peace. In the breaking up of material beliefs, there will be famine and pestilence; want and woe, sin and sickness and death will assume new phases, and their nothingness will finally appear. These disturbances will continue until the end of error, when all discord will be swallowed up in spiritual Truth. . . . During this final conflict wicked minds will endeavor to find means whereby to accomplish more evil; but those who discern Christian Science will hold crime in check. They will aid in the ejection of error. They will maintain law and order, and cheerfully await the certainty of ultimate perfection." [1]

Nor is there any escape from this mental purgation. Every man must pass through it, either in this life, or in the world to come. For

"progress is born of experience. It is the ripening of mortal man, through which the mortal is dropped for the immortal. Either here or hereafter suffering or Science must destroy all illusions regarding life and mind, and regenerate material sense and self. The old man with his deeds must be put off. Nothing sensual or sinful is immortal. The death of a false material sense and of sin, not the death of organic matter, is what reveals man and Life, harmonious, real and eternal." [2]

The manner after which this purgation is to be made is briefly indicated in the following passage:

"Belief produces the result of belief; and the penalties it affixes last as long as the belief, and are inseparable from it. The remedy consists in probing the trouble to the bottom, in finding, and casting out by denial, the error of belief which produces a moral disorder, never honoring it with the title of law, nor yielding obedience to it." [3]

[1] *Science and Health*, p. 96.
[2] *Ibid.*, p. 296.
[3] *Ibid.*, p. 184. Cf. *No and Yes*, p. 27. "Surely the probation of mortals must go on after the change called death, that they may learn the definition

The result of this purgative process is properly speaking understanding, or Science, or spiritual sense. This involves a complete readjustment of our mental attitude. We enter into new conscious relations. The world is no longer for us what it was and, on the other hand, God is now to us what He never was before. He has become an ever-present help in all our needs, mighty in subduing the ebullitions of mortal sense, thus destroying sin, sickness and death.

"Spiritual sense, contradicting the material senses, involves intuition, hope, faith, understanding, fruition, reality. Material sense involves the belief that mind is in matter. This human belief, alternating between a sense of pleasure and pain, between hope and fear, between life and death, never reaches beyond the boundary of the mortal, or the unreal. When the real is attained which is announced by Science, joy is no longer a trembler, nor is hope a cheat. Spiritual ideas, like numbers and notes, start from Principle, and admit no materialistic beliefs concerning them. Spiritual ideas lead up to their divine origin, God, and to the spiritual senses." [1]

In some of these passages the founder of Christian Science has borrowed the accent of the ancient inspired seers, and there is in her tone a glow of cheerful assurance which is not without effect on the minds of her followers. Such passages help to maintain the fiction of a new revelation, and to reconcile the Christian Scientist to the many open contradictions scattered throughout the book. Men love a certain amount of mysticism: it warms and cheers the dullness of everyday life, and if it adds no special burdens to man's duties, large circles of our population will welcome it.

Mrs. Eddy has largely succeeded in supplying this need of the many unchurched, and of such among church members as do not find in their congregations anything equivalent to this

of immortal being; or else their present mistakes would extinguish human existence. How long this false sense remains after the transition called death, no mortal knoweth. . . . Of his intermediate conditions—the purifying processes and terrible revolutions necessary to effect this end—I am ignorant."

[1] *Science and Health*, p. 298.

soft and easy mysticism. It would be idle to say that there is no truth at all in this. It may be only a half-truth, but this half-truth, coupled with other characters of Christian Science, helps to explain in part its success. In so far as this conception of the universe implies a habitual realization of the presence of God, it represents a distinct gain in the daily practice of religion. Were it not for the many and serious errors inextricably bound up with Mrs. Eddy's pantheism, we could sincerely rejoice in this renovation of a practice constantly and urgently advocated by all Catholic spiritual writers.

We cannot agree with the author when she declares that God cannot create matter, or that matter is essentially evil, or that sin, sickness and death are purely mental, either in their essential character or even only in their origin, or that they are merely material beliefs, or that mind can cure all disease; but we cannot deny that the description of the world as divine ideas, even while falling far short of the true and full concept of Creation, at least embodies one of its essential elements. While regretting the absence of the other element, namely that of a Divine Will freely enacting, so to say, the Divine idea, we do agree that God's creative act is not one which, having taken place once for all, leaves the world to itself and its laws. God continues, and will continue unto the end of time, to govern the world as Divine Providence, thus maintaining—we could almost say, continually creating—the world He has called into being. There is in God a Divine Life which is His very essence, inherent, immanent and immutable: of this we catch a glimpse, and only a glimpse, in the mystery of the Blessed Trinity; but beyond this, there is in Him an activity that cannot be called necessary: of this we have a palpable proof in the existence of the world. Mrs. Eddy recognizes the former, and extends it beyond its limits, and rejects the latter.

It is easy to recognize in Mrs. Eddy's errors the influence of that liberalizing movement in Protestant theology which, in the first half of the nineteenth century, transformed New England from the rigid ancient unorthodox "orthodoxy" of Calvinism into a stronghold of Unitarianism. The days of a Cotton Mather (1663-1728) and of a Jonathan Edwards (1703-1758) were gone. Unitarianism had captured not only single individuals, but whole congregations, of which some had been among the strongest supporters of Calvinism. Harvard College was definitively aligned with this liberalizing, or, to speak more correctly, naturalizing current. This spirit Mrs. Eddy consciously and unconsciously inhaled, and incorporated into her religious system. From this source she obtained some of the arguments met with in her writings; their doctrines are her doctrines, except in so far as they were incompatible with her *discovery*.

Excess marks every one of Mrs. Eddy's utterances. She knew not how to keep the golden mean. We must reject, as contrary to fact, her claim of the absolute One-ness of Mind. There are minds many, as there are beliefs many. There are created minds, as there is created matter. Mrs. Eddy's own exposition of the progress from mere belief, through faith, into understanding is unintelligible except on the supposition that there are many minds. This is not to materialize mind, or to claim intelligence for matter, a belief which Mrs. Eddy gratuitously imputes to the theist. A future chapter will make this clearer; meanwhile we must turn our attention to the subject of malicious animal magnetism, which occupied such a large space in the life of Mrs. Eddy.

CHAPTER VI

MALICIOUS ANIMAL MAGNETISM

New Thought being without official textbook or creed, there is no uniformity of teaching to be found among its adherents. Most of the doctrines, however, explained in the previous chapter are received by the great majority of them in substantially, if not absolutely, the same form. But when we come to what Mrs. Eddy has dubbed malicious animal magnetism, the case is different; both the name and the thing are Mrs. Eddy's invention and property. Whether all Christian Scientists follow the Leader into this field of her metaphysics, may be considered doubtful; yet so closely interwoven with the whole fabric of Christian Science is this doctrine of mental malpractice, that it is difficult to see how any one can reject it and still honestly call himself a loyal follower of Mrs. Eddy.

The dogma of malicious animal magnetism has an interesting history. The expression animal magnetism came to Mrs. Eddy from Mesmer who, as we have seen, defended the existence, in man, of a fluid akin to natural magnetism and for that reason called animal magnetism. Mrs. Eddy, with her craving for the occult, her delight in the marvelous, and her pursuit of what was novel, became early in life interested in mesmerism. Her first acquaintance with it dates back to the Tilton days. There the Baker family-physician who looked after Mary Baker in her many nervous attacks was experimenting in this new-fangled science and found in his patient an interested and responsive subject. Animal magnetism continued to attract her until something more sensational, spiritism, came to supplant it. Mrs. Eddy not only visited professional spiritists, but she repeatedly acted, or pretended to act, as a medium—even after Quimby had given yet another direction to her thought.[1]

[1] Milmine: History of Christian Science in *McClure's Magazine*, Vol. XXIX, p. 108. Mrs. Eddy at one time claimed "that, because of her

Quimbyism itself was close enough to mesmerism to continue —without putting much faith in them—certain practices which originally purported to transmit the magnetic current. Mrs. Eddy, in her earlier days, treated in exactly the same manner. "She always instructed her students, after treating their patients mentally, to rub their heads. In addition Mrs. Eddy would dip her hands in water and lay them over the stomach of the patient repeating, as she did this, the words 'Peace, be still.' " [1]

But now two events occurred which were to change this indulgent compromise into rabid hostility. One of her former students, Wallace W. Wright, who had gone to Knoxville, Tennessee, as a pioneer in Christian Science, soon "began to question the propriety of calling this treatment *moral science* instead of mesmerism," and returning East, he charged Mrs. Eddy publicly in the daily press with teaching, under a new name and at an exorbitant fee, nothing more original than mesmerism. Mrs. Eddy defended herself spiritedly, but the sting remained in her bosom.[2] About the same time (1872) Richard Kennedy, the young student, who had helped so much to make Mrs. Eddy's theories known and appreciated, left her, which angered Mrs. Eddy to such an extent "that she wished to repudiate him and his methods, and to do this, it was necessary to repudiate what she herself had taught." She now declared solemnly that Kennedy's treatment, the one which she had taught him and which had made her own success, was a pernicious practice based on mesmerism [3] and had her students change their manuscripts to this effect by striking out the following passage:

". . . and wetting your hand in water, rise and rub their head. This rubbing has no virtue; only as we believe and

superior spiritual quality, and because of the purity of her life, she could only be controlled in the spirit world by one of the Apostles and by Jesus Christ." On another occasion she pretended to receive messages from her deceased brother Albert for Mrs. Crosby at whose home she was staying at the time. *Ibid.*, Vol. XXVIII, p. 352.

[1] Milmine: *op. cit.*, p. 94.
[2] Mr. W. W. Wright was a brother of Carroll D. Wright, at one time U. S. Commissioner of Labor. His attack was published in the *Lynn Transcript*, Jan. 13, 1872, quoted in *McClure's Magazine*, Vol. XXIX, p. 107.
[3] Milmine: *op. cit.*, in *McClure's Magazine*, Vol. XXIX, p. 113.

others believe, we get nearer to them by contact, and now you would rub out a belief, and this belief is located in the brain. Therefore, as an M. D. lays a poultice where the pain is, so you lay your hands where the belief is to rub it forever out." [1]

After thus putting the stigma of her disapproval on manipulation, as she called it, Mrs. Eddy found some difficulty in explaining away her own earlier practice. In 1876, in a booklet entitled *The Science of Man*, she pleaded ignorance:

"When we commenced this science, we permitted students to manipulate the head, ignorant that it could do harm, or hinder the power of mind acting in an opposite direction, viz., while the hands were at work and the mind directing material action. We regret to say it was the sins of a young student that called our attention to this question for the first time and placed it in a new moral and physical aspect." [2]

Still later, emboldened by her success, she put the whole blame on the incapacity of her students:

"My students at first practiced in slightly differing forms. Although *I* could heal mentally, without a sign save the immediate recovery of the sick, my students' patients, and people generally, called for a sign—a material evidence wherewith to satisfy the sick that something was being done for them; and I said 'suffer it to be now,' for thus saith our Master. Experience, however, taught me the impossibility of demonstrating the Science of metaphysical healing by any outward form of practice." [3]

Fastening the note of infamy on her followers, with whom for some reason or other she grew dissatisfied, by branding them as malpractitioners or mesmerists was not for Mrs. Eddy as innocuous a diversion as it might seem. Like a boomerang, this weapon rebounded and hit her that handled it with terrific force. She unwittingly educated herself into a firm belief in the possibility of the crimes which she imputed and into the conviction that they were actually being attempted against

---

[1] Cf. facsimile of Mr. Spofford's copy in *McClure's Magazine, ibid.,* p. 109.
[2] Milmine: *op. cit.,* p. 95.
[3] Eddy: *Miscellaneous Writings,* p. 380.

her, with untold mental anguish to herself. From the day that
she put the ban on manipulation till *Science and Health* appeared, three years elapsed during which her belief in animal
magnetism sufficiently evolved to have an entire chapter devoted
to it. The full bearing of her teaching on this point can be
gauged from the following quotation:

"In coming years," she writes, "the person or mind that
hates his neighbor will have no need to traverse his fields to
destroy his flocks and herds and spoil his vines, or to enter
his house to demoralize his household. For the evil mind
will do this through mesmerism, and not *in propria per-
sonae* (?) be seen committing the deed. Unless this terrible
hour be met and restrained by Science [Christian Science, of
course], mesmerism, that scourge of man, will leave nothing
sacred when mind begins to act under direction of conscious
power." [1]

Later on she claimed divine warrant for inserting this chapter on Animal Magnetism into her book.

"My reluctance," she says, "to give the public in my first
edition of *Science and Health* the chapter on animal magnetism, and the divine purpose that this should be done, may
have an interest for the reader and will be seen in the following circumstances. I had finished that edition as far as that
chapter, when the printer informed me that he could not go
on with my work. I had already paid him seven hundred
dollars and yet he stopped my work. All efforts to persuade
him to finish my book were in vain. After months had passed,
I yielded to a constant conviction that I must insert in my
last chapter a partial history of what I had already
observed of mental malpractice. Accordingly I set to work,
contrary to my inclination, to fulfil this painful task, and
finished my copy for the book. As it afterwards appeared,
although I had not thought of such a result, my printer resumed his work at the same time; finished printing the copy
he had on hand, and then started for Lynn to see me. The
afternoon that he left Boston for Lynn, I started for Boston
with my finished copy. We met at the Eastern depot in
Lynn and were both surprised—I, to learn that he had

[1] *Science and Health* (1st ed.), p. 123, quoted in *McClure's Magazine,*
Vol. XXIX, p. 338.

printed all the copy on hand and had come to tell me he wanted more—he, to find me *en route* for Boston to give him the closing chapter of my first edition of *Science and Health*." [1]

In Mrs. Eddy's thought Kennedy was indissolubly associated with this conception of life. Often in her lectures she would wander away from her subject and would devote half the lesson to bitter invective against the treacherous Kennedy. He pursued her, she would tell them 'as a hound pursues its prey' and unloaded on her the diseases of the patients he cured. To him she began to attribute not only her illnesses, but all her vexations and misfortunes, any lack of success in her ventures and any difficulties with her students. The following apostrophe to be read in the 1881 edition of *Science and Health* applies to him:

"The Nero of to-day," she writes, "regaling himself through a mental method with the tortures of individuals, is repeating history, and will fall upon his own sword, and it shall pierce him through. Let him remember this, when, in the dark recesses of thought, he is robbing, committing adultery, and killing; when he is attempting to turn friend away from friend, ruthlessly stabbing the quivering heart; when he is clipping the thread of life, and giving to the grave youth and its rainbow hues; when he is turning back the reviving sufferer to her bed of pain, clouding her first morning after years of night; and the Nemesis of that hour shall point to the tyrant's fate, who falls at length upon the sword of justice." [2]

We sometimes feel inclined to ask in wonderment whether Mrs. Eddy could really believe what she wrote, and yet there cannot be the slightest doubt that she did with an intensity of feeling sufficient at times to demoralize her entirely.

"This malpractitioner," she says of Kennedy in the 1881 edition, "tried his best to break down our health before we learned the cause of our sufferings. It was difficult for us to credit the facts of his malice or to admit they lie within the pale of mortal thought."

[1] *Retrospection*, p. 46.
[2] Cf. Milmine: *op. cit.*, pp. 218-232. *Science and Health* (1881), p. 38.

And again:

"We say that he did these things because we have as much evidence of it as ever we had of the existence of any sin. The symptoms and circumstances of the cases, and the diagnosis of their diseases proved the unmistakable fact. His career of crime surpasses anything that minds in general can accept at this period." [1]

This dread of mental malpractice, variously known by Mrs. Eddy's intimates as the Red Dragon, malicious animal magnetism or (abbreviated) M.A.M., accompanied the discoverer of Christian Science throughout her life, finding vent in all her writings. In 1887 a department devoted to malicious animal magnetism became one of the regular features of the *Journal*, and continued for some years. At the head of this department regularly occurred the following quotation from Nehemiah: "Also they have dominion over our bodies and over our cattle at their pleasure, and we are in great distress." [2]

Even in the latest editions of *Science and Health* we find such effusions as these:

"Whosoever uses his developed mental powers like an escaped felon, to commit fresh atrocities as opportunity occurs, is never safe. God will arrest him; divine justice will manacle him. His sins will be millstones about his neck, weighing him down to the depths of ignominy and death. The aggravation of the error foretells its doom, and confirms the ancient axiom 'Whom the gods would destroy, they first make mad.' From ordinary medical practice the distance to Christian Science is full many a league in the line of light; *but to go from the use of inanimate drugs in healing, to the criminal misuse of human willpower, is to drop from the platform of common manhood into the very mire of iniquity, to work against the free course of honesty and justice and push vainly against the current running heavenward.*" [3]

We almost fancy ourselves back in the full swing of Paganism, when we find such sentiments proposed in all seriousness to

---

[1] Milmine: *op. cit.,* in *McClure's Magazine,* Vol. XXIX, p. 338.
[2] *Ibid.,* p. 692.
[3] *Science and Health,* pp. 105-106.

men as a guiding principle of their conduct. What difference, after all, is there whether we live in continual fear of infernal demons, always ready to pounce on us and harm us in life and limb, or whether we dread the same things performed in much the same way from our human fellow-beings? How this Pagan superstition could regain its hold, and become a leading tenet in a system that pretends to be scientific and Christian is only another illustration of the oft-repeated assertion that as soon as one forsakes the safe path of faith, one strays away into the vagaries of superstition.

It may not be out of place here to inquire how Mrs. Eddy could square her *Science* with her superstitious fear of animal magnetism. If God is All-in-all, where does malicious animal magnetism come in? We might answer with truth in Miss Milmine's words that

> "when the original Science of Man, as she (Mrs. Eddy) had learned it from Quimby and as she had first taught it, no longer met the needs of her own nature, Mrs. Eddy simply went ahead and added to her religion out of the exuberance of her feelings, leaving justification to the commentators—and she has rapped them soundly, whenever they have attempted it."[1]

And yet, it may be doubted whether the doctrine of mental malpractice is as inconsistent with Christian Science as it appears on the surface. Let us review the situation historically: Mesmerism had entered early into Mrs. Eddy's life; but it was only after she began to teach Christian Science that it developed into that overmastering fear which obsessed her for the remainder of her life, and made her quake helplessly before these invisible terrors that could act independently of space and matter by the power of a malevolent mind alone. Was this fear completely an adventitious one, entirely out of keeping with her teaching? In short, was it a mere personal *mortal belief* of Mrs. Eddy's without basis in fact and without place in *Science?* The fact that Mrs. Eddy has assigned to it such a prominent place in all her writings, and defends it against all

[1] Milmine: *op. cit.*, p. 227.

comers, seems to warrant a negative answer. And indeed, though *mortal mind* and *erroneous beliefs* have no *real* existence in Mrs. Eddy's sense of the word, they are, nevertheless, *very real* to her in the ordinary sense of the word. Now, absent treatment often at great distances, is a specialty with modern mind-healers in general, and with Christian Science in particular. Need we wonder, then, that the counterpart of divine Mind which is always good, namely mortal mind which is always evil, should also be believed to act at will for considerable distances? Thus, rightly or wrongly, malicious animal magnetism has taken its place among the fundamental tenets of Christian Science.

This parallelism once established, be it even unconsciously, the importance of animal magnetism was bound to grow in Christian Science lore. Not only did Mrs. Eddy impute to all her disaffected or rejected students the fell design of exercising this nefarious power against herself, whom she thought they could not but regard as their enemy; not only did she assign to this subject a prominence out of all proportion in her doctrinal teaching, but she made it also the subject of direct legislation. We find the following regulations in the *Church Manual:*

Art. VIII, *sect.* 8: Members will not intentionally or knowingly malpractice, inasmuch as Christian Science can only be practiced according to the Golden Rule: "All things whatsoever ye would that men should do to you, do ye even so to them." (Matt. 7:12) A member of The Mother Church, who mentally malpractices upon, or treats our Leader, or her staff, without her or their consent, shall be disciplined, and a second offense as aforesaid shall cause the name of said member to be dropped forever from The Mother Church.[1]

Art. XI, *sect.* 9: Members of this Church shall not learn hypnotism on penalty of being excommunicated from this Church. No member shall enter a complaint of mental mal-

---

[1] As Mrs. Eddy in another article had laid down the rule that "If the author of *Science and Health* shall bear witness to the offense of mental malpractice, it shall be considered a sufficient evidence thereof," it can be imagined what arbitrary powers these by-laws placed in her hand. She used these unstintingly to the discomfort of all her fancied enemies and of all apostates from her Church.

practice for a sinister purpose. If the author of *Science and Health* shall bear witness to the offense of mental malpractice, it shall be considered a sufficient evidence thereof.

Art. XXIV, *sect. 3*: Teachers shall instruct their pupils how to defend themselves against mental malpractice, never to return evil for evil, but to know the truth that makes free, and thus to be a law, not unto others, but to themselves.

Mrs. Eddy went further. She would have liked to see the strong arm of the law of the land lifted up against these *mental assassins*.

"Courts and juries," she wrote, "judge and sentence mortals, in order to restrain crime, to prevent deeds of violence, or to punish them. To say that these tribunals have no jurisdiction over mortal mind, would be to contradict precedent, and to admit that the power of human law is restricted to matter, while mortal mind which is the real outlaw defies justice and is recommended to mercy. Can matter commit a crime? Can matter be punished? Can you separate the mentality from the body over which courts hold jurisdiction? Mortal mind, not matter, is the criminal in every case, and human law rightly estimates crime, and courts reasonably sentence it according to its motive." [1]

This was no mere empty rhetoric, witness the famous witchcraft trial which created such an amount of surprised merriment, back in 1878. When Mr. Spofford, who had brought Mr. and Mrs. Eddy together; who had so laboriously disposed of the first edition of *Science and Health;* who had been on such intimate terms with his teacher as to deserve to be called by her Harry (Harrison) and to receive her letters signed simply Mary; when this man at last lost his place in the sun and was ignominiously expelled for "immorality," that means disloyalty to Mrs. Eddy, he fell at once into the category of mesmerists or "mental marauders." The higher the place he had occupied in Mrs. Eddy's affections, the deeper the resentment which now rankled in her breast. Only Kennedy was more sincerely hated. In the case of Spofford the most formidable attack took the form of a legal prosecution.

[1] *Science and Health*, p. 105.

A certain Lucretia Brown, cured for a time by one of Mrs. Eddy's students, had suffered a severe relapse. Mrs. Eddy being consulted had the solution of this mystery on the tip of her tongue: "Spofford was bewitching her." She did more than just pronounce sentence; summoning to her house the apostolic number of twelve, she began to treat Spofford "adversely." "She required each of these twelve students, one after another, to take Mr. Spofford up mentally for two hours, declaring in thought that he had no power to heal, must give up his practice, and so forth."

When this novel form of intensified absent treatment proved unavailing, she asked her lawyer to draw up in Miss Brown's name a bill of complaint in which Spofford was accused of being a mesmerist, of controlling "by his said art and the power of his mind the minds and bodies of other persons . . . for the purpose of injuring the persons and property and social relations of others," and in particular of having "at divers times and places, wrongfully and maliciously and with intent to injure the plaintiff, caused the plaintiff . . . great suffering of body and mind and severe spinal pains and neuralgia and a temporary suspension of mind." [1]

The trial was set for May 14, 1878. On that memorable day Mrs. Eddy and Mr. Arens, her new ephemeral favorite, who himself was soon to be classed among the mesmerists, both under power of attorney for Miss Brown, and attended by some twenty witnesses appeared at the opening session of the Supreme Judicial Court in Salem to lay this case before the judges of the Bench. As might have been expected, the case was demurred to, and was dismissed by the judge with the smiling remark "that it was not within the power of the courts to control Mr. Spofford's mind."

Miss Milmine comments as follows on this case:

"So, after a lapse of nearly two centuries, another charge of witchcraft was made before the Court in Salem village. But it was an anachronism merely, and elicited such ridicule that it was hard to realize that, because of

[1] Cf. Milmine: *op. cit.*, pp. 239-243.

charges quite as fanciful, one hundred and twenty-six persons were once lodged in Salem jail, nineteen persons were hanged, and an entire community was plunged into anguish and terror. . . . Mrs. Eddy's attempt to revive the witch horror was only a courtroom burlesque upon the grimmest tragedy in New England history. It is interesting only in that it demonstrates how surely the same effects follow the same causes. When Mrs. Eddy had succeeded in overcoming in her students' minds the tradition of sound reasoning of which they and their century were the fortunate heirs, when she had convinced them that there were no physical causes for physical ills, she had unwittingly plunged them back into the torturing superstitions which it had taken the world so long to overcome. . . . Among this little group of people who had been friends and fellow-seekers after God, there broke out in a milder form that same scourge of fear and distrust which demoralised Salem from 1692–1694. In the attempt to bring the glad tidings of emancipation from the operation of physical law, which is sometimes cruel, Mrs. Eddy had come back to the cruelest of all debasing superstitions, that of attributing disease and misfortune to a malevolent human agency." [1]

The terrors with which the belief in the reality of animal magnetism inspired Mrs. Eddy are pathetic in the extreme. In the course of time she came to distinguish between various brands of this nefarious power. "All mental malpractice," she now declared, "arises from ignorance or malice aforethought." She defines it as "the action of one mortal mind taking control of another, without the other's knowledge or consent." It is practiced from either "mistaken or wicked motives," and, consequently, it is either ignorant or malicious.[2] At first she accounted for her repeated fits of illness by the theory that she

---

[1] Milmine: *op. cit.,* 243-244. Mr. Spofford appeared again in court in October of the same year (1878), this time as a complainant against Mr. Eddy and Mr. Arens charging both with conspiracy to murder him. The details of this sensational trial can be read in Milmine, *op. cit.,* pp. 250-261, and Peabody, *The Religio-Medical Masquerade,* pp. 185-188. Mrs. Eddy and Mr. Arens were indicted, but for some unexplained reason this indictment was never prosecuted, but, *upon the payment of costs by Mr. Eddy,* was *not prossed.*

[2] *Science and Health,* p. 451.

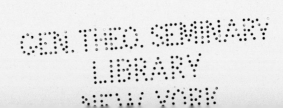

bore in her own person the ills from which she released her patients. But time brought different views:

> "By 1877 Mrs. Eddy not only believed that she suffered from the physical ills from which her students were released, but declared that her students followed her in thought and selfishly took from her to feed their own weakness. The work upon the second edition could not go on, because they nourished themselves upon her and sapped her powers." [1]

Sometimes Mrs. Eddy is near despair. She must flee from Lynn, because mesmerism is waxing too powerful there; she must abandon Boston for the same reason; even as late as 1908 when Mrs. Eddy was eighty-seven years old, she has to give up Pleasant View, driven away by the same mysterious force. Mrs. Eddy was sure that mesmerism interfered not only with her health, but also with her property.

> "Mesmerism caused the water-pipes to freeze and the wash-boiler to leak. She was convinced that all the postal clerks and telegraph operators in Boston had been mesmerized, and on one occasion, when she was sending an important telegram to Chicago, she sent Luther M. Marston, one of her students, to West Newton, to dispatch it via Worcester, so that it need not go through Boston at all." [2]

On another occasion she ordered the publisher of the *Christian Science Journal*, "to take the magazine and flee with it at once into some other city; if he stayed in Boston a month longer, she declared, mesmerism would wreck the periodical." Mr. Dixon, the publisher, went to Philadelphia, but hardly had he found a suitable office and printer, when he was ordered to bring the *Journal* back to Boston at once. [3]

Not all of Mrs. Eddy's troubles came from her supposed enemies. She knew that her friends were causing her untold sufferings. In course of time she came to feel absolutely certain who it was that caused her a particular affliction. It was on the strength of these feelings that Mrs. Eddy inserted in her *Church Manual* this arbitrary ruling that "if the author of

[1] Milmine: *op. cit.*, p. 214.
[2] *Ibid.*, p. 301.
[3] *Ibid.*, in *McClure's Magazine*, Vol. XXX, p. 584.

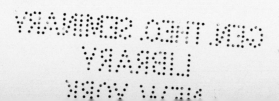

Science and Health shall bear witness to the offense of mental malpractice, it shall be considered a sufficient evidence thereof." [1]   So also she wrote to Spofford:

". . . those who *call on me mentally* in suffering are in belief killing me! . . . Tell this to Miss Brown, Mr. McLauthlen, Mrs. Atkinson and Miss Norman, but do not let them know they *can call* on me thus, if they are doing this ignorantly; and if they do it consciously, tell *McLauthlen* and *them all* it would be no greater crime for them, to come directly and thrust a dagger into my heart; they are just as surely in belief killing me and committing murder." [2]

Another letter belonging to the same period and addressed to the same person breathes exactly the same spirit:

"I am in Boston today feeling very, very little better for the five weeks that are gone.   I cannot finish the Key [3]; yet I will be getting myself, and all of a sudden I am seized as sensibly by some others' belief as the hand could lay hold of me.   My sufferings have made me utterly weaned from this plane, and if my husband was only willing to give me up, I would gladly yield up the ghost of this terrible earth plane and join those nearer my Life." [3]

As long as Mrs. Eddy adhered to the belief that malicious animal magnetism was inseparably bound up with manipulation, there was some limit set to her anxieties; but when she threw Mr. Spofford overboard, this restriction, too, had to go. "Mesmerism," she now wrote, "is practiced through manipulation—and without it.   And we have learned, by new observation, the fool who says 'There is no God' attempts more evil without a sign than with it." [4]   After this final pronouncement Mrs. Eddy's dread of mental malpractice grew apace.   If her friends, unwittingly, could draw from her vital forces and, thus, become a source of acute suffering, need we wonder that she lived in daily and deadly awe of her supposed enemies?   She suffered from the obsession of persecution which alone can ac-

---

[1] *Church Manual,* Art. XI, sect. 9.
[2] Milmine: *op. cit.,* p. 214. Italics are Mrs. Eddy's. Cf. p. 49.
[3] *Ibid.,* p. 215. The "Key" referred to is the *Key to the Scripture,* part of *Science and Health.*
[4] *Science and Health* (ed. 1878), quoted by Milmine, p. 226.

count for some of her strange actions, and which affected her whole surrounding and all her teaching.

"The atmosphere of Mrs. Eddy's house," writes Miss Milmine, "derived its peculiar character from her belief in malicious animal magnetism which exerted a sinister influence over every one under her roof. Her students could never get away from it. Morning, noon and night the thing had to be reckoned with, and the very domestic arrangements were ordered to elude or to combat the demoniacal power. If Mrs. Eddy had kept in her house a dangerous maniac or some horrible physical monstrosity which was always breaking from confinement and stealing about the chambers and hallways, it could scarcely have cast a more depressing anxiety over her household. Those of her students who believed in mesmerism were always on their guard with each other, filled with suspicion and distrust. Those who did not believe in it, dared not admit their disbelief. If a member of that household denied the doctrine, or even showed a lack of interest in it, he was at once pronounced a mesmerist and requested to leave." [1]

An even more drastic and personal estimate is given us by Mr. Peabody who writes:

"I have talked with a gentleman who years ago with his family lived for some six months in the house with Mrs. Eddy; and he said to me with great earnestness, 'I lived there six months *and, I tell you, Sir, I* rather would spend ten years in hell than another six months in Mrs. Eddy's company. She nearly drove my children into frenzy with her malicious animal magnetism business.' " [2]

Mrs. Eddy, driven to bay, as it were, declared that she had to protect herself by treating her enemies adversely. Convinced that she could tell from whom the magnetic influence came, she would ask her students at that particular time to treat so and so adversely. This treatment became an important feature in Mrs. Eddy's home.

"A regular society was organized among Mrs. Eddy's most trusted students and was called the P.M. (Private Meet-

[1] Milmine: *op. cit.,* p. 301.
[2] Peabody: *op. cit.,* p. 173.

ing). This society met daily after breakfast in the morning and after supper at night, gathered in Mrs. Eddy's parlor and 'took up the enemy' in thought. Mrs. Eddy was not always present at these sittings, but she usually gave out the line of treatment. She would say for example: 'Treat Kennedy. Say to him, Your sins have found you out. You are affected as you wish to affect me. Your evil thought reacts upon you. You are bilious, you are consumptive, you have liver trouble, you have been poisoned by arsenic. . . .' " [1]

It seems to have been especially at night that this animal magnetism came to torment Mrs. Eddy. Her nocturnal illnesses became more frequent and more violent with the years, and one of the principal duties of the resident students was to treat Mrs. Eddy for these attacks.

"These seizures usually came on about midnight. Mrs. Eddy would first call Mr. Frye, and he, after hurrying into his clothes, would go about the house, knocking at the doors of all the students, and calling them to dress immediately and hurry down to Mrs. Eddy's room. After arousing the inmates of the house, he would hasten through the deserted streets, summoning one after another of the healers whom Mrs. Eddy considered most effective. When they arrived at the college, they would find a group of sleepy men stand· ing in the hall outside Mrs. Eddy's door, talking in low tones. They were called, one by one, by Miss Bartlett or Mr. Frye, and admitted singly into Mrs. Eddy's chamber. Sometimes she lay in a comatose condition, and would remain thus for several hours, while each student, in his turn, sat beside the bed and silently treated her for about twenty minutes. He then left the room by another door than the one by which he had entered, and another student took his place. . . ." [2]

This picture of the new freedom which Christian Science was bringing into the world ought to open the eyes of those who still speak of Christian Science as a religion of healthy-mindedness. The bane of this fear manifested itself not only in Mrs. Eddy, but also in those that had to live with her. As

[1] Milmine: *op. cit.*, p. 304.
[2] *Ibid.*, pp. 301-302.

Asa Gilbert Eddy was the closest associate of his wife in her life work, so also was he most impressed by the dreadful possibilities of this subtle malignant power. He may not have believed in it more sincerely than his wife, but with less power of reaction and recuperation, his health suffered more under the strain. He sneaked through the city streets like one whose every step was dogged by unknown pursuers. He spoke in a whisper and anxiously looked round about when transacting any business even of little importance, afraid that a mesmerist might be there to cross his purpose. Especially after his arrest Mr. Eddy fell into an ever deepening gloom, and became literally the victim of his own fears. Christian Science treatment was of no avail in his case: the fear it had instilled did its slow but deadly work and was not counterbalanced by that spirit of optimism and that joy of life which is popularly believed to be the badge of Christian Science. He lingered on for some years. Even the eyes of a Christian Scientist could not help feeling that he was failing. At last Mrs. Eddy, thoroughly alarmed, threw all her science to the winds, and, in open contradiction with herself and her teaching, she summoned a regular physician to his bedside, who diagnosed his illness as a very common form of heart disease. But Mr. Eddy was beyond human help: he died on June 3, 1882, after only five and a half years of wedded life. Mrs. Eddy was beside herself from fear. All her worst suspicions she found verified in the case of her deceased husband. The mesmerists who had been haunting her so persistently had at last found a victim in her husband. She was convinced, or pretended to be convinced, that animal magnetism had killed him. To prove this to the world, she violated another fundamental rule of her organization, a rule which only the year before she had inserted in her *Church Manual,* and which reads: "A metaphysician never gives medicine, recommends or trusts in hygiene, or believes in the ocular or *the post-mortem examination of patients.*" In the same edition of *Science and Health* she had declared that "many a hopeless case of disease is induced by a single post-mortem examination." [1] Despite these strong words, Mr. Eddy was no sooner

---

[1] *Science and Health* (ed. 1881), p. 269 and p. 163.

dead than Mrs. Eddy, with her customary inconsistency, telegraphed for a physician to come and perform an autopsy. By this post-mortem examination the doctor proved to Mrs. Eddy that her husband had died of organic heart disease. Notwithstanding this testimony and the evidence submitted to her, Mrs. Eddy on the very same day sent out the following statement:

> "My husband's death was caused by malicious animal magnetism. Dr. C. J. Eastman (a Christian Scientist) who attended the case after it had taken an alarming turn, declares the symptoms to be the same as those of arsenic poisoning. On the other hand, Dr. Rufus K. Noyes, late of the City Hospital, who held an autopsy over the body to-day, affirms that the corpse is free from all material poisoning, although Dr. Eastman still holds to his original belief. *I know it was poison* that killed him, not material poison, but mesmeric poison. . . ." [1]

Here we may close this subject of animal magnetism. By introducing it into her teaching, Mrs. Eddy nullified and stultified her doctrines concerning God, the universal Mind, Life, Love and only Reality. By it she opened the floodgates through which poured in all kinds of superstitious fears, groundless suspicions and unwarranted judgments. It led to practices which in reality voided her religion of that love which in theory she preached. Hatreds, embittered feelings, false aspersions, and criminal attempts are the natural fruits of this scandalous doctrine. "The opponents of Christian Science must be charitable," writes Mrs. Eddy, "if they would be Christian. If the letter of Christian Science appears inconsistent, they should gain its spiritual meaning." [2] How can we better attain to this spiritual meaning than by its practical application. The test proposition "by their fruits you shall know them" which Mrs. Eddy wants to have applied to her successful cures, we must also apply to her failures, and first of all, to her mental and moral failures. There can be nothing more damning than this test when applied to the doctrine of malicious animal magnetism.

[1] Milmine: *op. cit.,* p. 286.
[2] *Science and Health,* p. 354.

And yet, Mrs. Eddy could not well have done without it. She needed it to round out her system; she needed it to answer objections; she needed it to explain her own teaching concerning human beliefs; she needed it, above all, to justify in the eyes of her own followers her frequent lapses into sickness which, according to her teaching, has no real existence. This test alone will satisfy every earnest seeker after truth, even if it fail to influence the declared partisan of a movement.

CHAPTER VII

THE FACT OF MENTAL CURES

"COMING down to more recent times," wrote Thomson Jay Hudson some thirty years ago, "we find that cures seemingly miraculous are as common today as at any period of the world's history. In fact, one unbroken line of such phenomena is presented to the student of psychotherapeutics which extends from the earliest period of recorded history to the present time. At no time of the world's history has there been such a widespread interest in the subject as now, and the hopeful feature is that the subject is no longer relegated to the domain of superstition, but is being studied by all classes of people, from the ablest scientists down to the humblest peasants."

Of the various schools of mental healing he says: ". . . all these schools effect cures of the most wonderful character, many of them taking rank with the miracles of the Master." [1]

It goes without saying that Christian Science and New Thought both agree in claiming these honors for themselves. Says Mrs. Eddy:

"By thousands of well-authenticated cases of healing she (the author) herself and her students have proved the worth of her teachings. These for the most part have been cases abandoned as hopeless by regular medical attendants. . . . Today there is hardly a city, village, or hamlet, in which are not to be found living witnesses and monuments to the virtue and power of Truth, as applied through this Christian system for healing disease." [2]

Mr. Evans, who in some respects may be considered the founder of New Thought, goes so far as to express a belief that the mental healer will eventually oust the regular physician:

[1] Hudson: *The Law of Psychic Phenomena* (Chicago, 1893), p. 147.
[2] *Science and Health,* Preface, p. x and p. 149.

109

"The first," he says, "somehow brings into action the divine principles of faith and imagination and directs their force upon the body, and the world accepts the result as almost, if not quite, miraculous. The time may come when there will be an entire revolution of public opinion, and the now unorthodox physician, who appeals, whether he knows it or not, more directly to the principles that in the highest degree influence the bodily condition, will be accepted as the man who is legally authorized to prescribe for 'the ills that flesh is heir to.' He who can best minister to a mind diseased, and control and direct these mental forces so as to modify the corporeal condition, is the best physician. And if he is 'constrained by the love of Christ' or the same benevolent impulse that actuated him, he is in the regular line of apostolic succession, even though no mitred priest has laid hands upon his head and consecrated him to a work, the importance of which the ecclesiastical functionary understands but little or nothing." [1]

The problem, therefore, which presents itself now, is whether and how far, these pretentious assertions are based on facts: for evidently there is no room for any hypothesis purporting to explain the manner of the cures until the reality of the cure is first established.

I.   THE CURES OF CHRISTIAN SCIENCE [2]

Reports of cures by Christian Scientists are abundant. A full chapter in *Science and Health* is consecrated to them; every issue of the *Journal* contains a number of them; even in the *Congressional Record* is found a well-selected list of them.

We may at once discard the cures, eighty-four in all, recorded in the textbook. Even overlooking the fact that the reports are unsigned and that most of them are extremely vague, it is plain from the nature of these testimonials that they

---

[1] Evans: *The Divine Law of Cure* (Boston, 1881), p. 211.

[2] Consult on this subject *Science and Health, passim,* especially chapter xviii; any issue of the *Christian Science Journal; Congressional Record,* Vol. LII, Part I, pp. 1039 ff. Also Huber, in *Popular Science Monthly,* 1899, p. 755, article: "Christian Science from a Physician's Point of View." Cabot, in *McClure's Magazine,* Vol XXXI, p. 472 ff. article: "One Hundred Christian Science Cures." Powell: *Christian Science, the Faith and the Founder* (New York, 1907). Paget: *Faith and Works of Christian Science* (New York, 1909).

obtained their honorable position in the textbook for no other purpose than to promote its sale. In almost every instance the cure is ascribed directly to the reading of the book.[1]

The cures reported in the *Journal* enjoy over those just mentioned the advantage of not being anonymous, full name and address being given in every instance. Some of these reputed cures are plainly ridiculous; most of the others can easily be accounted for on very natural grounds; a few of them might deserve a more minute discussion. Dr. Paget has examined scientifically two hundred such cases reported between April and August, 1908, and Dr. Cabot one hundred others, both of these authorities finding very little in them to arrest their attention.[2]

But we have a better selection in the *Congressional Record*. In the year 1915 Senator Works, a convinced Christian Scientist, spoke against extending further governmental protection to the medical profession, and, in the course of his argument, called the attention of his colleagues to the works and principles of Christian Science, giving as documentary evidence fifty-seven reports, some of which, twenty-one in number, he had selected "from the experience of people of his own acquaintance," and the others had been obtained for him by "a good and reliable friend. They are," he adds, "so convincing of the efficacy of Christian Science healing that I cannot see how any fair and candid mind can continue to doubt it." [3]

The selection is evidently made with great care, and, as far as outward appearance goes, can leave little to be desired. Not only are the names and addresses of the patients given, but in many cases also those of the physicians under whose care they

---

[1] For a more detailed examination consult Searle: *The Truth about Christian Science* (New York, 1916), pp. 246-293.

[2] Christian Scientists not only cure themselves, but also their animals by means of their Science. A ludicrous case is reported in the *Journal* of October, 1887. It is as follows:

"DEAR JOURNAL: Our dog was bitten by a rattlesnake on the tongue a short time ago, and the verdict, as is usual in such cases, was death; but through the understanding of God's promise that we shall handle serpents and not be harmed, if we but believe, I was able to demonstrate over the belief in four days. The dog is now as well as ever." This is not the only case of its kind. Cf. Paget: *op. cit.,* pp. 101-129. Cabot, in *McClure's Magazine, op. cit.,* pp. 472 ff.

[3] *Congressional Record,* Vol. LII, Part I, p. 1034.

were. Physicians would, undoubtedly, find the description of the symptoms in many cases insufficient; but the lay mind cannot but be impressed by the reading of them, especially as Senator Works owed his own strong feelings in the matter to his personal experience: "I was healed," he testified, "in Christian Science, when death was near, and after all hope of relief from medical practitioners had been abandoned after long and faithful trial of such remedies." [1]

It is clearly impossible to give here more than a summary of the diseases of which these persons claim to have been cured, and the full report of one or two of the more remarkable cases in a collection where all are remarkable. I disclaim in advance any intention of passing judgment on their intrinsic merit, as only physicians have the necessary qualifications for such a task. If I quote any at all, it is partly to bring them to the attention of persons that are interested in these studies, partly to acquaint the reader with the nature of the material on which the physicians, whose verdict will be quoted later, base their judgment.

FIRST CASE [2]

Miss Julia C. Meek—*Chronic Myelitis*

About eight years ago, at the age of thirteen, I was taken with what physicians called chronic myelitis, which gradually developed in intensity until it extended over the entire length of the spinal column, in consequence of which my entire body, except the right arm, became absolutely useless. My head and knees were drawn so closely together that the only way I could take food was by having my knees forced apart and being fed by means of a tube. Every physician who was employed pronounced my case incurable, and in consultation they agreed that it was impossible for me to live, and positively would never be well. After failing to receive any help or get any encouragement from the several physicians, I turned to Christian Science, and through its efficacy was completely healed. The following doctors were employed: Dr. C. O. Bernhardt, Sr., 506 Eighteenth Street, Rock Island, Ill.; Dr. George Eyster, 1109 Second

---

[1] *Congressional Record, loc. cit.,* p. 1028.
[2] *Ibid.,* p. 1036 (case 17).

Avenue, Rock Island, Ill.; Dr. J. F. Meyers, 2926 Fifth
Avenue, Moline, Ill.; Dr. V. A. Berland, 1721½ Second
Avenue, Rock Island, Ill.

Respectfully yours,

(Miss) JULIA C. MEEK,

912 Seventeenth Street, Rock Island, Ill.

The narrative of this young lady bears on its face the
marks of sincerity and truth. Yet how careful one must be
about accepting testimonies may be illustrated by another case
reported by Senator Works. Christian Science makes the
claim that its treatment can benefit little children through the
thoughts of their parents, and testimonials to this effect find a
conspicuous place in every collection of cures. The following
represents one such case:

CASE 26 [1]

Child of Mr. and Mrs. A. K. Wine—*Crippled and Deformed
from Birth*

WASHINGTON, D. C.

September 19, 1914.

Our youngest daughter, born July 15, 1912, was mis-
shapen at birth, having curvature of the spine, and both arms
and legs constantly remained in an unnatural position, one
arm being drawn down to the side and back in a twisted
position, the other arm being drawn up back of the head;
both legs were drawn up in an unnatural position. The
child had convulsions from the day of her birth, sometimes
as many as eighteen in a day and night. Every particle of
food she attempted to eat would bring on convulsions. She
never had a natural movement of the bowels. We tried every
means that we could, but her condition never improved.

On August 1, 1913, we took her to Johns Hopkins Hospital, in Baltimore. The surgeons told us that the child
had been injured at birth and had a clot of blood on the
brain; that she was an idiot and could not live; that if it
were possible for her to live, she would never be able to walk,
because her legs were drawn out of shape. They also said
that one shoulder was dislocated. She was in such a mis-
shapen condition that this had never been discovered. We

---

[1] *Congressional Record*, Vol. LII, Part I, p. 1037.

brought the child home, and the end seemed to be at hand. The local physician, Dr. William P. Wood, said that she was nearly gone, and we began to make arrangements for the funeral. She revived, however, and continued to live. Some friends then called our attention to Christian Science and advised us to give it a trial. We did so, and as soon as the treatment in Christian Science commenced, the convulsions stopped and the bowels began to act normally, and have done so ever since. One day when bathing her and moving as carefuly as possible the dislocated arm, it suddenly snapped into place with considerable noise. It has remained in place ever since. She is now able to stand on her feet, her legs are straight, and she is learning to walk and talk, and is not an idiot.

Before being healed in Christian Science she had cut several teeth. They were all without enamel, so soft and chalky that they could be flaked off with the finger nail. Since her healing the teeth that she has cut have been covered with enamel, and enamel is forming at the roots of the teeth that came before she was healed.

The surgeons at the Johns Hopkins Hospital stated, among other things, that a rib had been broken and grown together. There was a disagreeable-looking lump where the break had occurred. The lump has entirely disappeared. Her back is also perfectly straight.

Mrs. MAUDE A. WINE,
A. K. WINE,

116 Third Street, N. E.

An affidavit is added:

This is to certify that I have this day seen the daughter of Mr. and Mrs. A. K. Wine, referred to in the accompanying statement. The appearance of the child bears out the statement of the parents. The child appears bright, active and happy.

WILLIAM S. CAMPBELL,

The Burlington.

This certainly reads like a most remarkable case of the power of mind over the bodies of others. To make assurance doubly sure, I wrote to the parents of the baby and received the following reply:

My Dear Sir: Your letter dated October 25, received and the questions noted. I can only say in reply, that the statement concerning the condition of our baby girl as found in the *Congressional Record*, Vol. II, Part I, p. 1037, is absolutely correct.

The case was thoroughly investigated and proven, before being given out by the California senator on the floor of the senate. Sincerely,

Mrs. A. K. Wine.

Two of my questions remained unanswered, namely (1) whether this child was still living at the time of my inquiry, and (2) whether I might be permitted to see her. As I did not receive satisfaction on these two points, I continued my investigations and ascertained that the child must have died shortly after being reported cured. She had never been known to be able to walk or to talk and was carefully secreted from the view of the neighbors. This shows with how much distrust such testimonials must be read. Without in any way accusing anybody of bad faith, it is evident how easy self-deception is in these matters, and how the whole truth is not, as a rule, printed in testimonials given out in favor of a particular school or sect.

In all the cases reported by the Senator, so far as we are able to judge, the cure was a gradual one. There is perhaps one exception, the case of Dr. Burton, an alumnus of Rush Medical School, Chicago, who after his cure gave up his medical practice in order to devote himself to Christian Science healing. He describes his physical condition as follows:

"About twelve years ago I was advised . . . that I must go to Arizona, if I would take my one chance for life, as I would soon die with consumption otherwise. . . . When I went to Arizona I tried to stop the drug, but found that I had a well-founded opium habit and that, when I attempted to break it, which I did several times, the lung trouble became too serious to be borne. . . . To make a long and miserable story as short as possible, these three things—alcohol, morphine, and cocaine—became my food and drink . . . until toward the end I was taking such quantities as no one has ever recovered from, so far as I know. For weeks I took on an average of more than one hundred grains each of these two drugs hypodermically, and consumed between one and two quarts of whisky daily. I became entirely demented and a menace to those about me."

At this point the patient was near his end. Five of his fellow-physicians told his wife at a time, when he had been unconscious for forty-eight hours, that he could not live more than three or four weeks, and that this time must be spent under the strictest restraint. It is then that the cure occurred:

"At the request of a friend whose husband had been benefited by Christian Science, Mrs. Burton was induced to allow a Christian Science practitioner to call to see me. Again to make a long story short, he came and spent three hours with me. I have no memory of his coming or of his going, but he left me asleep, and I woke on the following morning free from all of these habits, normal in brain and nerve, hungry, energetic, clear-headed and happy. I knew the moment that I awoke that something had happened to me, and that, whatever had done it, I was free from the awful things that had bound me. But I did not know what it was that had done it until I was told."

His cure was a complete and lasting one.

"That was nine years ago, the twentieth of April of this year. From that moment I have never felt the slightest appetite for any opiate, cocaine or alcohol in any form, have never felt any symptom of lung trouble, and have been mentally sound and clear. Nor was there a moment of convalescence. My bowel condition was normal. My nerves were steady and quiet. I gained 30 pounds in weight the subsequent month, and within ten days from this memorable morning I undertook and carried to a successful issue the most strenuous piece of work, from both mental and physical standpoints, that I have ever done. . . ."

This cure induced the doctor to give up his medical practice, and devote himself entirely to the cause of Christian Science:

"I have spent over nine years in constant study of Christian Science, and seven years in its practice. I was most enthusiastic in the practice of surgery, and was a Pharisee of the Pharisees as to its virtues. I gave it up only after being most thoroughly convinced that there was something better. I have learned to my entire satisfaction, knowing both sides of the question, that Christian Science is a science, and not only that, but also that it is an advance step—and a long one—beyond medicine and surgery, and that time will prove this to the whole world. I have seen many cases of disease healed by it after they had been pronounced hopeless and dying by the best physicians. I have seen disease healed through it in a few minutes where it would have run days or weeks, according to medical prognosis. And although it is not the practice of Christian Science practitioners to attempt the healing of broken bones without the aid of surgery, I have seen dislocated joint and broken bone healed within a few days without the use of splint or bandage." [1]

Senator Works concluded his presentation of the case for Christian Science in the following words:

"MR. PRESIDENT: To summarize the cases of healing I have presented to the Senate, and the number of each of the mentioned diseases, they include fifty-seven cases, covering thirty-six distinct diseases, and the number of each kind shown to have been healed are almost if not all of them—regarded as incurable by medicine and surgery, and diagnosed as such by competent physicians. They are as follows:

Tuberculosis	7	Insomnia	1
Drink Habit	3	Diabetes	2
Drug Habit	2	Pemphigus	1
Kidney disease	6	Lead Poisoning	1
Cancer	10	Valvular heart disease	1
Tumor	7	Paralysis	1
Double curvature of spine	2	Chronic Myelitis	1
Asthma	1	Gallstones	1
Nervous Prostration	1	Lung trouble	1
Neuralgia	1	Bright's disease	1
Organic heart disease	1	Multiple Neuritis	1
Rheumatic Gout	1	Tobacco heart	1
Ulceration of Stomach	1	Rheumatism	3
Accidental injuries	1	Blindness	1
Locomotor ataxia	3	Deafness	2
Malformation of Children	3	Necrosis of chest bones	1
Chronic Constipation	2	Epilepsy	1
Indigestion	1	Appendicitis	1

[1] *Congressional Record, ibid.,* pp. 1028-1029.

"Many good people," he continued, "who do not believe in Christian Science concede willingly that it is doing great good in bringing consolation and good cheer to the bereaved and disconsolate, allaying fear and healing functionary or imaginary diseases, but deny its power to heal organic diseases. For these they still believe resort to the medical practitioner is necessary. In the cases I have given, not one (?) is of the kind to which it is thus conceded Christian Science may successfully minister. Of such as these, cases by the thousands might be cited. But they can be healed by the medical doctor with his drugs or his bread pills. The great work of Christian Science, as I have shown, is in the healing of organic diseases given up by the doctors as incurable." [1]

Senator Works has had the courage of his conviction and has not hesitated to give fullest expression to it, though his knowledge of the distinction between functional disease and organic disease is extremely vague.

Out of his personal experience grew the belief that healing "is as much a religious rite as redemption from sin."

"I, in my own experience and by later observations," he says, "have been convinced that drugs and other material alleged remedies do not heal, and that there is a remedy that, if rightly applied, will heal all our diseases. I have been the more reluctant to enter upon this discussion, because it necessarily leads in an indirect way into a discussion of religion because of the conscientious belief on my part, and of thousands of others, that the healing of disease is as much a religious rite as redemption from sin, and that the same principle that regenerates the sinner, applied in precisely the same way, heals the sick." [2]

II.   EXPERT OPINIONS ON MENTAL HEALING

In view of facts like those here presented Professor William James all too enthusiastically exclaims:

"To my mind, a current far more important and interesting than that which sets in from natural science to-

[1] *Congressional Record*, ibid., p. 1039.
[2] *Ibid.*, p. 1022.

wards healthy-mindedness is that which has recently poured over America and seems to be gathering force every day . . . and to which, for the sake of having a brief designation, I will give the title of the Mind-cure movement. There are various sects of this *New Thought*—to use another of the names by which it calls itself—but their agreements are so profound that their differences may be neglected for my present purpose. . . . The leaders in this faith have had an intuitive belief in the all-saving power of healthy-minded attitudes as such, in the conquering efficacy of courage, hope and trust, and a correlative contempt for doubt, fear, worry, and all nervous precautionary states of mind. Their belief has in a general way been corroborated by the practical experience of their disciples; and this experience forms today a mass imposing in amount. The blind have been made to see, the halt to walk; lifelong invalids have had their health restored. The moral fruits have been no less remarkable. . . . These general tonic effects on public opinion would be good, even if the more striking results were non-existent. But the latter abound, so that we can afford to overlook the innumerable failures and self-deceptions that are mixed in with them. . . . The plain fact remains that the spread of the movement has been due to practical fruits; and the extremely practical turn of character of the American people has never been better shown than by the fact that this, their only decidedly original contribution to the systematic philosophy of life, should be so intimately knit up with concrete therapeutics." [1]

To oppose the claims of Christian Science by producing evidence that it has signally failed in many cases, or by asserting that the sicknesses in the cases mentioned were more imaginary than real, or that the cure was merely temporary, or that it should be attributed to causes not at all connected with Christian Science looks very much like refusing to see what one does not care to admit. The question is not whether Christian Science succeeds all the time, but whether it has to its credit a certain number of well-accredited cures. Competent persons that have studied the subject at first hand grant this unhesitatingly.

[1] William James: *The Varieties of Religious Experience* (New York, 1910), pp. 92-94.

"While there are many," writes Dr. Eleanor M. Reed, "who are inclined to scoff at all the reported cures by Christian Science, and to ascribe the supposed results to imagination, or hypnotism, or mere suggestion, this is not true of those who have honestly investigated available evidence. Such students all acknowledge that among those with whom this so-called religion has become a matter of genuine personal conviction, there are occasionally wonderful cures of real organic disease, and very frequently relief from the less serious, but only slightly less discomforting difficulties known as functional and nervous diseases." [1]

Of the greatest weight, on this subject, especially among us Catholics, must be the opinion of Dr. James J. Walsh, as his important contributions to the study of psychotherapy place him in the front rank among contemporary investigators of mental healing. Under date of February 8, 1909, he writes in the *Catholic Mind:*

"During the last year or two the air has been full of discussion of psychotherapy. The reason for this is well known. Christian Scientists have found that by denying the existence of evil and of disease of all kinds . . . they have succeeded in relieving many people of ills with which they have been afflicted often for long years. These ills have almost as a rule been under the care of physicians who have failed to relieve them. The consequence has been a calling of attention to this new mode of viewing disease. Until the last couple of years this awakening of attention was confined to Christian Science circles. Christian Science was found, however, to be making such serious inroads on the membership of Protestant churches, that the question not unnaturally occurred of taking up some of the Christian Science ideas with regard to the healing of disease by changing the mental attitude of people toward their ailments, in order to prevent further defections from Protestantism, and even perhaps to attract people who had not been seriously interested in religion up to that time. It is universally conceded that this is

[1] Dr. Reed, in *Pan-Anglican Congress Report,* 1908, Vol. III, sect. B; article: "Christian Science and the Contrasting Christian Truth." S. B., pp. 8-17.

the origin of the present very lively interest in psychotherapeutics or mental healing." [1]

III.   EXTENT OF MENTAL HEALING

The possibility of healing real diseases by merely mental
influence being granted, it remains to be seen to what extent
these mental influences can be effective. Is mind influence curative in all kinds, or even in all cases of disease? Does it cure
chronic and malignant sickness? Is it effective in organic diseases, or must it be limited to functional disorders? Sentiments
differ and it is perhaps as yet impossible to give any definite
answer.

It is well known that men of science, including the greater
portion of the medical profession, narrow down the usefulness
of mental influence to nervous ailments, and deny that mind
can cure organic disease, Dr. Sadler declares:

"It should be recalled that *a great many* diseases can be
wholly produced and completely cured by mental influences
alone. *Such diseases, of course, are purely functional.* Other
chronic and organic diseases, as such, cannot be produced by
exclusive mental influences, neither can they be fully cured
by unaided psychic power." [2]

In a similar strain Dr. Walsh says:

"Of course mental influence cannot affect organic disease. A crumpled heart valve can no more be helped by an
idea than can an amputated limb. An ulcerated lung can no
more be cured in this way than can an ulcerated eye." [3]

No less an advocate of the power of suggestion than Bernheim on the whole supports this contention. In his work *De la
Suggestion et de ses Applications à la Thérapeutique* he denies
that psychotherapy is able to reconstruct damaged tissues of
the human organism, and declares that suggestion "is almost
entirely restricted to functional diseases." [4]

---

[1] *Catholic Mind,* February 8, 1909, p. 31.
[2] Sadler: *The Psychology of Faith and Fear* (Chicago, 1912), p. 301.
[3] James J. Walsh in the *Catholic Mind,* February 8, 1909, article: "Psychotherapy," p. 44.
[4] Il est vrai que la suggestion est une thérapeutique presque exclusivement
fonctionnelle.

The authors of the Emmanuel movement share these views:

"We believe," writes Dr. Worcester, "in the power of the mind over the body, and we believe also in medicine, in good habits, and in a wholesome, well-regulated life. In the treatment of functional nervous disorders we make free use of moral and psychical agencies, but we do not believe in over-taxing these valuable aids by expecting the mind to attain results which can be effected more easily through physical instrumentalities. . . . For this reason we have confined our practice to that large group of maladies which are known today as functional nervous disorders. Although a sound psychical and moral method is a valuable adjunct in every branch of medicine, yet, viewed as an independent remedial agent, the legitimate sphere of psychotherapy is strictly limited. It is in the field of the functional neuroses that all its real victories have been won. Here again our conception of our mission differs from that of our predecessors. In answer to their taunt, 'If you believe in God's power to cure disease, how dare you place any limit to that power?' we are content to reply: 'We believe God has power to cure all disease, but we do not believe God cures all disease by the same means. At all events *an authentic instance of recovery from organic diseases through psychical means is what we are waiting for.* While we do not believe that any man knows all that is to be known on this subject, or that we are in a position to affirm dogmatically what the mind can or cannot accomplish, yet we are surely safe in accepting as to this the overwhelming weight of scientific opinion, and in confining our practice to a field in which it is known to be efficacious.' " [1]

Such restrictions are not, of course, acknowledged by persons of the stamp of Mrs. Eddy.

"The author never knew a patient," she declares, "who did not recover when the belief of the disease was gone. Remove the leading error and governing fear of this lower mind, and you remove the cause of any disease, as well as the morbid and excited action of any organ. You also remove in this way *what are termed organic diseases as readily as functional difficulties.*[2] . . . The author has cured what is

[1] Worcester-McComb-Coriat: *Religion and Medicine* (New York, pp. 3-5).
[2] *Science and Health,* p. 377.

termed organic disease as readily as she has cured purely
functional disease, and with no power but the divine Mind.
. . . Working out the rules of Science in practice, the author
has restored health in cases of both acute and chronic disease, and in their severest forms.   Secretions have been
changed, the structure has been renewed, shortened limbs
have been elongated, cicatrized joints have been made supple,
and carious bones have been restored to healthy conditions.
I have restored what is called the lost substance of lungs, and
healthy organizations have been established, where disease
was organic.   *Christian Science heals organic disease as
surely as it heals what is called functional;* for it only requires a fuller understanding of its divine Principle, to
demonstrate the higher rule." [1]

Although modern mind-healers scoff at the idea of limiting
the power of mind, they admit certain limits; but these are determined not by our bodily constitution, but by the limitations
of our mind.   Could we but realize the true *gnosis*, the full
understanding of the reality of our spiritual nature, no disease,
they claim, could resist this demonstration.   This assertion,
let us note, is not based on experience, but is a bold profession
of faith in the supreme reality of mind and in its universal ap-
plicability to the healing of all disease.   The sweeping claims
of Mrs. Eddy stand only as long as there is question of consistent theorizing.   In practice, her repeated boasts of personal
success must be largely discounted on the ground that she remained an indifferent healer, who could not prevent her husband,
her grandchild and her favorite niece from dying relatively
young.   Moreover, at the end of the Preface of every edition of
Science and Health she inserts the following note: "The author
takes no patients, and declines medical consultation."

Those students of Mrs. Eddy's who took her instructions
too literally, got themselves occasionally into very trying circumstances, not a few deaths resulting from sheer lack of proper
medical attention.   Mrs. Eddy, of course, had an explanation
for failure as well as for success.   When she did not blame it
on the lack of understanding on the part of patient or prac-

[1] *Science and Health,* pp. 149, 162.

titioner, she blamed it on that mysterious non-entity, called
Malicious Animal Magnetism. But Mrs. Eddy was not content
with theory: as she grew older, she grew wiser and when disagreeable facts could no longer be varnished over with accom-
modating theory, she flung her theories to the winds and met
fact with fact. While officially maintaining with all the assurance of revealed truth that "Christian Science is always the
most skillful surgeon," she prudently admonished her practitioners to leave "the adjustment of broken bones and disloca-
tions to the fingers of a surgeon" and to confine themselves
"chiefly to mental reconstruction and the prevention of in-
flammation." [1]

In a statement published in the *Christian Science Journal*
December, 1902, she advises that "until public thought becomes better acquainted with Christian Science," Christian
Scientists should decline "to doctor infectious or contagious
diseases." She warns them earnestly against taking "a case of
malignant disease," before considering well their ability to
cope with the case, reminding them "that there are those lying
in wait to catch them in their sayings" and "that in their practice, whether successful or not, they are not specially protected
by law." [2] Queer physicians these who refuse to doctor infectious diseases and think twice before they venture to help a case
of malignant disease! Truly, truth is stranger than fiction!
After all that Mrs. Eddy has written about the omnipotence
of Mind in the healing of disease, and against the dangers of
consulting M. D.'s (doctors of medicine) and employing medicine, she coolly veers about and incorporates into her *Church
Manual* the following by-law:

Art. VIII, *sect*. 23: If a member of this Church has a patient whom he does not heal and whose case he cannot fully
diagnose, he may consult with an M.D. on the anatomy involved. And it shall be the privilege of a Christian Scientist
to confer with an M.D. on Ontology, or the Science of being.

[1] *Science and Health,* p. 401. Cf. on this subject Paget: *Faith and Works
of Christian Science,* pp. 130-190. Peabody: *The Religio-Medical Masquerade,* pp. 103-120. Milmine: *op. cit.,* pp. 324-326, 354 ff.
[2] Cf. Snowden: *The Truth about Christian Science,* p. 237.

When Mrs. Eddy inserted this concession into the fundamental laws of her Church organization, she must have entirely
forgotten her former "revealed" statements concerning the
dire consequences of any diagnosis whatever. As Christ never
diagnosed, so a Christian Scientist was never to resort to such
a practice. As all disease was unreal, what would a diagnosis
profit? "We never read," she says, "that Luke or Paul made
a diagnosis of a disease, in order to discover some means of
healing it. Luke never asked if it were acute or chronic." [1]
And still more plainly: "The moral and spiritual facts of
health, whispered into thought, produce very direct and marked
effects on the body. A physical diagnosis of disease—since
mortal mind must be its cause if it exists—generally has a tendency to induce disease." [2]

Thus, through the whole gamut of condemnations, medical
diagnosis is outlawed and execrated as unchristian and dangerous, until Mrs. Eddy herself has recourse to it, and recommends
it to her students. In like manner she condemned the medical
profession again and again in arrogant and insulting tones,
until theoretically and practically she falls back on their assistance. She summons them to the bedside of her dying husband,
and grants to her students the privilege of consulting them. By
this inconsistency, on her own avowal, she has rendered herself
guilty of fostering "a tendency to induce diseases." It is,
therefore, evident that her sweeping affirmations are but a
label to her stock in trade and describe its contents with more
zest than truth. This trade brings her and her opponents ap-
preciably nearer together.

When these deny the possibility of mentally healing organic
disease, they commonly qualify this statement and render it
less absolute. Bernheim limits the power of suggestion "*almost
exclusively*" to functional disorders, thus allowing a certain
influence even on organic disease. Sadler, after stating that
such diseases as can "be wholly produced and completely cured
by mental influences alone" are, of course, purely functional,
qualifies this by adding:

[1] *Science and Health,* pp. 369-370.
[2] *Ibid.,* p. 370.

"We are forced to recognize two great classes of physical disorders: one, in which the mind is a powerful factor in both the cause and the cure; the other—the organic diseases— *in which the mind exerts but a minimum influence.* In addition to these two great classes of diseases there may be recognized a third class of physical disorders in which the mind exerts a varying and uncertain influence, both as to causation and cure." [1]

In like manner Dr. Walsh acknowledges that

"with all of the organic diseases there comes a series of symtoms that are often even harder to bear than those due directly to the disease itself. These symptoms are the results of the discouragement, the depression and the lowered state of mental activity which comes with incurable disease. This mental depression may be the most important factor in causing loss of appetite and various digestive disturbances. It may be the most prominent element in that general disturbance of the patient which makes all the functions of the body run at a much lower capacity than they ought to, and which, consequently, disturbs general vitality, weakens the patient very seriously, and leads to intercurrent disease. *All of these symptoms may be influenced very much and very favorably by psychotherapy.*" [2]

These explanations seem to narrow the discussion down to one of terminology. It is admitted, on the one hand, that organic disease can be indirectly helped by psychotherapy: mind treatment can clear the way, remove the obstacles, and establish favorable conditions which either through medicine or through nature enable the cure to proceed unchecked. On the other hand, it is also demonstrably certain that not all diseases, not even all functional diseases, can be fully cured by unaided psychic power.

"The sharpness of this distinction between organic and functional troubles," writes Dr. Cabot, "is somewhat blurred by the fact that a functional or nervous affection, such as insomnia, may lead, both directly and through loss of appetite, to a loss of weight or to a considerable deterioration in

[1] Sadler: *op. cit.,* p. 302.
[2] Walsh: *op. cit.,* pp. 44-45.

the body tissues. Here we have what might be called *organic disease produced by functional disease*, and such organic disease as this is often cured by Christian Science or by some more rational method of mental healing." [1]

Christian Science, consequently, is not what Mrs. Eddy calls it, a panacea for "all the ills human flesh is heir to," and the testimonials, printed in the textbook, the *Journal*, and elsewhere, are at best a thoroughly one-sided presentation of the evidence.

"The vast majority of these testimonials," writes Dr. Paget, "are not worth the paper on which they are printed. What are kidney trouble, lung trouble, heart trouble, liver trouble, eye trouble? They are not chronic nephritis, phthisis, valvular disease, cirrhosis and cataract. Bowel trouble is ordinary constipation; stomach trouble is ordinary indigestion and aversion from food; spinal trouble is ordinary backache. These are not testimonies, but testimonials; every advertisement of a new quack medicine publishes the like of them. We all know Mr. A and Mrs. B and Miss C who bear witness to So-and-So's Pills. They had spinal trouble and kidney trouble. There is a rough sketch of them doubled up with pain or weeping at the family tea table. And it is certain that the pills did them good. . . . Again, many of these witnesses are not telling the truth . . . not wilfully, but from sheer inability to be accurate. Again, we all know that no statement is more inaccurate than the average statement of what the doctor said. . . . Again, what is the good of proclaiming that Christian Science heals diseases which get well of themselves. Time heals them." [2]

Hence, Mrs. Eddy's discovery comes to this: she obtained from P. P. Quimby her fundamental principles which, as long as there was no opposition, she stretched to extremes and embellished with various adventitious doctrines. Then she posed before the world as God's chosen instrument to usher in the new era of universal health and general prosperity. When defending her system, she is boundless in her pretension of curative powers, but when dealing with hard fact and fearing

[1] Cabot: *op. cit.*, p. 473.
[2] Paget: *op. cit.*, pp. 131-133.

the arm of the Law, which does not allow unwarranted theories to endanger the lives of the people, she compromises with theory and covers her tracks as best she can, on the whole, talking and acting surprisingly much like the rest of the world who believe in real matter and real disease. The theory was made to attract believers; the practice was modified to escape its dangerous consequences.

As early as 1884 Dr. Townsend of Boston University printed the following challenge to Mrs. Eddy:

"If you, or the president of your College, or your entire college of doctors, will put into place a real case of rip or ankle dislocation without resorting to the ordinary manipulation, or without touching it, I will give you $1000. Or if you, or your president, or your entire College, will give sight to one of the inmates of South Boston Asylum for the Blind, that sightless person having been born blind, I will give you $2000."

To this challenge Mrs. Eddy replied in the *Journal of Christian Science* under date of February 7, 1885:

"The article of Prof. Townsend . . . published in *Zion's Herald*, December 3, came to my notice not until January 9. In it he offered the President of the Metaphysical College in Boston, or one of her students, the liberal sum of $1000, if she would reset certain dislocations without the use of her hands, and $2000, if she would give sight to one born blind. Will the gentleman accept my thanks due to his generosity; for, if I should accept his bid, he would lose his money. Why? Because I performed more difficult tasks fifteen years ago. At present *I am in another department of Christian work, where 'there shall be no sign given them,'* for they shall be instructed in the Principle of Christian Science that furnishes its own proof." [1]

'Tis a pity Mrs. Eddy did not see fit, either personally or through one of her students, to take up the challenge of Dr. Townsend, at least as an act of pure charity, and as a means of making converts innumerable, seeing it was such an easy task for her!

[1] Townsend: *Faith-Work, Christian Science and Other Cures* (Boston, 1885), pp. 56-57.

CHAPTER VIII

Mental-healing methods are continually forming. They vary with every individual, almost with every cure. Yet, through them all runs an unmistakable family likeness marking them all with the Quimby impress of thought. The Quimby system soon outgrew its original simplicity; like the doctrine of evolution it branched out into various systems which all tend to become complete philosophies of life. No longer confined to the treatment of disease, they promise to establish in man's life perfect harmony, contentment and happiness. Their treatment against disease maintains its place of honor; but other treatments, like the so-called prosperity treatment, line up beside it. New Thought, in particular, lays great stress on the larger aspects of its teaching and on the experiential value of the facts of life.

As this broadens out the underlying principles, so it also modifies the current methods of treatment. On the whole, their practice is considerably more conservative than their theory. In theory they may hold with Mrs. Eddy that food, climate and hygiene have nothing to do with the health of man, even that any attention paid to hygiene and to climatic conditions is full of dreadful dangers; in practice, they will be quite as sensitive as the rest of us to the changes in temperature, quite as particular about bodily comfort, quite as fully alive to the daily need of food. We are still waiting for the Christian Science hunger-striker who would be willing to demonstrate the truth of his religion by renouncing that scandalously material process known as eating. Mrs. Eddy herself took care to guard against any such extension of her teaching. "It would be foolish," she writes, "to venture beyond our present understanding, foolish to stop eating until we gain perfection and a

129

clear comprehension of the living Spirit. In that perfect day of understanding we shall neither eat to live nor live to eat." [1]

Mrs. Eddy was less reserved with regard to hygiene. "The less we know or think about hygiene," she declares, "the less we are predisposed to sickness." [2] Physical comfort received no consideration from her in theory. In practice, however, it is well known, that the luxury of Mrs. Eddy's home became a scandal to her followers.[3] When she fled from that imaginary demon *Animal Magnetism* to Barre, Vermont, she stayed there only a short while, because the town band would not, as requested, stop playing on the square in front of her house.[4] Later on, when at Concord, she had her piazza enclosed with heavy sailcloth, to protect herself against the unreality of the chilly autumn air.[5] Thus the lives of the founder and of the whole school of Christian Scientists daily belie in a thousand different ways their solemn profession of immateriality, a clear proof that whatever truth Christian Science possesses is like a tiny grain of gold buried under an immense heap of rubbish.

But this is the negative side of mental healing. On its positive side, it is almost true to say that there are nearly as many methods as teachers and practitioners. These methods, however, can easily be reduced to a few well-defined types. Thomson Jay Hudson classifies them as follows:

"1. *Prayer and Religious Faith*, as exemplified in the cures performed at Lourdes and at other holy shrines. To this class also belong the cures effected by prayer alone, the system being properly known in this country as the *faith-cure* and the *prayer-cure*.[6]

---

[1] *Science and Health*, p. 388.

[2] *Ibid.*, p. 389.

[3] Milmine: *op. cit.*, p. 342. "In the Christmas holidays of 1887 Mrs. Eddy moved from her dwelling in Columbus Avenue to a more pretentious house at 385 Commonwealth Avenue. The fact that some of the members of Mrs. Eddy's own Boston Church began to murmur texts about the foxes having holes and the birds of the air having nests . . . augured ill for the year that was just beginning."

[4] *Ibid.*, p. 387. "Mrs. Eddy suddenly left Boston, driven from home, so she declared, by malicious Mesmerism."

[5] *Ibid.*, p. 411.

[6] For the sake of completeness this passage is quoted in full. We do not imply by this that we ascribe to prayer and to shrines no other than merely mental efficacy.

"2. *The Mind-Cure.*—'A profound method of healing which rests upon the suppositions that all diseased states of the body are due to abnormal conditions of the mind, and that the latter (and thus the former) can be cured by the direct action of the mind of the healer upon the mind of the patient.' [1]

"3. *Christian Science.*—This method of healing rests upon the assumption of the unreality of matter. This assumed as a major premise, it follows that our bodies are unreal, and, consequently, there is no such thing as disease, the latter existing only in the mind, which is the only real thing in existence.

"4. *Spiritism*, which is a system of healing based on the supposed interposition of spirits of the dead, operating directly, or indirectly through a medium, upon the patient.

"5. *Mesmerism.*—This includes all the systems of healing founded on the supposition that there exists in man a fluid which can be projected upon another, at the will of the operator, with the effect of healing disease by the therapeutic action of the fluid upon the diseased organism.

"6. *Suggestive hypnotism.*—This method of healing rests upon the law that persons in the hypnotic condition are constantly controllable by the power of suggestion, and that by this means pain is suppressed, function modified, fever calmed, secretion and excretion encouraged, etc., and thus nature, the healer, is permitted to do the work of restoration." [2]

Leaving aside for the present the cures of Lourdes and other Catholic shrines, and waiving also the question in how far these six groups of healing systems are identical and in how far they differ, we shall turn our attention to the methods employed by Christian Science and New Thought. Both these aim directly at curing the soul, confident that a healthy soul necessarily means a healthy body. Whether in the abstract they admit the reality of the body or not, is immaterial, since they agree that disease must be reached from within, not from without. Sin and sickness, being exterior manifestations of some lurking interior shortcoming, must vanish as soon as this

---

[1] Definition quoted from the *Century Dictionary.*
[2] Hudson: *The Law of Psychic Phenomena* (Chicago, 1893), p. 150.

interior defect is cured. Such is their basis for this work of
reformation. This apparently so grand conception of life, on
its positive side, sins by attributing excessive powers to the
soul; and, on its negative side, by denying altogether, or at
least greatly underrating, the physical basis of life.

Their methods are largely, though not exclusively, based on
this false principle. To begin with Mrs. Eddy, we find her
whole system built on the demand of perfect faith on the part
of both practitioner and patient. Many of her counsels need
not be despised: they are such as might be given by any one to
a prospective nurse. For Mrs. Eddy was above all practical:
whenever she comes down to hard fact, her theories recede into
the background, and commonsense takes their place. Theory
is not forgotten, but hedged in to such an extent by other regulations that it becomes effective largely through these. Her
instructions, wisely enough, begin with the mental and moral
preparation of the prospective healer. Two qualities, moral
rectitude and gentleness, she strongly inculcates.

> "The metaphysician [1] should first cast moral evils out of
> himself, that he may thus attain the spiritual freedom, which
> will enable him to cast physical evils out of his patients. . . .
> An ill-tempered and complaining person should not be a
> nurse. The nurse should be full of cheerfulness, faith, light,
> —a believer in God, Truth, Life and Love. . . . The tender
> word and Christian encouragement of an invalid, pitiful pa-
> tience with his fears, and the removal thereof are better
> than hecatombs of gushing theories, stereotyped borrowed
> speeches, and the doling of arguments which are but so many
> parodies on legitimate Christian Science aflame with divine
> Love." [1]

Beautiful words these, which, if Mrs. Eddy had heeded, her
book *Science and Health* would either never have been written,
or would be very different from what it is.

From these subjective dispositions, essential in a healer,
Mrs. Eddy passes on to those which must be called forth in the
mind of the patient, and insists in a very special manner on two

---

[1] *Science and Health,* pp. 366 and 395. A metaphysician in Mrs. Eddy's
terminology is a Christian Science practitioner or healer.

things: strong faith and complete dismissal of the thought of illness.

"One should never," so she teaches, "hold in mind the image of disease, but efface all its forms and types in thought both for one's own sake, and for the patient's. Avoid talking illness to the patient. Make no unnecessary inquiries relative to feelings or disease. Never startle with a discouraging remark about recovery, nor draw attention to certain symptoms as unfavorable, nor speak aloud the name of the disease. Never say beforehand how much you have to contend with in a case nor encourage in the patient's thought the expectation of growing worse before the crisis is passed." [1]

The reason for these rules of conduct is obvious. Every physician knows that lack of courage aggravates disease. Persons of a nervous, quick, imaginative, and impressionable nature, obsessed with the fear of death, are placed at a disadvantage and frequently are unequal to the task of fighting the germs of ill-health. Any suggestion as to the gravity of the situation lowers to that extent his chances of recovery. What is peculiar to Mrs. Eddy's teaching on this subject is not the good advice given, but the mold in which it is cast. Even the image of disease in the minds of those who attend the sick is considered dangerous, irrespective of the fact whether it finds utterance in speech or not. But to utter the name of the disease aloud, for some unexplained reason, might prove disastrous. The same remarks must be made on the counsels of calmness and discretion which Mrs. Eddy gives.

"The sick are terrified by their sick beliefs," she says emphatically, "and sinners should be affrighted by their sinful beliefs; but the Christian Scientist will be calm in the presence of both sin and disease, knowing as he does that God is Love and God is All.[2] . . . If they ask about their disease, tell them only what is best for them to know, Assure them that they think too much about their ailments and have already heard too much about that subject. Turn their thoughts away from their bodies to higher objects. Teach them that their bodies are sustained by spirit, not by matter,

[1] *Science and Health,* p. 396.
[2] *Ibid.,* p. 366.

and they will find rest in God, divine Love, more than in oblivious sleep." [1]

In addition to these helps to a speedy recovery, Mrs. Eddy, true to her principles in this case, recommends also a thorough spiritual house-cleaning.

"Include moral as well as physical belief in your efforts to destroy error. Cast out all manner of evil. . . . A moral question may hinder the recovery of the sick. Lurking error, envy, revenge, malice or hate will perpetuate, or even create disease. Errors of all sorts tend in this direction. Your true course is to destroy the foe and leave the field to God, Life, Truth and Love, remembering that God and His ideas are real and lasting." [2]

If Mrs. Eddy does not go so far as to recommend the sacrament of Penance as suitable to her purposes, others have not hesitated to point out the supposed physical advantages of this Catholic practice. Says Mr. Evans:

"We ought to ascertain, so far as practicable, the precise nature of the disordered mental state, or fixed mode of thought, that is the spiritual root of the patient's malady, and which has crystallized, through the law of correspondence, into an organic expression in the body. This should be attacked by the psycho-therapeutic force from every point of approach. The patient should himself freely aid in the spiritual diagnosis of his case. *The Roman Catholic Church maintains the Divine order, when it makes confession a necessary antecedent of absolution, or a being released.* The sin—the error, the falsity, as the word means—should be remitted or sent away." [3]

These are very general considerations, too general and sweeping to be of much practical value. Yet they do form the gist of Mrs. Eddy's instructions. She must stay in generalities and allow others to work out the details. It makes it easier for her to defend herself in case of failures, and failures in

---

[1] *Science and Health,* p. 416.
[2] *Ibid.,* p. 418.
[3] Evans: *The Divine Law of Cure* (Boston, 1881), p. 281. We may note the similarity of these views with those of the Psychoanalysts.

the shape of death or relapse were bound to come. For such emergencies her prescription was as follows:

"If your patient from any cause suffers a relapse, meet the cause mentally and courageously, knowing that there can be no reaction in Truth. Neither disease itself, sin, nor fear has the power to cause disease or relapse. . . . A relapse cannot in reality occur in mortal minds, for there is but one Mind. . . . If it is found necessary to treat against relapse, know that disease or its symptoms cannot change forms, nor go from one part to another, for Truth destroys it. . . . Instruct the sick that they are not helpless victims; for, if they will only accept truth, they can resist disease and ward it off, just as positively as they can the temptation to sin. This fact of Christian Science should be explained to invalids when they are in a fit mood to receive it,—when they will not array themselves against it, but are ready to become receptive of the new idea. . . . If it becomes necessary to startle mortal mind, in order to break its dream of suffering, vehemently tell your patient that he must awake. Turn his gaze from the false evidence of the senses to the harmonious facts of Soul and immortal being. Tell him that he suffers only as the insane suffer, from a mere belief. The only difference is that insanity implies belief in a diseased brain, while physical ailments (so-called) arise from belief that some other portions of the body are deranged." [1]

These methods, taught and employed by Mrs. Eddy, were more fully developed by her students, especially by those among them who, in point of Church affiliation, followed an independent course. All aimed at instilling in the hearts of the sick that spirit of faith, trust and confidence which, in the words of William James, creates a state of healthy-mindedness. Where a hypnotic doctor would be satisfied to suggest, under hypnosis, states of health, or remedies for disease without ever aiming at the reconstruction, on an entirely new basis, of his patient's mental life, the modern mind-healer, true to his philosophy, would aim mainly at inspiring an entirely changed outlook on life. Even Dr. Quimby, though his method was simplicity itself, had this larger aim.

[1] *Science and Health,* pp. 419-420.

"Instead of putting the patient into a mesmeric sleep," writes his son, Mr. George Quimby, "Mr. Quimby would sit by him, and after giving a detailed account of what his troubles were, he would simply converse with him, and explain the causes of his troubles, and thus change the mind of the patient and disabuse it of its error and establish the truth in its place, which, if done, was the cure." [1]

Since then methods have multiplied. To bring some sort of order into them, we may form them into groups and treat successively of what may be termed the tactual or sympathetic method, the visual method, the silent and telepathic methods and the verbal method.

Tabooed by Christian Scientists and tolerated by Quimby, the tactual method finds itself defended by others of the mind-healers. It is thus explained by Mr. Evans:

"There is a tendency in the minds of two persons who are in tactual contact towards a oneness of thought and feeling. This takes place through a universal principle of human nature denominated psychometry but which I prefer to call *the sympathetic sense*. . . . When the hand is placed on the head of a patient, at the point of impact, your mind comes into contact, as it were, with his mind: for sensation is not in the external organ, but in the spiritual organism. If he is receptive or, in any degree, impressible, your thoughts and healthy emotional states can be transmitted to him or, more properly, excited in him, as they do not pass out of your mind in coming into his. An impulse towards a healthy action can in this way be imparted to any organ of his body. This has been established by experiment. Here is the philosophy of the method of cure by the imposition of hands, which, as the primitive, instinctive means of cure, is again restored to the healing art. It was practiced by Jesus, the Christ, and his disciples, or scholars, which ought to be enough to give it currency among those who assume his name and profess to copy his life." [2]

The visual method, according to the same author, also has Scriptural support. It was employed by St. Peter and St.

---

[1] Quoted in Dresser's *History of the New Thought Movement,* p. 39.
[2] Evans: *op. cit.,* p. 273.

John in the cure of the lame man at the gate of the temple when, *fastening their eyes upon him, they said "look on us"* and bade him rise and walk.[1] This method need not detain us as it is not in common use except perhaps as an auxiliary that may add to the effectiveness of other ways of healing.

The silent method enjoys at present a considerable vogue. It consists either in silent meditation, or in silent but direct intercourse with the patient's mind, without the aid of external bodily organs, according as it is employed in one's own behalf, or in behalf of some one else. Mrs. Melinda E. Cramer thus elucidates silent meditation: "Going into the silence," she explains, "does not fully express what is meant to be conveyed by the statement; it simply means being still mentally for the purpose of realizing the truth of the power and possibility of Being."[2]

Silent healing is described by Evans as follows:

"When a patient is in a passive and, consequently, impressive and receptive mood, *and with his eyes closed,* so as to shut out from his mind all sensational images of external things, our thoughts may be imparted to him, or, at least, we can change the character and direction of his thinking. This can be done either when in actual tactual contact with him or at a distance. In addition to a state of passivity, he should be in a state of sympathy with his physician. These conditions being fulfilled, his mind becomes a *tabula rasa* or clean slate on which our thoughts may be written, and even without the intervention of spoken words. What we imagine and believe and think, will be transferred to him; for the stronger and more active mind will control the other. Thought is an interior speech or inward word. It is the proper language of souls, the universal language of spirit. . . . It is the idea, the thought, that imparts to a word a sanative virtue."[3]

As an example of this method I select from Dr. Dresser's *Handbook* the following excerpt:

[1] Evans: *op. cit.,* p. 277.
[2] Cramer: *Divine Science and Healing* (2d ed., San Francisco, 1907), p. 129.
[3] Evans: *op. cit.,* p. 279. The Psychoanalysts likewise insist on such a state of sympathy between physician and patient.

"The healer, sitting in silence by the patient, would put his mind through a process somewhat as follows, addressing his thought to the patient's inmost self: 'Peace be with you. I come as a messenger of peace to bring freedom and happiness. Let us realize the peace and goodness of God. You are God's child, perfect in ideal, strong, well and free. In God there is perfect peace and harmony, no discord at all. Let your fears and doubts go that you may know His peace and love. There is nothing to fear. Now your fears are going; you are becoming restful, trustful and free. You are settling down, down into quietness and repose: the disturbance is subsiding, the tension is lessening. Now God's perfect ideal is being realized. You are at peace; you are well; you are healed.' " [1]

When this silent treatment is undertaken from a distance by means of telepathic thought-transference, it is called distant treatment. This distant treatment, believed in by practically all modern mind-healers, becomes the source of many superstitious fears; for, if the human mind can influence the minds and bodies of others at will, regardless of distances, there is absolutely no reason why it could not exert an influence for evil as well as for good. Of this conviction was born Mrs. Eddy's lifelong dread of malicious animal magnetism. This faith or, rather, blind belief in the possibilities of absent treatment, is an unfounded assumption. It is assumed to be true, just as the exclusive reality and sole existence of God is assumed to be true. Yet mind-healers will believe in it with a conviction worthy of a better cause. Distant treatment has been developed into a regular trade, witness the accompanying reproduction of an advertisement printed in *Unity*, the monthly issued by Unity School of Christianity, Kansas City, Missouri:

Society of Silent Unity

Be still and know that I am God

INSPIRED BY THE SPIRIT OF TRUTH

Silent Unity represents the Healing Department of the Unity School, and it ministers unto those needing help, with-

[1] Dresser: *Handbook,* p. 61.

out seeing them personally. Jesus Christ spoke the Word and healed the centurion's servant and others.

We are glad to help all who have faith in the Power of God, no matter what the need may be, whether physical, financial, mental or spiritual. If everything else has failed we will take your case. "With God all things are possible."

Silent Unity will pray for you and instruct you how to pray to the Father in secret, and the Father who sees in secret will reward you openly.

The expenses of the Silent Unity work are met entirely by the free will offerings of those to whom we minister. "Give, and it shall be given unto you, good measure, pressed down, shaken together, running over."

All letters are strictly confidential.[1]

UNITY SCHOOL OF CHRISTIANITY

SILENT UNITY DEPARTMENT

We come now to the verbal method. It needs no explanation as to the form it takes, and can best be illustrated by paying attention to its contents. It goes without saying that this subject covers a wide range of ideas. Yet the one common aim is constant and is well characterized by the title chosen by Mr. Horace Fletcher for one of his books on mental science, namely *Happiness as Found in Forethought Minus Fear-thought*.[2] No less constant is the one common way that leads to this coveted goal, described by Dr. Sadler as the *Masterkey to Mental Healing*, namely faith, meaning thereby psychological faith which comprises optimism, contentment, self-confidence, certainty, trust and other cheerful dispositions.[3]

All mental healing, consequently, consists in denying audibly or otherwise the existence, and, thereby, destroying the disposition, of fear, and in affirming motives of trust, self-confidence, self-exaltation. The following treatment is taken from Fillmore's well-known book entitled *The Science of Being and Christian Healing* in which through six successive stages corresponding to the six days of Creation he professes to lead men out of

[1] *Unity* (Magazine), November, 1920, p. 451.
[2] Chicago, 1897.
[3] *Loc. cit.*, p. 106.

the land of servitude and error into perfect harmony with Truth. These six stages are:

"1. The mind perceives and affirms truth to be a universal Principle.
"2. Faith in the working power of Truth is born to consciousness.
"3. Truth takes definite form in mind.
"4. The Will carries Truth into acts.
"5. Discrimination is quickened and the difference between Truth and error discerned.
"6. Every thought and word is expressed in harmony with Truth."

The following invocation is to precede each day's treatment:

"I acknowledge thy presence and power, O blessed Spirit, and in thy Divine wisdom now erase my mortal limitations, and from thy pure substance of Love bring into manifestation my world according to thy perfect law."

The following treatment for Tuesday is submitted as a sample of the whole process of reasoning to which the mind is subjected. Its positive and negative aspects are indicated by the words *deny* and *affirm*.

"Deny—I deny the belief that I have inherited disease, sickness, ignorance or any other mental limitations whatsoever. I deny all belief in evil; for God made all that really is and pronounced it good. Therefore, no such deception as a belief in evil can darken my clear understanding of Truth. Those with whom I associate can no longer deceive me with their words of consideration and sympathy. I can no longer deceive myself with such weakness.

"Perish from my world these silly beliefs of darkened ignorance. I am now free from them all, and by my powerful word hereby destroy them wholly.

"Affirm—God's Life is my life and I vibrate with harmony and wholeness. I am free with the knowledge that all is good; I am, therefore, perfectly whole and well."

Thus the author leads his client through a different exercise every day until by the end of the week he is ready to declare and believe that he is unlimited in power. Here are a few short extracts of Saturday's treatment:

"Deny—. . . I now in the sight and presence of Almighty God unformulate and destroy *by my all-powerful word* every foolish and ignorant assumption that may impede my march to perfection. *My word is the measure of my power.* I have spoken and it shall be so.

"Affirm—. . . I am unlimited in my power and have increasing health, strength, life, love, wisdom, boldness, freedom, charity and meekness now and forever. . . . I am one with, and now fully manifest, Infinite goodness and mercy. Peace floweth like a river through my mind, and *I thank thee, O God, that I am one with thee.*"

Sunday's enigmatical treatment covers just part of a line and reads: "Be still and know that I am God." [1]

These citations show better than any words of ours could do the peculiar mentality of the modern mind-healer. Its pantheistical strain is obvious to even a casual observer. The Christian mind cannot be fitted into it. The necessity of a re-translation of our popular hymns into this *New Tongue* is a consequence; the sentiments of our saints and doctors are grossly erroneous in the light of these new discoveries. For instance, that well known children's rhyme which begins with the words *Now I lay me down to sleep*, receives the following version in the textbook of the Colorado College of Divine Science.

> Now I lay me down to sleep
> *I know* that God his child does keep
> *I know* that God, my life, is nigh:
> I live in him, *I cannot die.*
>
> *God is my Health; I can't be sick*
> God is my strength, unfailing, quick;
> God is my All, *I know no fear*
> Since Life, and Love, and Truth are here.

"If you will learn these lines," the author adds, "and repeat them every night, you will find help in them." [2]

[1] Fillmore: *Christian Healing*, pp. 261-266. Italics are mine to bring out more clearly the author's characteristic views. The same applies elsewhere, unless otherwise noted.

[2] James, Fannie B.: *Truth and Health* (3d ed., Denver, 1905), p. 51.

An objection also is considered. "Suppose," says the objector, "a child is sick. How can she say 'God is my help, I can't be sick?'" The author replies: "Let her say it then ten times instead of once. She is sick because she has forgotten that God is her health. Claiming God as her health will remind her of the Truth and drive away the false belief. This is the prayer of faith that heals the sick." [1]

We have seen enough of these methods to understand their general drift and specific character. They are not mere makeshifts, to be administered when needed, and relegated to oblivion when not wanted; they are rules of life, and as rules of life they appeal to many. This spiritualized life must be lived daily; at stated hours a loyal menticulturist is expected to take his mental medicine, if this expression be allowed. How deeply this affects their whole life, permeates their mentality, and influences their actions, is manifested in their cheerful dispositions and frequently enough in their improved health. These results are not affected by the fanciful character of their religious and philosophical principles. In the case of some of them at least, the theoretical denial of the individuality of the soul leaves them, theoretically, no mind to cultivate, and the denial of the existence of the material world leaves them, theoretically again, no body to cure. Thus, always theoretically speaking, their systems are self-destructive, and their practices meaningless.

Their unguarded actions, however, are a refutation of their philosophical beliefs and a vindication of our common sense philosophy. For us, in truth, as for all unsophisticated men, the reality of the material world is beyond dispute. It is the touchstone of all our concepts and ideas. No reasoning that begins with denying the reality of our senses, or the objectivity of their data, can meet with our approval. Nor can the followers of the modern mind movements point to results as the proof of the truth of their philosophical tenets; they would first have to show that no other explanation for their alleged cures is valid. But we are convinced that another explanation does exist, and to prove that, we now turn to a consideration of the interrelations of mind and body.

[1] James: *op. cit.,* p. 51.

CHAPTER IX

MIND AND BODY

I

A THOROUGH study of the interrelations of mind and body, though of great interest to the modern mind, cannot be undertaken in this connection. We propose, however, briefly to review the traditional Catholic teaching on this subject. For it is our firm conviction that it alone, among all the various psychological systems, takes squarely into account the full bearing of all the phenomena of life. Confronted with the problem of matter and spirit, the philosophers of the golden age of Scholasticism—unlike our modern idealists,—did not cut the Gordian knot by denying the reality of matter, or by making it a purely mental state. Such extreme views may please certain minds that love to live in paradoxes, but will find no favor with the common people, to whom of all realities matter is the most obvious.

With the best minds of classical antiquity, the Schoolmen opposed a materialistic conception of the world with as much determination as the most pronounced idealist; but, at the same time, they no less carefully avoided ultra-idealism. Matter for them was real, and so was mind. But reality did not mean identity. Thinking matter or material mind were both inconceivable, an evident contradiction in terms. But the reality of both mind and matter were primary facts, not dependent on any speculation, but plain postulates of reason which no man in his right senses could venture to question.

The reader will probably be surprised to learn how the Scholastics reconciled their teaching concerning a material body and a spiritual soul by maintaining the closest possible union of mind and body. Body and soul, in their view, are substances essentially different from each other, but so closely united that the concept of a living body includes that of the

143

soul. In spite of its essentially spiritual nature, the soul is not contrasted with the body as with something hostile or foreign. When spiritual writers depict in glowing colors the uninterrupted struggle between man's material and spiritual parts, and, with St. Paul, declare that there is a law in their members fighting the law of the mind and captivating them in the law of sin, they do not run counter to the scholastic teaching, which, far from denying this struggle, explains it on the very ground of the intimate union of the material and the spiritual elements in man.

1. For them the soul is the "forma substantialis" of the body, its energizing power, even its architect and organizer, so that the body is actuated and becomes a human body only through the energizing and organizing action of the soul. This action never ceases; it, so to say, perpetually creates the body which it permeates, communicating to it whatever faculties the latter possesses. The soul is the force that organizes the material out of which the body is constructed; that indwells and vivifies these material elements, and works in, with, and through them. The intellectual soul is, therefore, the source, not only of its intellectual activities, but even of what we conceive to be specifically bodily functions, like nutrition, sense-perception, and locomotion. In the words of St. Thomas:

"We must assert that the intellect, which is the principle of intellectual operation, is the *form* of the human body. For that whereby primarily anything acts, is the form of the being to which the act is to be attributed. . . . Now it is clear that the first thing by which the body lives, is the soul. . . . For the soul is the primary principle of our nourishment, feeling and local movement, and likewise the primary principle whereby we understand." [1]

2. In man there is none but an intellectual soul, no inferior, no merely bodily *form* that would give the body an inde-

[1] St. Thomas: *Summa Theologica,* Pars I, q. 76, art. 1. "Necesse est dicere quod intellectus qui est intellectualis operationis principium sit humani corporis forma. Illud enim quo primum aliquid operatur est forma ejus cui operatio attribuitur. . . . Manifestum est autem quod primum quo corpus vivit, est anima. . . . Anima est primum quo nutrimur et sentimus et movemur secundum locum, et similiter quo primo intelligimus."

pendent existence. This is true to such an extent that an intense absorption, let us say in some intellectual pursuit, largely inhibits the exercise of other faculties, as for instance, hearing and seeing. A man, intensely interested in the reading of a book, will fail to observe what is going on around him. In such cases, the whole consciously controllable energy of the soul is riveted on the one object and everything else becomes blurred. In the words of St. Thomas:

"We do not say that there are two souls in one man . . . one, animal, by which the body is animated and which is commingled with the blood; the other, spiritual which obeys the reason; but we say that it is one and the same soul in man, that both gives life to the body by being united to it, and orders itself by its own rule." [1]

3. By holding this view, the Scholastics took issue with the Platonists, who, confirmed idealists that they were, could not admit that man's spiritual soul would stoop so low as to perform the very lowest bodily functions.

"Plato held that there were several souls in one body, distinct even as to organs, to which souls he referred the different vital actions, saying that the nutritive power is in the liver, the concupiscible in the heart, and the power of knowledge in the brain. . . . This is proved impossible by the fact that when one operation of the soul is intense, it impedes another, which could never be the case, unless the principle of action were one. . . .

"We must therefore conclude that in man the sensitive soul, the intellectual soul, and the nutritive soul are numerically one soul. . . . Thus the intellectual soul contains virtually whatever belongs to the sensitive souls of brute animals, and the nutritive souls of plants." [2]

[1] *Summa Theologica,* Pars I, q. 76, art. 3. "Neque duas animas esse dicimus in homine uno, unam animalem qua animetur corpus et immixta sit sanguini, et alteram spiritualem quae rationem ministret; sed dicimus unam et eandem esse animam in homine quae et corpus sua societate vivificat et semetipsam sua ratione disponit."
[2] *Ibid.,* Pars I, q. 76, art. 3: "Plato posuit diversas animas esse in corpore uno, etiam secundum organa distincta quibus diversa opera vitae attribuebat dicens, vim nutritivam esse in hepate, concupiscibilem in corde, cognoscitivam in cerebro. . . . Apparet hoc esse impossibile per hoc quod una operatio animae, cum fuerit intensa, impedit aliam, quod nullo

Here we have a principle of the highest importance for our present purpose. It will go far towards explaining all the cures we have enumerated in a previous chapter. For the same soul is intellective, sensitive, and nutritive all at once; it conceives through the intellect, perceives through the senses, and builds up the body it inhabits by means of nutrition, and yet it is essentially one and indivisible. From this it naturally follows that the closest possible union, the most intimate relations, exist between the rational soul and the material body. No accidental bond unites soul and body; the soul itself is the bond, the only link; it is the proprietor of the body in as much as the life of the body is its own, communicated to the body, but not lost to itself. Not only does it give life, but it gives an animal *existence* as well, to that organized body with which it finds itself united.

4. The soul is, consequently, the only controlling and manufacturing power in the human compound.

"Whence," says St. Thomas, "we must conclude that there is no other substantial form in man besides the intellectual soul; and that the soul, as it virtually contains the sensitive and the nutritive souls, so does it virtually contain all inferior *forms* (or powers), and itself alone does whatever the forms do in other things. . . . Therefore, while remaining one and the same, it perfects matter according to the various degrees of perfection. For the same essential form makes man an actual being, a body, a living being, an animal and a man." [1]

5. A consequence of this is that the soul finds itself in its entirety in the whole body and in every one of its parts. Yet, since some of its faculties entirely transcend the body, they do not reside in the body, but in the soul; others, on the contrary,

modo contingeret, nisi principium actionum esset per essentiam unum. Sic ergo dicendum quod eadem numero est anima in homine sensitiva et intellectiva et nutritiva. . . . Sic igitur, anima intellectiva continet in sua virtute quidquid habet anima sensitiva brutorum, nutritiva plantarum."

[1] *Summa Theologica,* Pars I, q. 76, art. 4: "Unde dicendum est quod nulla alia forma substantialis est in homine nisi sola anima intellectiva, et quod ipsa, sicut virtute continet animam sensitivam, ita virtute continet omnes inferiores formas, et facit ipsa sola quidquid imperfectiores formae in aliis faciunt."

can only be exercised through those parts of the body which are fitted for that purpose, hence they are properly said to reside in the body.

"Of the powers of the soul," says St. Thomas, "some reside in it, in so far as it transcends the whole capacity of the body, namely the intellect and the will; hence such powers are said to reside in no part of the body. But others are common to soul and body. Hence it is not to be said of any of these powers that it finds itself wherever the soul is, but only that it finds itself in that part of the body which is fitted out for the operation of such a power." [1]

This theory of the Scholastics avoids the shoals both of materialism and of false idealism. It explains intelligibly both the spiritual side of man and those relations between the psychic and the physical which remain unexplained in other systems. It helps to understand many phenomena which more one-sided philosophies gloss over, and which remain standing objections to their theories. Let us, then, pass on to inquire into the consequences flowing from this substantial union of body and soul.

II

The soul being the active principle in man, transcending the body by means of some of its faculties, but residing in it and depending on it by means of others, it virtually contains in itself two essentially distinct, but by no means independent, groups of powers. The higher of these may be comprehensively called *mind*, or in more abstract terminology, *the psychic;* the lower one may be designated under the term *the physical*. The higher group includes intellection and volition; the lower one, sensation and nutrition. Somewhere between these two groups, under the direct influence of both, the scholastic philosopher would place the *phantasia* or *imaginativa*, fancy or

[1] *Summa Theologica,* Pars I, q. 76, art. 8: "Potentiarum animae quaedam sunt in ea secundum quod excedit totam corporis capacitatem, scilicet intellectus et voluntas; unde huiusmodi potentiae in nulla parte corporis esse dicuntur. Aliae vero potentiae sunt communes animae et corpori. Unde talium potentiarum non oportet quod quaelibet sit, in quocumque est, sed in illa parte corporis, quae est proportionata ad talis potentiae operationem."

imagination.   Without imagination it is impossible for the
intellect to think, as it is impossible for the imagination to be
active without a previous or subsequent sensation.   The former
truth is asserted by St. Thomas in the following passage:

> "It is impossible for our intellect, in the state of our
> present life in which it finds itself joined to an impressionable
> body (*passibili corpori*), to understand a thing as really
> existent, except by turning to the mental images (*phantas-
> mata*). . . . The reason for this is that the faculty of
> knowledge is proportioned to the thing to be known. . . .
> Now the proper object of the human intellect is the essence
> (*quidditas*) or nature existing in a body.   But it belongs
> to the very concept of this nature that it should exist in an
> individual . . . hence the nature of a stone or of any ma-
> terial object cannot be fully or truly known, except in so far
> as it is known to exist in a particular thing; but the particu-
> lar we apprehend through sense and imagination.   Hence,
> it is necessary that the intellect, in order to know its proper
> object, should turn to the mental images." [1]

Of greater importance for us, at present, is the truth that
imagination is built on sensation and always accompanied by
sensation.

> "The body is naturally changed by the imagination of the
> soul," says St. Thomas, "and so much more changed, the
> stronger the soul's imagination. . . . If the imagination be
> strong, the body obeys naturally in some things . . . for
> instance, as regards alteration in heat and cold and their
> consequences.   For the passions of the soul whereby the
> heart is moved, naturally follow the imagination, and thus,
> by commotion of the spirits the whole body is altered. . . .
> but other corporeal dispositions, which have no natural rela-
> tion to the imagination are not transmuted by the imagina-

---

[1] *Summa Theologica,* Pars I, q. 84, art. 7: "Impossibile est intellectum
nostrum, secundum praesentis vitae statum quo passibili corpori coniungitur,
aliquid intelligere in actu, nisi convertendo se ad phantasmata. . . . Huius
autem ratio est quia potentia cognoscitiva proportionatur cognoscibili. . . .
Intellectus autem humani qui est coniunctus corpori proprium objectum est
quidditas sive natura in materia corporali existens. . . . De ratione autem
huius naturae est quod in aliquo individuo existat . . . unde natura lapidis
vel cuiuscumque materialis rei cognosci non potest complete et vere nisi
secundum quod cognoscitur ut in particulari existens; particulare autem
apprehendimus per sensum et imaginationem."

tion, however strong it is . . . for instance, the shape of hand or foot or such like." [1]

This alteration of the body, at times hardly perceptible, at other times extends very far.

"By the apprehension of the human soul," says St. Thomas, "the human body is changed as to heat and cold, as appears when a man is angry or afraid. Indeed, this change sometimes goes so far as to bring on sickness and death." [2]

Thus we find the philosophical and scientific principles of the modern systems of healing clearly and comprehensively stated by the Schoolmen. True, they were chary about practical inferences flowing from them. So many occult practices, so many strange and unreasonable hypotheses, were then, as now, blazoned forth as facts in the name of science, that only specialists, men well versed in medicine and psychology, could see their way dimly through this labyrinth of facts and fancies. The Scholastics condemned as *divinatio* (sorcery) or *vana observantia* (vain observances) whatever appeared to them as plainly superstitious; but what was believed to be capable of a natural explanation was permitted to pass uncondemned until time and observation should clearly manifest its nature. In these matters the early Scholastics showed themselves eminently judicious, limiting themselves to the enunciation of broad principles that could serve as a guide and safeguard to all inquirers into the mysteries of Nature. Men were left free to use their natural powers and abilities in the pursuit of natural effects; but to introduce anything superstitious was condemned as sinful.

[1] *Summa Theologica,* Pars III, q. 13, art. 3: "Ad imaginationem animae naturaliter corpus immutatur; et tanto magis, quanto magis anima fuerit fortis imaginationis. . . . Imaginationi, si fuerit fortis, naturaliter obedit corpus quantum ad aliqua, puta . . . quantum ad alterationem quae est secundum calorem et frigus et alia consequentia, eo quod ex imaginatione consequenter natae sunt consequi animae passiones, secundum quas movetur cor, et sic per commotionem totum corpus alteratur; aliae vero dispositiones corporales quae non habent naturalem ordinem ad imaginationem, non transmutantur ab imaginatione, quantumcumque sit fortis, puta, figura manus vel pedis vel aliquid simile."

[2] *Ibid.,* Pars I, q. 117, art. 3: "Per apprehensionem animae humanae immutatur corpus humanum ad calorem et frigus . . . et quandoque etiam haec immutatio pervenit usque ad aegritudinem et mortem."

"If natural objects," says St. Thomas, "are simply employed to bring about some effects, for which they are believed to have some natural virtue, it is not superstitious or illicit; but if there be added to this either some characters or some words or any other vain observances which manifestly do not possess naturally any efficacy, it will be superstitious and illicit." [1]

Such principles were faithfully adhered to in the Church, and found their application in the works of theologians and physicians. Their necessity is clearly evinced by the facts of history. For the lack of this sound basis, the new impulse given to these studies at the time of the Renaissance failed to discriminate between what was based on natural law and what was mere fancy, between what was certain and what probable or doubtful. There came to be made the wildest claims regarding the curative power of either mind or body. A look, a word, an application of some indifferent matter by a privileged person, came to be looked upon as a powerful vehicle of either good or evil. This opened the door for many superstitious beliefs and practices, the hidden forces of nature being made to sponsor many a fraud in the name of science, even as in our days the extravagant claims of many a patent-medicine vender and so-called miracle worker are unhesitatingly accepted as the last word in medicine. Since herbs, stones, animals, contain curative powers, so they argued, why should not similar virtues exist in men that were born under favorable conditions?

All this goes to show that science and superstition are close neighbors; superstition will always appeal to the hidden, the mysterious, the unknown forces of nature, to gain thereby some show of respectability. But the extravagant fancies of the superstitious cannot invalidate the careful conclusions of the student of nature. That the powers of mind have been exaggerated will not justify our rushing to the opposite extremes.

---

[1] *Summa Theologica,* Pars II, II/æ q. 96, art. 2, ad primum: "Si simpliciter adhibeantur res naturales ad aliquos effectus producendos, ad quos putantur naturalem habere virtutem, non est superstitiosum vel illicitum; si vero adiungantur vel characteres vel aliqua nomina vel aliae quaecumque observationes quae manifestum est naturaliter efficaciam non habere, erit superstitiosum et illicitum."

Monism, be it materialistic or idealistic, will not give us the true explanation of the forces at work in and around us. The truth is to be found in that golden mean which does not give too much either to matter or to mind.

"Everybody knows from experience," says Dr. Walsh, "how a violent passion affects the whole body. Anger, fear, disgust, worry, passionate love, and a number of similar mental states, registrate themselves automatically throughout man's physical body. So, likewise, dread of disease, and, generally speaking, any excessive preoccupation for bodily health and vigor has an effect on the whole system, which suffers and is rendered weak under the weight of a preoccupied mind."

So true is it that sickness, sorrow, and sin ramify into each other, as would the branches of trees in close proximity. Even very ordinary states of mind may be reflected in man's bodily constitution, and, vice versa, ordinary physical conditions may affect man's spiritual nature. Certain mental states are favorable to a general healthy development; others, on the contrary are injurious.

Enough has been said to enable us to judge intelligently concerning the admitted fact of successful mental cures. On general principles, the possibility of mental healing cannot be rejected. The fact itself cannot be denied. Just as the mind can be the real cause of real disease, so we know that it can be the real cause of real cures. The question, however, remains whether the cures now under discussion are, as a matter of fact, explainable on this hypothesis, or whether we have to adopt any of the other explanations that have been proposed. This will be the subject-matter of the next chapter. Provisionally we may indorse the following sentiments of Mark Twain:

"No one doubts, certainly not I, that the mind exercises a powerful influence over the body. From the beginning of time the sorcerer, the interpreter of dreams, the fortune teller, the charlatan, the quack, the wild medicine-man, the educated physician, the mesmerist and the hypnotist have made use of the client's imagination, to help them in their work. They have all recognized the potency and availability of that force. Physicians cure many patients with a bread pill: they know that where the disease is only a fancy, the patient's confidence in the doctor will make the bread pill effective. *Faith is the doctor.* Perhaps that is the entire thing. It seems to look like it. In old times, the king cured the king's evil by the touch of the royal hand. He frequently made extraordinary cures. Could his footman have done it? No!—not in his own clothes. Disguised as a king, could he have done it? I think we may not doubt it." [1]

[1] Mark Twain: *Christian Science,* p. 34.

CHAPTER X

EXPLANATION OF MENTAL CURES

I

IT is with a great display of earnestness that Mrs. Eddy ascribes Christian Science cures to the direct action of God. Neither drug nor doctor, neither nature nor hygiene, neither regular rules of life nor confidence, neither mesmerism nor spiritism, neither mortal mind nor faith nor will power, nor any material cause whatever, according to her, effects a cure, but solely the all-pervading, ever-active, all good, and all real, Divine Mind, which is more a negation of disease than a cause of cure. For there is no such thing as sickness; there are only symptoms, beliefs and illusions of sickness, and he that rids himself of these, rids himself also by that very fact of all disease.

Christian Science explains its cures as follows: All things come from God, not only indirectly—that no one will deny—but directly and immediately; they are the thoughts of God, divine ideas. Now, it would be a sacrilege, so argues the Christian Scientist, to ascribe to God the three-fold error of sin, sickness, and death; hence, it follows that these are mere illusions of mortal mind which must cease as soon as we cease to believe in their reality. "If mankind would relinquish the belief that God makes sickness, sin and death, or makes man capable of suffering on account of this malevolent triad, it would sap the foundations of error and insure its destruction." [1]

The Christian Scientist explains the cessation of evil by stating that evil never existed.[2] He does not deny the exist-

---

[1] *Science and Health*, p. 357.

[2] "The origin of evil is the problem of ages. It confronts each generation anew. It confronts Christian Science. The question is often asked, If God created only the good, whence comes the evil? To this question Christian Science replies: *Evil never did exist as an entity*. It is but a

153

ence of the *belief in evil,* despite certain phrases that seem to imply this; on the contrary, it is precisely this belief that is the cause of the world's misery and wretchedness, and not vice versa. In the logical order, the belief is first, and the wretchedness follows, but in the real order the belief itself is the wretchedness.[1]

Destroy, therefore, this belief, and you insure for yourself perpetual health, happiness and immortality. If you can sincerely believe that there is no sickness, because man is incapable of sickness; that there is no sin, because sin is unreal; and that there is no death, because God, Life, could not create death—this triad of errors will vanish, according to the promises of Mrs. Eddy, and leave the world in the condition of a veritable Paradise.

The apparent simplicity of this remedy is appalling. This simplicity, however, disappears when it is realized that it implies the denial of all that is most obvious to the senses. To the Christian Scientist nothing is real, everything is unreal and evil except God and His ideas, which, being like God spiritual, must exclude matter and mortal mind, and all that is conditioned by them, namely sin, sickness and death.[2] Such ideas bring their own refutation with them. Vainly does Mrs. Eddy insist on the errancy of the senses that put us in touch with the material world, on the impossibility on the part of God, a Spirit, to create matter, the "antipodes" of Spirit, and on the incompatibility of the goodness of God with the existence of anything that is evil. These are not arguments; they are assertions with nothing to show their truth beyond the bare

belief that there is an opposite intelligence to God." *Miscellaneous Writings,* p. 346.

[1] "The sinner is not sheltered from suffering from sin; he makes a great reality of evil, identifies himself with it, fancies he finds pleasure in it, and will reap what he sows; hence the sinner must endure the effects of his delusion until he awakes from it" (*Ibid.,* p. 14).

"We should blush to call that real which is only a mistake. The foundation of evil is laid on a belief in something beside God" (*Science and Health,* p. 92).

[2] "The error which saith Soul is in body, Mind is in matter, and good is in evil, must unsay it, and cease from such utterance; else God will continue to be hidden from humanity, and mortals will sin without knowing that they are sinning . . . all because of their blindness, their false sense concerning God and man." *Science and Health,* p. 204.

word of the Founder of Christian Science. Such a complete knowledge of the Divine Nature as Mrs. Eddy and her followers pretend to possess has not only not been vouchsafed to man; it is contrary to both reason and revelation.[1]

Mrs. Eddy's final argument is always an appeal to the success of her healing methods; but plainly, if there is any other explanation of these cures, if there are parallel cases of healing which Mrs. Eddy both acknowledges and disowns—acknowledges inasmuch as they are real cures, and disowns, because in her judgment, they are not complete cures—if mental healing is not peculiar to Christian Science and New Thought, the argument loses all its force and is no more than a *petitio principii.* We may, therefore, safely pass on to an examination of the other explanations that have been advanced to account for mental healing, in general, and for the cures of Christian Science and New Thought in particular.

II

The problem that presents itself first is whether the modern mind-cures are natural or supernatural, whether they are due directly to natural causes or to supernatural beings. The possibility of a supernatural intervention on the part of God in behalf of believers that in good faith implore his help, cannot be gainsaid. Nor is the possibility excluded that He might allow evil spirits to seduce through wonderful cures such as are willing to be seduced. Jesus foretold that "there shall rise false Christs and false prophets and *shall show great signs and won-*

---

[1] The question of the existence of evil has been treated frequently, but to some minds it may always remain somewhat of a mystery. Catholic philosophy broadly speaking agrees with the Christian Scientists to the extent of declaring evil a non-entity, but it differs from them in maintaining that it is not the mere absence of being, but the privation of some being that should be present. It is, therefore, not a mere nothing, but it is a defect in something. Catholic philosophy does not deny the existence of evil, nor assert its incompatibility with the Goodness of God. True, God cannot be the author of moral evil: his sanctity prohibits this. But He can be the author of what to us seems evil without being absolutely evil. Moral evil does not come from God, but from the creatures; physical evil, including sickness and death, may come from God not as something evil, but as something accidentally connected with something good, past, present or to come. The whole question can be studied with profit in St. Thomas: *Summa Theologica,* Pars I, qq. 48 and 49.

ders in so much as to deceive (if possible) even the elect." This prophecy creates not merely a presumption, but a certainty that, at sometime or other, wonderful events will take place that must not be ascribed to God. Both possibilities consequently demand at least brief consideration, especially as both of them have been mentioned as possible solutions.

In harmony with the former supposition Father Searle says of the cures of Christian Science:

> "It is, of course, possible that in some of them the belief of the patients in the power of God to heal the sick without the help of drugs or surgery, which power every Christian acknowledges, may have been rewarded by Him; and such a result would be specially likely to occur in a materialistic age like this, when the possibility of it is so generally denied, not only by absolute infidels, but by non-Catholic Christians, who have been brought up to believe that the age of miracles has passed. Even incipient faith might be so rewarded. For they were not test cases, as it were, in which the issue lay between Eddyan ideas and normal Christian ones. . . . Outside of such test cases miracles are not necessarily restricted to the one true and complete faith; as we see, for instance, of the Syro-Phenician woman, recorded in Mark, chapter 7." [1]

Arguing from a diametrically opposite viewpoint, Father Woods concludes his study on Christian Science with these words:

> "We see, therefore, that the cures claimed for Christian Science, as a general rule, can be proved improbable in individual instances, and, in the gross, false; or else, they can be explained by perfectly similar causes. Still, it is neither impossible nor improbable that its votaries may be able, in the future, or even now, to bring forward some, not to be accounted for in the natural way. It must be remembered that, as has been shown, Christian Science is not a harmless craze. It is one of the most diabolical of anti-Christian systems, and in it the visible promoters are but tools of the prime mover, the devil. He goes about seeking to deceive

---

[1] Searle: *The Truth about Christian Science* (New York, 1916), p. 294.

men, and would gladly use all the powers of his angelic nature, to snatch souls from Christ. He is restrained in this, but he is not absolutely prevented. To try our faith, some manifestations are permitted him. But of these we have been warned." [1]

These explanations, both tentatively proposed as possibilities by our authors and advanced as the true solution by others,[2] are only acceptable, if no *natural* explanation exists. The only safe rule to follow in these matters is that a natural explanation must receive precedence over a supernatural one, because it is impossible to prove the supernatural character of anything where a natural explanation suffices. Though the supernatural may exist where its existence cannot be proved, yet it is at least very improbable that it exists in cases where natural forces explain and where no special character of the fact calls clearly for the intervention of supernatural beings. We, therefore, turn our attention to natural explanations.

III

The cures of Christian Science have frequently been identified with mesmeric or hypnotic cures. The temptation to do this lay near owing to its historical connection with mesmerism. Mrs. Eddy frequently had to defend herself against this identification, and she did this, as always, with spirit and an assumption of superiority that stood her in good stead with her followers. Hypnotism became the enemy which she attacked at every opportunity. Her followers were forbidden under threat of excommunication to study hypnotism.

"Sooner suffer a doctor infected with smallpox to be about you," she writes on one occasion, "than come under the treatment of one that manipulates his patient's head and is a traitor to Science. . . . There is but one way of doing wrong with a mental method of healing, and this is mesmerism, whereby the minds of the sick may be controlled with error instead of Truth. . . . For years we have tested the benefits

[1] Woods: in the *Catholic Mind,* May 22, 1918, p. 239.
[2] Not a few Protestant pamphleteers have represented Christian Science as the work of the devil.

of Truth on the body, and knew no opposite chance for doing evil through a mental method of healing, until we saw it traduced by an erring student and made the medium of error. Introducing falsehoods into the minds of the patients prevented their recovery, and the sins of the doctor were visited on the patients many of whom died because of this." [1]

Let us admit hypothetically this distinction. Between hypnotic cures and modern faith-cures there is a similarity; for both have their origin and source in the mind. Similarity, however, is not identity: both Christian Science and New Thought differ from hypnotism by the fact that they do not induce any hypnotic sleep. Both, however, agree with it in so far as they address themselves at times to what has been called the subconscious or subliminal mind, that nondescript entity which may perhaps be best paraphrased as the mind at rest, deprived of its normal conscious and personal direction and intellectual guidance, but subject to other influences, be these an unconscious influx from other faculties of the soul, or be they the work of other persons. The possibility that certain factors, active in hypnotism, are also brought into play in modern mind-cures, cannot be altogether excluded.

But let us examine another possibility, that which arises from the efficacy of suggestions even in the waking state. It is a matter of everyday experience that in man's ordinary concerns, without any special theatrical display and mystification, suggestions constantly influence the lives of men in some fashion or other. A look, a gesture, a word, a presence, may arouse or calm you, may inspire you with courage and noble aims or, on the contrary, depress you with a general apathy and weariness of life. Joy and sorrow, love and hatred, courage and pusillanimity—to mention only a few of the many affections of the human heart—are constantly open to, and under the sway of, conscious or unconscious suggestions. These affections, if prolonged or intense, may have a considerable bearing on bodily health and physical well-being. One group makes for good health, another for disease.

---

[1] Quoted in Milmine: *op. cit.,* p. 164. The student herein referred to is Richard Kennedy.

"I shall not now," writes Dr. Worcester, "rehearse the long list of physiological changes which can be effected by suggestion. I will mention only a few which have occurred under my own observation. The temperature of the body can be elevated or lowered, and the pulse quickened or retarded. Perspiration can be produced; the actions of the intestines can be stimulated, resulting in the removal of constipation. . . . Many forms of pain depending on functional or trophic disturbance can be removed, and parts of the body rendered insensible to pain. The sense of hearing in certain forms of deafness can be quickened. Some forms of eczema can be removed, and some forms of asthma can be checked at once. Stammering can be controlled, and nervous dyspepsia can frequently be cured. To this short list which is taken almost at random from our clinical notes, Bernheim, Forel, Bramwell and Dubois add many other similar examples in support of the physiological action of suggestion. They prove beyond question, that our subconscious mind acts through the instrumentality of our whole nervous system, both cerebrospinal and sympathetic, and that through this complex mechanism it can effect important changes in our physical functions." [1]

Active suggestion, however, on the part of the would-be healer, would be ineffective, did not the mind of the patient respond to this treatment, either consciously or unconsciously. The treatment requires an active, personal, subjective coöperation transforming a suggestion into a belief with a soothing, quieting effect on the nervous system. There is no transfer of power from the healer to the patient: the former merely suggests confidence and healing thoughts, but the results are directly due, not to him, but to the patient's improved outlook. A little sympathy goes a long way towards putting on his feet the man who is to all appearances down and out.

But if a patient could do for himself what another can do for him, that means, if he could rouse himself and react against mental depression, then, in many cases, this sort of auto-suggestion would be followed by exactly the same results. Writes Dr. Worcester:

[1] Worcester-McComb-Coriat: *Religion and Medicine,* p. 40.

"At bottom suggestion and auto-suggestion are the same. The mechanism of the brain which carries into effect the suggestion offered in a hypnotic or in a waking state, carries into effect also auto-suggestion. In the one as in the other case there is the same mental state of heightened suggestibility, and common to both are the same morbid and healing effects. Auto-suggestion may be defined, then, as a self-imposed narrowing of the field of consciousness to one idea, by holding a given thought in the mental focus to the exclusion of all other thoughts. This statement, of course, does not solve the problem of auto-suggestion; it is intended simply to express what is meant by the word. The thing itself, the psychical process covered by the word, remains— and it is likely to remain for a long time—the standing riddle of psychology. What it is in its ultimate nature, how it operates and what are its physiological or nervous concomitants, no man knows. That it is a reality, however, and a reality of the highest psychical and ethical significance, no man may doubt." [1]

The terms *suggestion* and *auto-suggestion* need perhaps a word of explanation. To the popular mind they represent something artificial and unreal, something rather of self-deception than of self-expression. Such a restriction of meaning is not warranted by the word: true or false, normal or abnormal, suggestion always remains suggestion and applies to all cases in which mind influences mind. It is commonly enough held to be of no avail as a therapeutic or curative agent, until it has become the property of the subconscious mind. If this means that suggestion acts independently of consciousness, so that our conscious states are unaware of the modes of its activity, or even may be a hindrance to an effective suggestion, the statement cannot be questioned. But if it is made to convey the impression that the suggestion itself must be conveyed unconsciously, the modern mind-healers can point to their practice as a refutation of this meaning.

The subconscious mind contains not only previously acquired knowledge, but also all unconscious states of the soul, whether or not these will eventually rise into consciousness. It

---

[1] Worcester-McComb-Coriat: *op. cit.,* p. 93.

includes, on the one hand, feelings of joy and contentment, the sense of satisfied desires, the sentiment of happiness, the pleasure of being alive and well, and, on the other hand, their opposites: discontent, dreads and fears of all sorts, melancholy, worry, anger, distrust, hatred, the belief of being ill and the fact of being ill-at-ease and out of place: these are a few of the many emotions that exert no mean influence over the health of the individual.

That all kinds of suggestions, deliberate or otherwise, have a decisive influence in molding the states of the subconscious mind, is a commonplace which requires here no more than a bare mention. Little does it matter whether the suggestion come from without or from within, whether it be intentional or not, whether it be brought home under ordinary or under extraordinary conditions, whether it be intense, even violent, or, on the contrary, feeble, but persistent. If there is not, on the part of a strong personality, a conscious and deliberate counteraction through will power, morbid states of mind will prove injurious, while pleasant thoughts and contented desires will prove beneficial to health.

IV

This leads up to an investigation of what might be called, in the absence of a better name, the mechanism of mental healing. Whatever be men's views concerning the nature of the faculties of the soul, all must distinguish between cognitive, affective and appetitive acts. Are these equally effective in man's physico-psychical life? Is an act of the understanding, as Mrs. Eddy would have it, the direct and only agent for mental, moral and physical health and well-being? Is the will a hindrance rather than a help? Do the affections have any part in preserving health, in causing and curing disease? These problems need to be looked into, though the treatment of them must be necessarily brief.

For Mrs. Eddy the human will is something radically evil. It is "but a product of belief," "an animal propensity, not a faculty of the Soul." It is "blind, stubborn and headlong and coöperates with appetite and passion. Thence arises its evil. Thence also comes its final powerlessness, since all power belongs to God, Good." [1]

This conception of the human will is in line with the Christian Science philosophy of the absolute All-ness of God. The belief in a free human agent with power to act for good or for evil would, indeed, be out of place there. Consequently, these assertions concerning the nature of the human will are worth just as much and just as little as the philosophy on which they depend. It may be, of course, that they have yet another foundation. For in spite of the fact that Mrs. Eddy had renounced Calvinism, her views of the total depravity of human nature in general and of the human will in particular are Calvinistic and seem to be a relic of earlier Calvinistic training.

Men of science take issue with Mrs. Eddy's diatribes on the human will. The most ordinary observation is sufficient to disprove the now antiquated contention of man's total depravity; the human will is not half as bad as the Reformers represented it to be. And when there is question of the will influencing bodily health and vigor, there is now an ever increasing group of men that present the will, almost in the same light in which Mrs. Eddy presents the understanding, as a panacea for all human ills.[2] These exaggerations are not likely to be wholly false; underlying them, there must be a foundation of truth which alone makes them possible. In fact, Dr. James J. Walsh, in his book entitled *Health Through Will Power*, has shown how the will or strong determination to live has sometimes lengthened life beyond all expectation, and how it helps even in such serious organic diseases as tuberculosis and cancer. A good illustration of the assistance that will power lends in the curing of the alcoholic habit is given by Dr. Austin O'Malley in his *Cure of Alcoholism*. Of 35 patients treated in a hos-

---

[1] *Science and Health,* p. 490.

[2] Works on the cultivation of the will for all kinds of concerns are very numerous. We may mention Haddock's Power-Book Library, the first and most important volume of which was in 1917 in its 135th edition. Its title is *Power of Will* (Meriden, Conn., 1907). Patterson's *The Will to be Well* (New York, 1901). Barrett, S. J.: *Strength of Will* (New York, 1915). We may recommend Walsh, *Health Through Will Power* (Boston, 1920) and *Religion and Health* (Boston, 1920).

pital where they were confined chiefly against their own will, 21.2 per cent remained abstinent after eighteen months, while 78.8 per cent reverted to drunkenness. On the contrary, of 375 patients who voluntarily submitted to the same treatment in a private hospital, 87.8 per cent remained sober, and only 12.2 per cent relapsed.[1]

Important as are the functions of the will in human economy, even in so material an aspect as physical health, yet they must not be exaggerated. The will is important in so far as it exercises a certain control, direct or indirect, over other faculties.[2] It can induce the mind to adopt cheerful curative dispositions; it can command the removal of obstacles that are in the way of a permanent cure; it can order the act of faith which accepts whole-heartedly the new philosophy of life, thus wielding undoubtedly a great influence in the regaining and conserving of health. Yet, this it does rather as the physician that prescribes than as the remedy that cures.

The will is also important, because, although it is the directive faculty, it is itself quite open to suggestion and to outside influences. It is the door through which the re-education of the inner life is made possible; hence the insistence with which psychoanalysts demand the good will and sympathy of their patients. On the other hand, it is equally true that if conscious effort under the influence of the will is sometimes useful, it is more frequently an impediment to a favorable turn of the disease. The will is, therefore, often of doubtful benefit, and experimenting with it may result in more harm than good.[3]

This brings us to the intellect or cognitive faculty, which word is here taken in a broad sense as the faculty which receives,

---

[1] O'Malley, *The Cure of Alcoholism* (St. Louis, 1913), p. 142.

[2] "In concluding the consideration of the will, it may be said that the great fact to be borne in mind in regard to the range of its operation is that, while it cannot influence (unless in a few rare cases) the organic functions directly, it can indirectly through its employment of other mental forces, and can exert immense influence over the irregular movements of the muscles and automatic cerebral action." Tuke: *Influence of the Mind upon the Body in Health and Disease* (London, 1872), p. 350.

[3] Dr. Pierre Janet admits that Charcot's experiments at La Salpêtrière resulted in an unskillful training in disease. "Charcot's hypnotism with its three phases . . . was never anything but a cultivated hypnotism." Janet: *Les Médications psychologiques* (Paris, 1919), Vol. I, p. 169.

weighs and classifies images and thoughts, supplied either by the external world through sense perceptions, or by our inner world of instinctive and temperamental experience. In this sense, the cognitive faculties comprehend not merely the intellect, but perception of mental images, conception and association of ideas, judgments and reasoning processes, memory and imagination. Mrs. Eddy ascribes all her success to understanding, restricting the meaning of this word to signify exclusively the adoption of, and belief in, her theories concerning the spirituality, the one-ness and goodness of God and the unreality of everything else. It goes without saying that we ascribe no special virtue to these concepts, and that we take the word understanding in its ordinary connotation.

Of singular interest for our present study is the fact that the intellect perceives things as either good, bad or indifferent. If it were not so, the intellect would probably have no influence whatever over bodily health. For experience shows that what the intellect perceives as a present good, invigorates, stimulates, restores and quickens the vital powers of man, while, on the contrary, what it believes to be a present evil, naturally depresses, saddens and frequently sickens him.[1] It matters not, as far as bodily health is concerned, whether these beliefs are in conformity with intellectual Truth: if the mind is convinced beyond cavil or doubt that it is in full possession of the true and the good, it is in the best possible condition for enjoying excellent health.

It is under this general concept of intellection that we must place the subordinate concept of imagination. The word has been purposely avoided so far, because but too often the popular mind associates it with the unreal. People speak of imaginary disease and of imaginary cures as of such that have no reality. Cures, according to that view, occur because in the first place the disease itself was only imaginary, that means unreal. How far this is from being the truth could be demonstrated by numberless examples. Imagination can be, and often

---

[1] An exception to this is the case when a joyful news so strongly affects the nervous system, and, through it, the action of the heart that it takes away life. Man's powers of endurance are limited in every direction.

is, the cause of very real bodily ailments, and so likewise, imagination can be, and often is, the cause of very real cures. As Dr. Dubray succinctly puts it in his excellent *Introductory Philosophy*:

"The importance of imagination, both for good and for bad, can hardly be overestimated; it is a useful, yet dangerous power. . . . Imagination exercises a great influence on the health of the organism, because ideas are not only representative, but also motor. Many illustrations of this could be given. Do we not see frequently imaginary ills leading to real sickness? To imagine that you are sick is one of the best ways to become truly sick, and to avoid thinking of your real sickness frequently proves to be a powerful help in the cure. The use of an appropriate remedy is in itself very beneficial, but the conviction that it is beneficial and that it will produce a certain result makes it twice as effective. Imagination without the remedy may even produce the desired result. Cases might be cited of persons who felt sure they had taken a certain medicine, and indeed experienced the result of it, and who later found the pill which, in fact, they had forgotten to take. There is a better chance for the man who has made up his mind to get well than for the one who imagines that he will die, and despairs." [1]

Far from being a new discovery the knowledge of this power of the imagination belongs, so to say, to the traditions of the *School*. The teaching of St. Thomas has already been outlined at some length. A few centuries later, the famous Jesuit writer Martin Delrio (1551-1608) gives us an instructive glimpse into the scientific mind of his period regarding the powers of the imagination.

"In this all agree that the power of the imagination is very great, and since this power can either be regarded in relation to the body of him who imagines, or in relation to the body of some one else, we must inquire separately into each case. All agree that the imagination has a very powerful influence on the body of him who does the imagining. . . . As to other bodies, some hold that the power of the imagina-

---

[1] Dubray: *Introductory Philosophy* (Longmans, New York, 1912), p. 79.

tion extends exceedingly far, so that it could fascinate or
cure persons even at great distances. . . ." [1]

Another testimony to the belief of past ages in the power
of the imagination will be of more than ordinary interest. In
his monumental work *De Servorum Dei Beatificatione*, Pope
Benedict XIV (1675-1758) discusses at great length the question how to discriminate real from merely apparent miracles.
Laying down as a basic principle that we must not call miraculous what can be explained by natural forces, he gives the following conclusions of his painstaking inquiry into the extent
of imagination:

> "It first appears," he says, "that certain diseases, spring-
> ing from the imagination, can be cured naturally by the
> power of the contrary imagination. . . . Secondly, it ap-
> pears that the imagination can often cause purgations and
> vomitings through which the sick man regains his health;
> . . . Thirdly, it appears that the natural power of the
> imagination can extend so far as to suppress for a time the
> sting of the pains that affect the body. . . . Fourthly it ap-
> pears that *even in grave diseases* the imagination can help
> along the cure which, however, will not be sudden, but grad-
> ual. . . . Finally, it even appears that *perhaps at times dis-
> eases can be cured instantaneously* by the power of the
> imagination, but that such a cure is not permanent, and that
> a relapse will follow." [2]

---

[1] Martin Delrio: *Disquisitionum Magicarum libri sex* (Munich, 1624), p.
14: In eo conveniunt omnes, imaginationis vim esse maximam; et quia vis
haec considerari potest vel quoad corpus ipsius imaginantis, vel quoad
corpus alterius, ideo de utroque seorsim disquirendum. Conveniunt omnes
quoad corpus proprium imaginantis plurimum in illud posse. . . . Quoad
corpus alienum nonnulli censent imaginationis vim se longissime porrigere,
adeo ut possit etiam remotiora fascinari vel sanare. . . .

[2] Benedict XIV: *De Servorum Dei Beatificatione*, etc. (Romae, 1749),
lib. IV, pp. 526 ff.: Primum dicendum esse videtur morbos quosdam, ab
imaginatione ortos, viribus contrariae imaginationis naturaliter tolli posse.
. . . Secundum dicendum esse videtur ab imaginatione saepe purgationes et
vomitus causari posse ex quibus aeger sanitatem consequatur. . . . Tertio
dicendum esse videtur posse vim naturalem imaginationis eo usque se
extendere ut impetum dolorum qui corpus afficiunt ad tempus reprimere
valeat. . . . Quarto dicendum esse videtur posse imaginationem in gravibus
etiam morbis sanitati prodesse, non momento tamen, sed paulatim obtin-
endae. . . . Dicendum tandem esse videtur, forsitan posse aliquando morbos

This analysis of the case, made long ago by Benedict XIV, can hardly be improved upon even in our own days. And yet the imagination does not seem to be the *immediate* factor in mental cures. It is only in so far as it arouses sense affections that it possesses any healing influence. Thought can be conceived as neutral, taking sides neither one way nor the other. It is thus that an egotist may view the concerns of others for whom he feels no special interest. But not so the affections. The affections directly and immediately link the spiritual to the animal man, the mental faculties to the bodily elements. They are the personal reflections of the mental states, stronger in some, less so in others. By means of their stimulating effect on the nervous system, and through it on the heart, they permeate, so to say, the whole organism and predispose it, as the case may be, either to sickness or to health. Thus, strong feelings, especially when frequently repeated, or when well-nigh continuous, are bound to reverberate throughout the body and have a marked effect on the general state of health.

The heart was long considered the very seat of emotional life. This conception has entered into the language of all nations. Every one speaks of men of large, mean, ardent, faint, strong hearts to indicate their personal characters. Even though modern science has instructed us as to the real constitution of the material heart, and properly describes it as a muscle, it must not be forgotten that it is a muscle *sui generis*, unique in its kind, with functions all its own. Through it pulses the life blood in a never ceasing rhythm, thus feeding at every second every section of the human organism. Long before there is even a trace of the brain in the embryo, the heart is formed and begins its work which will not cease till the soul departs. This sensitive organ is peculiarly open to affective impulses. Like a delicate needle it responds unconsciously to the varying impressions of the mind, and transmutes them, so to say, into material values. Thus it still remains preëminently the organ of the affections, and serves directly the interests of

momento sanari vi imaginationis, sanitatem tamen non durare, sed recidivam aut metastasim sequi. . . .

mental cures, as it is also directly responsible for diseases that
have their root principally in the mind.[1]

To quote Dr. Sadler:

"It is evident that faith and fear are able profoundly to
influence the nerve centers which regulate and maintain heart
action. The action of the heart is most natural and regular
when it is least thought of. The care-free mental state
favors natural heart action. On the other hand, fear and
every form of mental anxiety interfere with the natural action of the heart, in common with the action of all the other
vital organs. . . . The healthy heart beats quietly and regularly when the mind is at peace and free from fear. Faith
is the ideal and natural mental state, so far as healthy heart
action is concerned. Any agitation of the mind almost immediately produces a conscious thumping of the heart
against the chest wall. The relation between the mental state
and the heart muscle is direct, and the response of the heart
muscle to mental disturbance is immediate, well defined, and
clearly established." [2]

v

Now let us apply these considerations to the modern mind-
cure movements. They must originate a real revolution in the
minds of their followers. They must banish forever all discontent, since the fundamental tenet of their new religion is the
optimistic doctrine that God Who is All-in-all is the author of
all and infinitely good. The thought even of the possibility of
sickness cannot be tolerated, because this would be a violation
of one of the principal tenets of the newly found faith. This
changed mode of life, with the changed frame of mind, the
setting of all worries at defiance, the giving up of medicine,
the deliberate quietus put on the nerves, the continual mental
discipline, all this brings about a gradual improvement and,
finally, a real cure of real and not merely imaginary diseases.
On its negative side, this changed outlook on life does away
with those many mental disorders which weigh like an incubus

[1] Cf. Walsh, in *Catholic Mind*, February 8, 1909, p. 41, article "Psychotherapy."
[2] Sadler, *The Physiology of Faith and Fear*, p. 118.

on many a wretched soul, and on its positive side, it quickens and brightens life by considerations that render it full of cheer and happiness.

The results are of the most gratifying kind and add to the hopes engendered by the new faith. As Miss Reed graphically puts it:

"Deep-rooted in the heart of humanity is the conviction that it is God's original purpose that man should express human perfection; and if only we can set aside a few annoying facts of history, and the still more disquieting burden of personal experience, and see ourselves at once transformed into paragons of virtue and unerring expressions of divinity, surely, this conception must be both tranquilizing and stimulating.

"Such is the mental revolution which follows conversion to Christian Science. This happy consciousness of personal superiority is maintained by continual mental discipline. There is no suggestion of hypnotism about this, and it is unfortunate when their results are ascribed to a condition in which will-power is so conspicuously absent. In case after case the phenomena of healing by Christian Science disprove the theory, so generally accepted, that the subconscious mind is in more intimate relation to the functions of the body than the normal supraliminal mind; for they demonstrate that, where the reason is convinced of supernormal power or the impossibility of personal danger, the physical expressions of this conviction are as definite as under hypnotism.

"Let us now think of the physical effects of the Negations and Affirmations of a Christian Scientist. Take the case of a lady whose whole thought as well as that of her entire family is centered upon her physical condition, perhaps a truly pitiable one, and whose mental life is one of genuine terror: her mind concentrated on the possible deadly effect of each mouthful of food; afraid to try and live without drugs, yet thrown into a state of apprehension by each new prescription; afraid of the breath of fresh air, though convinced that her death is imminent because of the lack of it— such a patient (and what physician is not acquainted with this lady) decides to try Christian Science. She soon realizes that the first thing to do is to live up to the theory that there is no reality behind her former fears, and this she proceeds to do. Her mental determination would be of no therapeutic value, but the results which logically follow are of stupendous importance.

"The bath chair attendant is dismissed (there is often the most heroic courage exhibited in these first efforts) and regular exercise is taken; sufficient food is eaten, unsalted by tears and unaccompanied by dread. As she does not now acknowledge any cause for self-reproach or anxiety for herself or any one else, her sleep is sound and, therefore, refreshing. If we are told that such a convert has in a few months grown to look years younger, why on earth should we doubt it, when the physical explanation is so obvious?

"This practice of leading a normal life is not a spasmodic one, for she is undaunted by the actual pain which results, and both denies and ignores the reality. Every physician knows how trammeled Nature is by the self-limitations imposed by patients because of the discomfort experienced as the result of effort. This element of interference is wholly eliminated by the practices of the Scientist, and Nature which perhaps for years has been struggling to restore physical poise, but has been baffled at every point by the paralyzing effect of mental conditions, now finds itself working under the most ideal habits of mind and body.

"The body is so thankful to be relieved of this mental interference that it does not mind in the least that, in order to accomplish this, its very existence is hourly consigned to extinction. Whether the disease from which such a person has suffered is functional or organic, is irrelevant, so far as possible improvement is concerned. Nature makes no distinction in her efforts; were this not true, the physician's work would end with the commencement of structural changes. Up to the hour of death, there is always the chance that in spite of seemingly insurmountable obstacles, the vital power of restoration may respond to assistance and, if not entirely overcome the disease, at least prolong life." [1]

This long citation is not only applicable to Christian Scientists, but also to the followers of the New Thought movement.

[1] Reed: *Christian Science and Contrasting Christian Truth,* Vol. III, S. B. 8.

Their faith in a very literal sense contributes to make them whole. This accounts in no small degree for their extraordinary success. What appealed to the people is neither Mrs. Eddy's philosophy nor her religion, but the promise of being cured. The cures themselves really rest on an entirely different foundation; but many people do not take the trouble of distinguishing between the two. The new mind-movements promise to cure; at the same time they offer an explanation of their cures and assert that the cure is conditioned by their explanation. If the cure really takes place, the unreflecting multitude will accept the explanation along with the cure without any further ado. They are like a crowd eagerly watching a conjuror perform his tricks and accepting his explanation of how he does them, when, as a matter of fact, this explanation only served to distract their attention from what he was doing in reality. So also in the modern mind-cure movements fact and theory must be carefully kept apart. The facts we are ready to admit, but we maintain that the explanation of the cure does not lie with the systems that exploit the cure, but must be sought in certain natural principles.

CHAPTER XI

It has been seen that Mrs. Eddy held out religion as a bait that might make Quimbyism acceptable to the masses. This statement must not be taken to mean that Mrs. Eddy consciously commercialized religion for the mere purpose of success in her undertaking. True, she had the ambition to become a religious founder; she gloried in the hope that church bells might one day ring out her birthday, and repeatedly boasted that she was writing a bible: but so complex are the workings of the human mind that it is difficult to say to what extent the desires of the heart produced real conviction in the mind, and how far conviction exultingly anticipated success. Mrs. Eddy probably enough believed in her own teaching; she probably was convinced that Mind and God were one and the same and the only reality; she may even have persuaded herself (however unbelievable this may seem to us) that she was the divinely chosen instrument for establishing a new and more complete revelation. She no doubt believed in the possibility of mental cures; she must also be credited with sufficient shrewdness to realize the importance of religion in such an undertaking as hers. All her natural abilities were thus enlisted for the natural success of a natural cause. Religion came in as a means, but not merely as a means, but also as an end. For Mrs. Eddy's religious bent was such that it could not but find a prominent place in her system of healing.[1]

The same remarks may apply to the New Thought movement. Though it forms no distinct and united church organization and lays no claim to a new revelation, yet its basis is distinctly religious. Most of its followers accept a sort of Liberal

[1] Cf. *Miscellaneous Writings,* p. 311; Milmine: *op. cit.,* p. 138, 182.

Christianity, speak of God with great unction, and hold fundamentally the same beliefs as the Christian Scientists. We cannot help calling attention here to a curious anomaly. While apparently holding a most prominent place in these modern mind movements, religion, in reality, occupies a very inferior and secondary rank. If its prominence comes from the fact that it serves as a basis for their healing methods, its inferiority is due to the same fact; for it constantly remains subordinated to the supreme purpose of healing and mental culture.

This is at once its strength and its weakness. The pragmatist, for whom results alone count, and who makes practical usefulness the supreme test of truth, must endorse Christian Science and New Thought for the good they effect. But if results alone are not an infallible guide to truth, such a test is unacceptable. For those who believe that God has not left his creatures in mental darkness and anarchy, but has revealed to them His holy Will and has safeguarded this revelation against all danger of perversion, for such there can be but one measure of the truth of a religion, namely whether it conforms to the standard of the Gospel of Christ.

The modern mind-movements are not Christian. The most fundamental tenets of Christianity are slurred over, misrepresented, ignored or completely rejected. And those doctrines that have found a quiet nook within the sacred precincts of *Scientism* are mostly out of place; they appear like a stranger within the gate unheeded, unwelcome and unnecessary. They are there, because they were in the minds of the Christian Scientist, before he became an adept of Christian Science, and it was deemed either useful to retain them, or not worth while to reject them. There is one, and just one, religious doctrine that really seems essential in these modern cults, namely the doctrine of the spirituality and universality of God. To believe in God as the one reality and as essentially good is the summary of a modern mind-healer's creed. That in spite of their contempt of all doctrine these reformers should try to graft their metaphysical theories on the tree of historical Christianity was to be expected. To do otherwise would have been to invite relative failure from the very start.[1]   Of love for the Church or the churches there was none.   Mrs. Eddy never pretended to make Christian Science acceptable to the sects, but, on the contrary, compelled her followers to break with their former religious affiliations.[2]   The same more or less open hostility is evident in practically all prominent leaders of the movement.   None of them evinced any preoccupation to investigate the revealed truth fairly and historically.   They merely set up the word of a new master or leader against the teaching and leadership of Christ.   And if they did found new religious organizations that kept the name Christian, their main aim, it would seem, was to have a religion to offer to their prospective disciples which, by retaining the Christian name, would leave them under the illusion that they had not given up what they prized most.

With the possible exception of her idea of the inexistence of matter and evil, Mrs. Eddy took her Christianity as she found it in New England Unitarianism, with which it is in the main identical, neither better nor notably worse.   With the liberal and modernistic school of theology she proposes to serve Truth "independent of doctrines and time-honored systems."[3]   The open contradiction contained in this statement escapes them. People may reject such or such a doctrine or set of doctrines, but to reject all doctrinal teaching and still pretend to serve or teach truth is an impossibility.   Positive doctrines may be replaced by negative ones; this doctrine may be replaced by that one; but doctrinal teaching as such cannot be abolished.   Christianity, in particular, must always be doctrinal, or cease to be Christian.

---

[1] Cf. Dresser: *History,* p. 312: "The New Thought has doubtless played a part in emancipating people from the old theology.   The connection between the New Thought and religious liberalism has been more pronounced since 1895.   The first people to leave the Church and espouse mental healing were formerly orthodox.   But more Unitarians and other religious liberals changed over after a time.   The implied theology of the New Thought has always been liberal."

[2] *Church Manual,* Art. 4, sect. 2: "This Church will receive a member of another Church of Christ, Scientist, but not a church member from a different denomination until that membership is dissolved."

[3] *Science and Health,* Preface, p. vii.

Though minimizing traditional dogma, neither Christian Science nor New Thought is without doctrinal basis. We have insisted sufficiently on their fundamental dogmas of the One-ness and All-ness of God, of the inexistence of evil and the impossibility of matter. What remains to be noticed is their attitude towards the positive teachings of Christianity.

Christian Science has repeatedly been identified more or less with various ancient heresies. It has, in turn, been charged with being Manichean, Gnostic or Docetic in doctrine, and antinomian in ethics. The truth is that Christian Science cannot be identified with any one heresy, either ancient or modern, though undoubtedly it has incorporated elements that were distinctive of ancient sects as well as elements distinctive of modern thought. To judge only from appearances, nothing seems to be farther from the truth than an identification of Christian Science, with its insistence on the One-ness of God, and Manicheism, with its dualism of the two irreconcilable and eternal principles of Good and Evil. And yet, is not Mrs. Eddy's anomalous teaching concerning malicious animal magnetism, which is practically omnipotent, the nearest approach to Manicheism?

Again, Gnosticism, with its numberless *æons* and its hierarchy of spirits, seems to be a long way from anything that Christian Science teaches. And yet, Christian Science is akin to Gnosticism by making understanding or science its issue in opposition to faith. While the Christian Church has always exalted the act of faith as the essential act of religion, the Gnostics, and with them the Christian Scientists, depreciate faith, in order to exalt what they label gnosis, understanding or science, but what in truth is nothing but a figment of their fertile imagination. So, likewise, is it easy to see some analogy between the Gnostic *æons* that emanate from God, and Mrs. Eddy's conception of the divine ideas, which are thoroughly spiritual, and yet so real as to be the only reality we know. Finally, a group of Gnostics based themselves on the Bible as the word of God, but insisted on the absolute necessity of giving it an *allegorical* interpretation; thus does Mrs. Eddy advocate a *spiritual* interpretation which, while it neglects the literal meaning, is to her the real interpretation and the *Key to the Scripture.*[1]

Let us pass on to the charge of docetism leveled against Mrs. Eddy. The charge can only be true in the sense that Mrs. Eddy divides Christ. She made a real distinction between Jesus, the man, and Christ, the divine ideal that had taken possession of him. "Jesus is the human man, and Christ, the divine Ideal," says Mrs. Eddy; "hence the duality of Jesus, the Christ." In her Glossary, she declares Jesus to be "the highest human corporeal concept of the divine, rebuking and destroying error and bringing to light man's immortality"; and Christ she defines as "the divine manifestation of God which comes to the flesh, to destroy incarnate error."[2] The Christ can, therefore, be as readily in Mrs. Eddy as in the prophet of Nazareth.

From this it follows that Christian Science is anti-Trinitarian. It denies the divinity of Jesus, and of the Holy Ghost. The latter is for Mrs. Eddy "divine Science, the development of eternal life, Truth and love."[3] With this teaching disappear the very foundations of the Christian religion. It is all the more surprising that Mrs. Eddy should maintain against the Liberal theologians that Jesus was born of a virgin.

"The illumination of Mary's spiritual sense put to silence material law and its order of generation, and brought forth her child by the revelation of Truth, demonstrating God as the Father of men. The Holy Ghost, or divine Spirit, overshadowed the pure sense of the Virgin-Mother with the full recognition that being is Spirit. The Christ dwelt forever an ideal in the bosom of God, the divine Principle of the man

---

[1] "All gnostic systems are based on a kind of dualism of God and matter. But with the Platonists some regarded matter as *unreal* and without form, while others supposed it to be ruled by an evil principle, and hence to be directly opposed and hostile to God. The theogonic and cosmogonic process was explained on the principle of an *emanation*, by which from the hidden God a long series of Divine formations or *aeons* had emanated, whose indwelling divine potency diminished in measure as they removed from the original divine source." Kurtz: *Church History* (Philadelphia, 1878), Vol. I, p. 96.

[2] *Science and Health*, pp. 473, 583, 589.

[3] *Ibid.*, p. 588.

Jesus; and woman perceived this spiritual idea, though at first faintly developed in infant form. . . . Jesus was the offspring of Mary's self-conscious communion with God." [1]

This quotation, while it proves that Mrs. Eddy maintained the Virgin-Birth, proves at the same time that she did so in a manner quite out of keeping with orthodoxy. In this fact she believed she saw a confirmation of her theory of the immateriality of things. Also did she teach this Virgin-Birth not as a unique privilege, but as something which will become the rule as soon as men are sufficiently spiritual no longer to believe at all in the reality of matter. Mrs. Eddy loved to dwell on this idea. It was taught in her college, and expounded in her writings and private conversations. To find a basis for the act of generation in God, she transferred the ideas of both fatherhood and motherhood to Him, and loved to speak of Him as "our Father-Mother God." [2]

No system that remains Christian, even in name only, can neglect to treat of the fundamental mystery of Redemption or the Atonement, be it even merely to repudiate it. In this sense Mrs. Eddy acknowledges "Jesus' atonement as the evidence of divine, efficacious Love, unfolding man's unity with God through Christ Jesus, the Way-shower." [3] To keep the time-honored word of the Christian dogma, to empty it of its consecrated meaning, and to give it a new significance at variance with the traditional belief is a favorite method of Liberal and Modernistic theologians. Mrs. Eddy is thoroughly modern in this respect. By acknowledging the atonement as an evidence of Love, and as unfolding man's unity with God through Christ Jesus, she implicitly rejects the Christian dogma of Christ's vicarious death, for our sins. Mrs. Eddy consecrates a whole chapter to atonement and Eucharist. She puts down many a beautiful thought on Christ's sufferings, but the general trend of her teaching is this, that Christ by suffering and apparently dying has become to us an example of how to overcome the belief of suffering and how to "demonstrate" over death. "Let

[1] *Science and Health,* p. 29.
[2] *Ibid.,* p. 16.
[3] *Ibid.,* p. 497.

men think they had killed the body! afterwards He would show it to them unchanged. This should demonstrate that the true man, in Christian Science, is governed by God, by good, not evil, and is therefore not a mortal, but an immortal." [1] Elsewhere Mrs. Eddy puts this more plainly when she said that the crucifixion of Jesus and his resurrection served to elevate faith and understanding to perceive eternal Life—the allness of Spirit and the nothingness of matter." [2]

A further consequence of this teaching is that all the sacraments are given up. While the earlier Protestants kept two or three, Christian Science and New Thought reject them all and take special pains to explain away the deep spiritual significance of Baptism and the Eucharist.

"Our baptism," writes Mrs. Eddy, "is a purification from all error. Our Church is built on the divine Principle, Love. We can unite with this Church only as we are newborn of Spirit, as we reach the Life which is Truth and the Truth which is Life, by bringing forth the fruits of Love—casting out error and healing the sick." [3]

In a similar manner the Holy Eucharist is spirited away:

"Our Eucharist is spiritual communion with the one God. Our bread 'which cometh down from Heaven' is Truth. Our cup is the cross; our wine, the inspiration of Love—the draught our Master drank and commended to His followers. . . . The material blood of Jesus was no more efficacious to cleanse from sin when it was shed upon the accursed tree than when it was flowing in his veins, as he went daily about his Father's business. His true flesh and blood were His Life; and they truly eat his flesh and drink his blood who partake of the divine Life." [4]

Thus the issue is clearly drawn between Christ and Christian Science, between the plain and obvious meaning of Christ's

---

[1] *Science and Health,* p. 42.

[2] *Ibid.,* p. 497.

[3] *Ibid.,* p. 35.

[4] *Ibid.* Cf. also *Church Manual,* Art. XVIII, sect. 1: "The Mother Church of Christ, Scientist, shall observe no more communion seasons." Sect. 2: "The Communion shall be observed in the branch churches on the second Sunday in January and July of each year, and at this service the Tenets of The Mother Church are to be read."

words and the so-called spiritual interpretations of Christian Science. It would be useless to attempt a direct refutation of these views; for as long as any one can claim the right to put his own meaning into somebody else's words, it is useless to argue about the meaning intended by the author. We shall, therefore, proceed to illustrate Mrs. Eddy's concept of salvation.

"We acknowledge that man is saved through Christ, through Truth, Life and Love, as demonstrated by the Galilean Prophet in the healing of the sick and the overcoming of sin and death." [1]

Purposely ambiguous like the rest, these words of Mrs. Eddy might be interpreted in a sense not too far apart from the teaching of the Church. But in the light of Mrs. Eddy's teaching they implicitly deny the most fundamental truths of Christianity. For, to begin with, Christ here does not mean the man Jesus, but the divine Principle which is variously styled Truth, Life or Love or all three combined. Delete the word Christ from this proposition and you have lost nothing of Mrs. Eddy's meaning; on the contrary, it becomes clearer and a good deal more candid. Mrs. Eddy undoubtedly means this: "We acknowledge that man is saved through Truth, Life and Love." These principles of life, according to the modern mind healers, were demonstrated or exemplified by the Galilean Prophet, not in His teaching, His life, his prayers, His sufferings, but in the "healing of the sick, and the overcoming of sin and death." Once again Jesus is only the Way-shower to Christ or Christian Science, that is, to Truth, Life and Love.

"Man is saved through Christ." When we speak of salvation, we generally mean future and eternal salvation. Nothing would be farther from the mind of a Christian Scientist: for him salvation means primarily and exclusively salvation from sin, sickness and death, as he understands these. Salvation is merely a getting rid of some erroneous beliefs in the present life. The future interests them very little. As there is no future hell to be feared, and therefore no future evil from which man must be saved, so, in the opinions of Christian Scientists, a

[1] *Science and Health,* p. 497.

future heaven holds out very little attraction. It adds nothing
to the happiness of a Christian Scientist; it is merely the
present life continued in a different sphere. For this reason the
Christian Scientist focuses all his attention on the present life.
Says Mrs. Eddy:

" 'Now,' cried the apostle, 'is the acceptable time; behold,
now, is the day of salvation,'—meaning thereby, not that men
must now prepare for a future world-salvation or safety, but
that now is the time in which to experience that salvation
in spirit and life. Now is the time for so-called material
pains and material pleasures to pass away; for both are unreal, because impossible in Science. To break this earthly
spell, mortals must get the true idea and divine Principle of
all that really exists and governs the universe harmoniously.
This thought is apprehended slowly: and the interval between
its attainment is attended with doubts and defeats as well
as triumphs."

These are some of the more common religious affirmations
and negations which Christian Science and New Thought have
accepted. We should, however, labor under an erroneous belief, were we to hold that all Christian Scientists and all followers of the New Thought movement are united in a common
profession of faith. Perhaps nowhere can the fact of the
multiplicity of error in opposition to the unity of Truth be
better demonstrated than in this pretended rediscovery of
original Christianity. What one affirms, the other denies, and
yet all claim to be the very mouthpiece of Truth. Mr. Charles
Fillmore presents us with a sketch of the intellectual confusion
which reigns supreme among the followers of the new movements. He himself glories in this state of absolute individualism
and mental isolation:

"This, then, is really the foundation of the New Thought
movement," says he, "that its adherents shall each and all be
priest and prophet and stand alone with the inner Wisdom
as sole guide in matters religious. But not all are living up
to this free doctrine. There are leaders many, and schools
separating their followers into limitations of various degrees.
These are the natural divisions of the inner thought planes

finding expression without, and are, in a measure, necessary in the present race development.

"There are those in New Thought who are seeking to carry into the kingdom of heaven their earthly possessions. They are trying to use the newly discovered powers of the mind to bring up humanity on the old foundations. They proclaim the universality of the one Life and Intelligence, and that all necessary resting upon God must be good. . . .

"What may be termed the 'Mental Science' school holds that God is not a being of Love and Wisdom, but a force of attraction. They repudiate the Loving Father proclaimed by Jesus Christ, and hold that man is the highest form of self-consciousness in the universe. . . .

"There is another class of New Thought people who accept Christianity in its true sense, and try to live up to the teachings of Jesus Christ. . . .

"There are a number of schools, passing under the general name of New Thought, that adhere to this Christian interpretation, yet even among them there are minor differences. Each teacher tinges with his mental bias the philosophy he promulgates. Not one seems yet to have attained that place where the revelation from the Spirit of Truth, promised by Jesus to his followers, is wholly transparent. For this reason disciples are never safe in accepting the teachings of any school as final, or as having the unadulterated truth."[1]

These words show in what helpless confusion the New Thought movement already finds itself intellectually. By making her system an autocracy, Mrs. Eddy succeeded in keeping it better united, but here also there are many signs of disunion. In neither case is the doctrinal basis held to be of any great importance; for them all practice is the supreme test of truth.

[1] Fillmore: *The Science of Being* (Kansas City, 1912), pp. 250-252.

CHAPTER XII

ON PRAYER

I

THE most common view, entertained by the people about Christian Scientists, represents them as men, or rather as mostly women, who abhor the regular physician, who deny all healing power to drugs, who renounce, theoretically only, hygiene, and who cure, or hope to cure, all bodily ills by means of prayer. Now if this is true, if Christian Science can be credited with fostering the spirit of prayer, it deserves in this respect unstinted praise, no matter what objections can be raised against it on other grounds. The chapter on prayer now heads all others in the textbook, and its very first sentences lend color to the popular belief that nothing in Christian Science is more important than prayer.

"Regardless of what another may say or think on this subject, I speak from experience. Prayer, watching and working, combined with self-immolation, are God's gracious means for accomplishing whatever has been done successfully for the christianization and health of mankind." [1]

This value judgment on the importance of these acts in life deserves recognition; for as far at least as the spiritual life is concerned, it is wellnigh perfect and would deserve the highest commendation, were it not for the explanations that follow. As we read on, we are forcibly reminded of the Pharisee and the Publican. The Pharisee thanked God that he was not like the rest of men; but the Publican, "standing afar off, would not so much as lift up his eyes towards heaven, but struck his breast, saying, 'O God, be merciful to me a sinner.'" And

[1] *Science and Health,* p. 1.

Jesus adds: "I say to you, this man went down into his house justified rather than the other." [1]

According to Mrs. Eddy the Publican was entirely wrong to pray the way he did, and the Pharisee, to say the least, was much more nearly right. For

"prayer is not to be used as a confessional to cancel sin. This error would impede true religion. Sin is forgiven only, as it is destroyed by Christ, (that means) Truth and Life. *If prayer nourished the belief that sin is canceled, and that man is made better by merely praying, it is an evil. . . .* Temptation bids us repeat the offence, and woe comes in return for what is done. So it will ever be till we learn that there is no discount in the law of justice, and that we must pay the 'uttermost farthing.' . . . To suppose that God forgives or punishes sin, according as His mercy is sought or unsought, is to misunderstand Love, and make prayer the safety-valve for wrong-doing. . . . Do you ask Wisdom (that is, God) to be merciful and not punish sin? Then, ye ask amiss. Without punishment sin would multiply." [2]

Now plainly, Mrs. Eddy little understands the Christian teaching concerning sin and forgiveness. To ask God's forgiveness for our sins in her view is an evil. "Calling on him," she says, "to forgive our work, badly done or left undone, implies the vain supposition that we have nothing to do but to ask pardon, and that afterwards we shall be free to repeat the offense." [3] Mrs. Eddy could hardly have made this statement in good faith. She ought to have known that forgiveness is not a dispensation to commit sin. This may have been dinned into her ears as part of a standard vilification of the Confessional, but, surely, it was never the Church's teaching. Forgiveness is a pardon granted only to those who, in all sincerity, return to their Maker and are fully determined to keep His holy law. Nor does it ordinarily mean a full remission of all the punishment due to sin. While the eternal punishment of hell fire is always remitted with the guilt, temporal punishments, flowing

[1] Luke 18:10-14.
[2] *Science and Health,* pp. 20, 6, 10.
[3] *Ibid.,* p. 6.

from, or due to, sin—the only kind that Mrs. Eddy can acknowledge—are not as a rule entirely remitted along with the
guilt.

What, in Mrs. Eddy's mind, does forgiveness consist in?
It consists not only in giving up sinning, but also in overcoming
evil habits that have resulted from former sins, and even in
conquering concupiscence which is partly natural, and partly a
consequence of original sin and an inherited disposition. Though
Mrs. Eddy does not express her mind very clearly, there can be
little doubt that she labored under the error of the Reformers
that human nature is totally corrupt, and that concupiscence
and every evil habit is sinful. Now, sin does not consist in a
habit, but in an act, a deliberate, willful, lawless act, and it is
for such sinful acts, that God's forgiveness must be sought, a
forgiveness which can be obtained only by such as are truly
penitent and resolved to renounce their evil ways. Correcting
evil habits is something quite different from obtaining forgiveness; but for both the one and the other prayer must be pronounced of the highest utility and necessity. "Ask, and it shall
be given you; seek, and you shall find; knock, and it shall be
opened to you." [1]

In the light of this and many similar Scriptural statements,
weigh the following statements of the "new" revelation:

> "God is Love; can we ask Him to be more? God is Intel-
> ligence. Can we inform the Infinite Mind or tell Him any-
> thing He does not already comprehend? Do we hope to
> change perfection? Shall we plead for more at the open
> fount which always pours forth more than we receive? . . .
> Asking God to *be* God is a vain repetition. God is the same
> yesterday, today and forever, and He who is immutably right,
> will do right without being reminded of His province. The
> wisdom of man is not sufficient to warrant him in advising
> God. . . . How empty are our conceptions of Deity! We
> admit theoretically that God is good, omnipotent, omni-
> present, infinite, and, then, we try to give information to this
> infinite Mind, and plead for unmerited pardon and a liberal
> outpouring of benefactions. . . ." [2]

[1] Matt. 7:7.
[2] *Science and Health*, pp. 2-3.

Thus the founder of a new religion has succeeded in compressing into a small compass, and making her own, century-old objections raised in the first place by rationalists whose only object was precisely to raise objections and create difficulties in the way of belief, little interested themselves, if at all, in the solution of them. No other answer is required than the clear teaching of the Bible which Mrs. Eddy despite her textbook continued to accept "as our sufficient guide to eternal Life."[1] It may be proper, none the less, to point out here, without transgressing the limits imposed on us, some of Mrs. Eddy's unwarranted assumptions. She assumes that we pray to inform God of our needs, when, in point of fact, we pray because we have been ordered to do so by God Himself, who, thus, requires us to prepare ourselves for a more abundant outpouring of divine gifts by coöperating with His eternal designs. She assumes that the granting of our petitions is conditioned on a change in the Divine Will, when, as a matter of fact, from all eternity the granting of certain favors has been made dependent on prayer. She assumes that because God can give all and more than we need, He actually does so without our asking for anything, when daily experience proves the contrary. She becomes ludicrous, almost profane, when she assumes that prayers are for the purpose of reminding God of His duty, "of His province."

How easy it is to retort to Mrs. Eddy's rhetorical questions by an equal number of queries, similar in appearance, but more solid in contents, addressed now to Mrs. Eddy.

"God is our Lord and Master. Can we lay down laws for Him? God is Intelligence. Can we inform the Infinite Mind concerning the best ways of salvation? How can we presume that we know so perfectly the ways of Divine Providence as to be able to proclaim without hesitation that the granting of favors as a result of prayers must mean a change in the Divine Will? Is God at the mercy of his creatures, so that He is bound to pour out His blessings upon them, even when they refuse to accept them? Can he not bestow greater favors on a saint that prays than on a sinner that scoffs?

[1] *Science and Health,* p. 497.

Are not those dispositions that are essential to prayer, and the acts, which it necessitates, absolute requirements in the designs of the Divine Providence for the improvement and salvation of mankind? We admit theoretically that God is good, omnipotent, omnipresent, infinite, and then we try to bring Him down to the level of our puny intellect and to apply to Him the measure of our human prejudices and self-conceit."

This accumulation of questions goes to show how easy the game of raising objections in the form of question marks, quietly assuming from the start that they all must be answered in the sense that is uppermost in the mind of the questioner.

Mrs. Eddy is not satisfied with claiming that a prayer of petition is powerless, she maintains that it is injurious: it does not, in her opinion, make man better, it makes him worse; for it is a belief, an error, an illusion, which, if it benefits momentarily, will in the end do harm.

"The habit," she says, "of pleading with the Divine Mind, as one pleads with a human being, perpetuates the belief in God as humanly circumscribed—an error which impedes spiritual growth. . . . A mere request that God will heal the sick has no power to gain more of the Divine Presence than is always at hand. The beneficial effect of such prayer for the sick is on the human mind, making it act more powerfully on the body through a blind faith in God. This, however, is one belief casting out another,—a belief in the unknown casting out a belief in sickness. . . . Prayer to a corporeal God affects the sick like a drug, having no efficacy of its own, but borrowing its power from human faith and belief. The drug does nothing because it has no intelligence. It is mortal belief, not divine Principle or Love which causes a drug to be apparently either poisonous or sanative. . . . This common form of praying for the recovery of the sick finds help in blind belief; whereas help should come from the enlightened understanding." [1]

These words are cunningly calculated to undermine the experiential proof which all praying people have of the efficacy

[1] *Science and Health*, p. 12.

of prayer and of the Divine help it obtains. Not God, but nature is responsible for its results; it is not even God through nature, but simply nature based on error, on a kind of hallucination or self-delusion. Thus, the rejection of the plain evidence of daily religious experience is demanded of the Christian Scientist on no other warrant than that of Mrs. Eddy's unsupported word alone. As this, however, cannot outweigh the clear teaching of Christ and of His Church, we may dismiss the subject without further comment.

But we have not done as yet with the analysis of Mrs. Eddy's destructive theories. If she rejects all prayer of petition and propitiation, she particularly execrates audible and public prayers.

"Audible prayer is impressive," she says, "it gives momentary solemnity and elevation to thought; but does it produce any lasting benefit? Looking deeply into these things, we find that 'a zeal . . . not according to knowledge' gives occasion for reaction unfavorable to spiritual growth, sober resolve, and wholesome perception of God's requirements. The motives for verbal prayer may embrace too much love of applause to induce or encourage Christian sentiment. . . . The danger from audible prayer is, that it may lead us into temptation. By it we may become involuntary hypocrites, uttering desires which are not real, and consoling ourselves in the midst of sin, with the recollection that we have prayed over it,—or mean to ask forgiveness at some later date. Hypocrisy is fatal to religion. . . . A wordy prayer may afford a quiet sense of self-justification, though it makes the sinner a hypocrite. . . ."[1]

"In public prayer we often go beyond our convictions, beyond the honest standpoint of fervent desire. If we are not secretly yearning and openly striving for the accomplishment of all we ask, our prayers are *vain repetitions*, such as the heathen use. . . . Can the mere public expression of our desires increase them? Do we gain the omnipotent ear sooner by words than by thoughts? Even if prayer is sincere, God knows our needs, before we tell Him or our fellow-beings about it."[2]

[1] *Science and Health*, p. 7.
[2] *Ibid.*, p. 13.

In the midst of much that we must reject, we find here some
sentiments that we must applaud. Hypocrisy is undoubtedly
fatal to religion; religion is too much an affair of the exterior,
for some; by prayer some of us "may become involuntary hypocrites, uttering desires which are not real and consoling ourselves in the midst of sin." If the charge "that verbal prayer
may embrace too much love of applause" is true, it can apply
only to the Protestant practice of formulating new prayers
at every new service, not to the public prayers of the Catholic
Church. These observations are not without foundation and
would, indeed, be praiseworthy but for the spirit in which they
were made. For Mrs. Eddy uses these strictures not as an
argument to lead men to put their heart and soul into prayer,
but as a weapon of offense against prayer itself. But as the
abuse of anything cannot reprobate its proper use, so abuses
that may creep into public prayers do not vitiate the use of
public prayer when resorted to for mutual edification and social
worship. Why, forsooth, should Mrs. Eddy worry about audible
prayer? If her theories are true, and matter does not exist, or
exists only in belief, audible prayers do not take place, since
they evidently presuppose material organs and a material surrounding.

II

Prayer in Christian Science seemingly is neither for the
asking of forgiveness nor for the obtaining of favors. No
mention is made of prayer of adoration, and although thanks-
giving is mentioned, it is practically restricted to a grateful
behavior. "Are we really grateful for the good already received? Then we shall avail ourselves of the blessings we have,
and thus be fitted to receive more. Gratitude is much more than
a verbal expression of thanks. Action expresses more gratitude
than speech." [1] What, then, does prayer really mean in Christian Science? Is all prayer of petition absolutely excluded?
The answer lies in Mrs. Eddy's definition of prayer: "Consistent
prayer is the desire to do right. Prayer means that we desire

---

[1] *Science and Health*, p. 3.

to, and will, walk in the light so far as we receive it, even though with bleeding footsteps, and waiting patiently on the Lord, will leave our real desires to be rewarded by Him." [1] Such a prayer God will hear.

Mrs. Eddy chiefly objects, and rightly so, to mere "lip-service," but she teaches that the right kind of desires are a most efficient prayer; "Prayer, coupled with a fervent habitual desire to know and do the will of God will bring us into all truth. Such a desire has little need of audible expression. It is best expressed in thought and life." [2] While thus insisting strongly on the sincerity of prayer, even to the extent of pronouncing audible prayer useless, Mrs. Eddy does not neglect to point out a fitting object for our prayer: "What we most need is the prayer of fervent desire for growth in grace, expressed in patience, meekness, love and good deeds." [3]

There may be nothing new in all this, but we are glad to find it in *Science and Health*. What we criticize is not this strong insistence on the necessity of sincerely desiring what we ask for, but the fact that prayer is completely identified with this desire. Does it not appear as if Mrs. Eddy looked for the effects of prayer not in a supernatural assistance, but in that gradual mental education which the fostering of good desires must accomplish?

This explains why prayer occupies such an insignificant place in Christian Science Church services. The order of exercises—fourteen in number—that constitute the service, includes the singing of hymns, the reading of selections from the Bible and the textbook, which is followed by what is called silent prayer. After the audible repetition of the Lord's prayer with its so-called spiritual interpretation, another hymn is sung, and then follow in regular order the alternate reading, by the First Reader and the congregation, of an assigned selection from Scripture; the Lesson-Sermon, consisting of the reading of extracts from the Bible and the so-called correlative sections from *Science and Health;* the collection, and, finally,

[1] *Science and Health,* p. 9.
[2] *Ibid.,* p. 11.
[3] *Ibid.,* p. 4.

what is called the scientific statement of being, with its correlative Scripture text taken from the Gospel according to St. John, third chapter, verses 1-3.

The only strictly vocal prayer in this series of exercises is the Lord's prayer with its so-called spiritual interpretation. Even Mrs. Eddy was not bold enough to reject this prayer; but she caricatures it. Though its every statement is plain enough for a child to understand, Mrs. Eddy interprets it, and such an interpretation! It has varied considerably in the course of time, and for comparison two of its versions are here reproduced in parallel columns.

SCIENTIFIC INTERPRETATION OF THE LORD'S PRAYER [1]

Edition of 1881	*Later Editions*
1. Principal, Eternal and Harmonious.	Our Father-Mother God, all harmonious.
2. Nameless and adorable Intelligence.	Adorable One.
3. Thou art ever present and supreme.	Thy kingdom is within us; Thou art ever present.
4. And when this supremacy of Spirit shall appear, the dream of matter will disappear.	Enable us to know—as in heaven, so on earth—God is supreme.
5. Give us the understanding of Truth and Love.	Give us grace for today; feed the famished affections.
6. And loving we shall learn God, and Truth will destroy all error.	And infinite Love is reflected in love.
7. And lead us unto the Life that is Soul, and deliver us from the errors of sense, sin, sickness and death.	And Love leadeth us not into temptation, but delivereth us from sin, disease and death.
For God is Life, Truth, and Love forever.	For God is now and forever all Life, Truth and Love.

How Mrs. Eddy must have labored to pervert the plain and obvious meaning of these words, so beautiful in their grand

[1] Cf. *Science and Health*, p. 17; Mark Twain, *op. cit.*, p. 305.

simplicity! Four of the petitions have been changed into affirmations; the reference to the Divine Will, in which Mrs. Eddy does not believe, and to obedience to it has been dropped. The word bread which sounded too material has been replaced by a reference to grace and famished affections, and, finally, the change that shocks most of all, is the change of "Our Father" into "Our Father-Mother God," and of the reference to Heaven as His abode into the adjective "all harmonious."

Christian Science, it is now evident, is far from being essentially an association of prayer for the improvement of the human race.

CHAPTER XIII

ETHICS OF THE MODERN MIND-MOVEMENTS

I

The pragmatism of our days professes to put all things through the crucible of experience. It transfers to all fields of human life and endeavor the methods of research and experimentation which have proved so valuable in the laboratory. It has invaded the field of ethics and gives as the supreme norm of good and evil the rule that whatever works out well in practice, is true and good. Mrs. Eddy has appealed to this principle as the test of the truth of what she says. She points to the record of Christian Science at the sickbed, and boldly demands the application, in her case, of the Master's word: "By their fruits you shall know them." The opponents of Christian Science, on the other hand, accept the challenge, but apply the test not exclusively to the sickchamber, but to all the intellectual and moral aspects of this new religion.

The pragmatism of the modern mind-healing places the emphasis on the wrong values of life. They assign to bodily health absolutely the highest place. They do not deny, they do even insist on, the necessity of a moral life, but their final aim and object is bodily health and bodily comfort, with the practice of certain virtues thrown in, as a necessary means towards this end. A palpable paradox stares us in the face: these systems deny the reality of disease, and yet, make the healing of disease their first and main concern. On almost every page of *Science and Health* reappears the ghost of ill-health to exorcize which ever remains the chief purpose of Christian Science.

Another feature of these cults, to which a Christian will object, is the fact that they throw together in a common class evils which Christianity has constantly kept apart. Sickness and death belong together; but when sin is grouped with both, as though they all belonged to the same order, chaos is introduced into Christian ethics. Sin springs from a will that is free and issues into a state that is called guilt and, thus, occupies an absolutely unique position in human life. Physical ills, on the contrary, belong directly to the material, and only indirectly to the spiritual world. The consequence is that the treatment of them, if the term be allowed, cannot be the same for both.

Has not Christ been described as "the man of sorrows," and acquainted with infirmity, wounded for our iniquity, and bruised for our sins? Is it not stated in so many words that "the Lord was pleased to bruise him in infirmity"? [1] If this is so, sickness and suffering cannot be treated as absolutely evil. Mrs. Eddy herself, when there is question of Christian Science interests, at times recognizes this.

"Who that has felt the loss of human peace has not gained stronger desires for spiritual joy? The aspiration after heavenly good comes even before we discover what belongs to Wisdom and Love. The loss of earthly hopes and pleasures brightens the ascending path of many a heart. The pains of sense quickly inform us that its pleasures are mortal, and that joy is spiritual. . . . The pains of sense are salutary, if they wrench away false pleasureable beliefs, and transplant the affections from sense to Soul, where the creations of God are good, 'rejoicing the heart.' Such is the sword of Science, whereby Truth decapitates error, and mortality gives place to man's higher individuality and destiny." [2]

The inconsistency of these declarations with Mrs. Eddy's fundamental tenet, that physical suffering is unreal and essentially evil, need not be pointed out. Christian Science is entirely reared on the supposition that sickness is an unmitigated evil, and that it is the first duty of every Christian Scientist to root it up. How different the Christian view, which

[1] Isaias 53:3, 10.
[2] *Science and Health,* p. 265.

represents many of the saints as winning their eternal crown through a long martyrdom of pains and penances! The Christion faith looks upon physical evil as a means of grace, of expiation and merit, and, consequently, often as a blessing in disguise, while it condemns sin as the only unqualifiedly real evil. If, then, sickness lingers in spite of doctor, drug and prayer, the patient's mental make-up is not necessarily at fault, as the modern mind-healer must consistently assert, for sickness and sorrow undoubtedly have a mission to fulfill in the designs of divine Providence for the spiritualization of man's sensual nature and for the salvation of his soul.

II

That Christian Science is lowering the standard of morality by its peculiar teaching concerning sin is beyond dispute. Shall we, with many authors, go so far as to accuse it of antinomian tendencies? One writer says:

"Christian Science teaches that there is no such thing as sin. Sin has no reality. Over and over and over again its non-existence is affirmed, its actuality denied. Well, if that be true, Christian Science teaches that you can commit adultery, robbery, murder or any other of the numerous crimes we have always thought to be sinful and not be guilty of sin at all! Whatever these iniquities and others equally heinous be, they are not sin. Heaven pity us if our intelligence endorse such ethics as truth." [1]

Another one writes:

"On this theory sin is only a bad dream and all we need do to get rid of it is to stab ourselves broad awake. This doctrine of the nothingness of matter and of sin is of ancient Gnostic lineage and it has lost none of its antinomian tendencies. It is allied to the pantheistic doctrine of illusion that saturates the Orient and is so productive of immorality. This denial of the very possibility of sin logically sweeps away all barriers against the flesh and opens the gate for sensuality

---

[1] Biederwolf: *The Unvarnished Facts about Christian Science*, p. 29.

to flood the soul. If Christian Scientists do not give way
to this tendency, it is because they are better than their
doctrine." [1]

Quotations might be multiplied, to prove these contentions;
yet, owing to Mrs. Eddy's peculiar terminology, such quotations would be misquotations. In all fairness we must admit,
that, in theory, Mrs. Eddy does not directly minimize the great
evil of sin. If she calls it an unreality, a belief, an illusion, she
does not mean that sinful acts are not really sinful, but that
they have no lasting substance; that they do not belong to the
real and eternal order of God's Creation, but are defects in
the order of being; they have no existence in the eternal
Mind, but form part of the "mortal mind," which, in the
nature of things, must disappear sooner or later with all its
contents. For Mrs. Eddy, both sickness and sin are unreal
in the peculiar sense which Mrs. Eddy gives to this word, but
they are superlatively real in human experience. In this sense
Mrs. Eddy says:

"If mortals would keep proper ward over mortal mind,
the brood of evils, which infest it, could be cleared out. We
must begin with this so-called mind, and empty it of sin and
sickness, or sin and sickness will never cease. The present
codes of human systems disappoint the weary searcher after
a divine theology, adequate to the right education of human
thought. Sin is thought before it is acted. You must control it in the first instance, or it will control you in the
second." [2]

Mrs. Eddy even declares that the cure of sin is harder than
the cure of disease:

"It is easier to cure the most malignant disease than it
is to cure sin. The author has raised up the dying, partly
because they were willing to be restored; while she has
struggled long, and perhaps in vain, to lift a student out of
a chronic sin. Under all modes of pathological treatment,
the sick recover more rapidly from disease than the sinner

[1] Snowden: *The Truth about Christian Science* (Philadelphia, 1920), p. 29.
[2] *Science and Health*, p. 234.

from his sin. . . . The fear of disease and the love of sin
are the springs of man's enslavement." [1]

How sin succeeds by degrees in enslaving the whole man, and
then rushes him on to his punishment is at times graphically
described by the founder of Christian Science.

"The belief of sin," she writes, "which has grown terrible
in strength and influence, is an unconscious error in the beginning,—an embryonic thought without motive; but afterwards it governs the so-called man. Passion, appetite, dishonesty, envy, hatred, and revenge ripen into action, only to
pass on from shame and woe to their final punishment." [2]

Here it may also be recalled that Mrs. Eddy insists on the
moral regeneration of a patient as a prerequisite for a final
cure of his physical illness. The reason given by her is that
disease often grows out of sin. "The soil of disease," she says,
"is sinful mortal mind, and you have an abundant or scanty
crop, according to the seedlings in that mind, unless they are
uprooted and cast out." [3]

If there is danger of antinomianism in Christian Science,
the danger lies not, therefore, in Mrs. Eddy's avowed sentiments regarding sin, but in her disregard of the sanctions that
God has attached to the violation of the Divine Law. The fear
of the Lord has been entirely eliminated. "The fear of the
Lord is the beginning of Wisdom," says Holy Writ; for the
modern healers' fear is more nearly the beginning of all evil,
for from fear spring evils innumerable. As all fears must be
banished, hell, logically enough, must be ruled out of existence,
no matter what the Bible teaches. How little, after all, does
Scripture count in the lives and thoughts of many who proclaim
it as their sufficient and only guide to salvation! Mrs. Eddy
does not so much as take the trouble of disproving the existence
of hell; she everywhere takes its non-existence for granted.

---

[1] *Science and Health*, p. 373. The sin of which Mrs. Eddy here speaks is
Richard Kennedy's defection from her. Whenever Mrs. Eddy used particularly strong language, there was generally a personal consideration in
the matter.
[2] *Ibid.*, p. 188.
[3] *Ibid.*, p. 188.

The word itself receives from her hands a singular connotation; hell means "mortal belief, error, lust, remorse, hatred, revenge, sin, sickness, death, suffering and self-destruction, self-imposed agony, effects of sin, and, finally, that which worketh abomination or maketh a lie." [1]   Now to deny the existence of hell is to remove one of the safeguards of virtue. It is a matter of common experience that passions are not overcome by the mere knowledge that they are evil, and, despite the high-sounding praises lavished on a morality with virtue as its own reward, the Bible truth still remains true today, that "the fear of the Lord is the beginning of Wisdom."

"The belief of sin is punished as long as it lasts," says Mrs. Eddy.[2] This does not mean, as it ordinarily should, that not sin, but only the belief in sin is punished; that not sin, but the belief in sin is evil; or that if one overcomes the belief that such or such an action is sinful, no punishment will ensue. It means that sin which is a "belief" (in Mrs. Eddy's vocabulary) is punished, but punished only as long as that belief lasts. Nor does this mean that the punishment ceases, as soon as the sinful act is accomplished; for Mrs. Eddy, sin is a state or lasting disposition rather than an act. Hence it follows that the punishment is commensurate with this lasting disposition and will not cease until this disposition has been done away with.

This interpretation of Mrs. Eddy's mind removes still further the danger of antinomianism. The immoral teaching often ascribed to Mrs. Eddy does not flow from her principles; the imputation of such teaching is entirely due to the erroneous interpretation given to her words by critics. Unfortunately her words lend themselves but too easily to such an interpretation and it is not impossible that the day may come when her words, rather than her meaning, will be accepted by some of her followers. Christian Science is still young, its members are still afire with the zeal of neophytes, still enthusiastically devoted to the mission which they believe it possesses. What is best in it is brought to the fore. Will it be so in fifty or a

---

[1] *Science and Health,* p. 497.
[2] *Cf. ibid.,* p. 35 ff.

hundred years from now? Will not the second or third generation of Scientists draw from Mrs. Eddy's premises conclusions
vastly different from those of their fathers?

As a matter of history, Mrs. Eddy's own sense of sin was
none of the strongest. Hers was not a delicate conscience.
Her most violent outbursts against sin were always occasioned
by some fancied wrong on the part of her students towards
their teacher and Leader.

The attempt to improve on her teaching, or even merely to
explain it, even with the best of intentions, was one of the
worst crimes that could be committed; to become disloyal to
the Founder or the Church,—an offense of which Mrs. Eddy
was the sole judge—was "immorality." No scruples stopped
Mrs. Eddy on her chosen path. After condemning, in the
most unmeasured terms, mental malpractice, she unblushingly
resorted to it herself, and organized others to resort to it, by
hurling back, mentally, on her imaginary enemies all those evils
which, as she thought, they were fastening on her.[1] In how far
such sentiments resulted from her religious beliefs, and in how
far they were the manifestations of a naturally intolerant and
vindictive spirit, may be an open question. One thing is certain: Christian Science did nothing to render such excesses impossible. "By their fruits you shall know them."

III

Mrs. Eddy's teaching concerning marriage has been much
under fire. It sounds strange to be told that a woman after
marrying three times and personally choosing her third husband, should disparage the institution of matrimony. She went
so far as to call it "legalized lust" and spoke of it as of an
evil, the toleration of which only the present backward state
of human progress could justify. How flippant she could be
on this subject is seen from her answer to the question: "What

---

[1] Mr. Peabody ends his *Masquerade* with an account of the suicide of a
young lady, which he ascribes directly to the demand made on her "to treat
Mrs. Eddy's own son and his lawyer in hostile fashion—by sending arsenical
poison into their veins (mentally, of course), or otherwise putting them to
death." *The Religio-Medical Masquerade*, pp. 192-194.

do you think of marriage?" She replied in *Miscellaneous Writings* "that it is often convenient, sometimes pleasant, and occasionally a love affair." "Marriage," she continued, "is susceptible of many definitions. It sometimes presents the most wretched condition of human existence. To be normal, it must be a union of the affections that tends to lift mortals higher." [1] In these words we discover an echo from Mrs. Eddy's own marriage ventures. But she was not always flippant when treating of this subject. In the chapter devoted to it in *Science and Health* are voiced many noble sentiments. She tells the married people that, "infidelity to the marriage covenant is the social scourge of all races," that "after marriage it is too late to grumble over incompatibility of disposition," that "the propagation of the human species is a greater responsibility, a more solemn charge than the culture of your garden, or the raising of stock to increase your flocks and herds."

Unfortunately these platitudes seem more like an introduction to the peculiarities of her teaching than an exhortation to fidelity. Why should Mrs. Eddy drag in marriage at all, when this subject seems so foreign to her purpose? The fact is that this theme possessed for her a strange fascination, as it offered her a splendid opportunity to draw out some of the consequences flowing from her theories. It also afforded her an occasion to bring forward, among others, her views on the rights of women, on the education of children, on the granting of divorce, and on heredity. But what has attracted the greatest attention is her statement that the time will come,—not in the hereafter, but in the present life,—when marriage will give way to a better state, as a direct result of the teaching of Christian Science. As soon as the world is prepared for this, men shall neither marry nor be given in marriage.

"The time cometh," she says, "of which Jesus spake, when He declared that in the resurrection there should be no more marrying nor giving in marriage, but man should be as the angels. Then shall Soul rejoice in its own, wherein passion has no part. Then white-robed purity will unite in one

[1] *Miscellaneous Writings*, p. 52.

person masculine wisdom and feminine love, spiritual understanding and perpetual peace." [1]

Still more enigmatic are the words which follow:

"The scientific fact that man and the universe are
evolved from Spirit—God—and so are spiritual and good, is
as fixed in divine Science, as is the proof that mortals gain
the sense of health and heaven only as they lose the sense of
sin, disease and matter. Mortals can never understand God's
creation while believing that man is a creator. His children
already created will be cognized only as man seeks and finds
the truth of his own being. Thus it is that the real, ideal man
appears in proportion as mortals, or the false and material,
disappear. *To 'no longer marry or be given in marriage'*
neither closes man's continuity, nor his sense of increasing
number in God's infinite plan. Spiritually to understand
there is but one creator,—God,—unfolds his creation, confirms the Scriptures, brings the sweet assurance of no part-
ing, no pain, and man perfect and eternal." [2]

Marriage and material generation smacked too much of
that non-entity, matter, not to fall under the ban. By speaking
on it as "one having authority" and by timely appeals to the
Virgin-Birth of Christ, she impressed her first followers with a
sense of awe and religious reverence. But even Mrs. Eddy
hardly expected that her words would be taken too literally by
her students.

"Until it is learned that God is the father of all, let marriage continue, and let mortals permit no such disregard of
law as may lead to a worse state of society than now exists.
Honesty and virtue ensure the stability of the marriage covenant. Spirit will ultimately claim its own, all that really is;
and the voices of physical sense be forever hushed." [3]

Little did Mrs. Eddy suspect that even in her own lifetime
a student might lay a claim to having exemplified this bold
teaching of the new "Science" concerning spiritual generation.

[1] *Science and Health*, p. 64.
[2] *Ibid.*, p. 68.
[3] *Ibid.*, p. 64.

In June, 1890, Mrs. Woodbury, who had been associated with Mrs. Eddy since 1879, and had been one of her foremost healers and teachers, claimed that her baby boy was the result of an immaculate conception and, consequently, a demonstration of Mrs. Eddy's theory of mental generation. Mrs. Woodbury named the child "The Prince of Peace" and baptized him at Ocean Point, Maine, in a pool which she called Bethsaida.

"Mrs. Woodbury would not permit the child who was called *Prince* for short, to address her husband as 'father,' but insisted that he address Mr. Woodbury as 'Frank' and herself as 'Birdie!' The fact that he was a fine, healthy baby, and was never ill, seemed to Mrs. Woodbury's disciples conclusive evidence that he was the Divine Principle of Christian Science made manifest in the flesh. It was their pleasure to bring gifts to 'Prince,' to discover in his behavior indications of his spiritual nature; and they professed to believe that when he grew to manhood, he would enter upon his Divine ministry." [1]

This romantic tale, as so many other ventures in which Mrs. Eddy was concerned, ended in the law courts and in a suit for libel on the part of Mrs. Woodbury. In an article published in the *Arena*, May 1899, Mrs. Woodbury vindicated her honor against Mrs. Eddy's insinuations and at the same time exposed Mrs. Eddy's teaching in the following strong language:

"The substance of certain instructions given by Mrs. Eddy in private is as follows: 'If Jesus was divinely conceived by the Holy Ghost or Spirit, without a human father, Mary not having known her husband,—then women may become mothers by a supreme effort of their own minds, or through the influence upon them of an Unholy Ghost, a malign spirit. Women of unquestioned integrity who have been Mrs. Eddy's students testify that she has so taught, and that by this teaching families have been broken up; that thus maidens have been terrified out of their wits, and stimulated into a frenzy. . . . Whatever her denials may be, such was Mrs. Eddy's teaching while in her college; to which she added

[1] Milmine; *op. cit.,* p. 430 ff.

the oracular declaration that it lay within her power to dissolve such motherhood by a wave of her celestial rod.' " [1]

Here we may leave this subject appealing once more to Mrs. Eddy's favorite motto: "By their fruits you shall know them."

IV

If it is true that Mrs. Eddy did not altogether deny the reality of sin, but rather looked upon sin as an evil worse even than sickness, it does not follow that her standard of morality was a very exalted one. Her moral code was vague and indefinite and could, at best, be an unsafe guide for regulating human life. But it may be rejoined that for the modern mind-healers the Bible is an official and an inspired book; that, in consequence, they cannot be accused of lacking a safe and sound rule of life. To this we reply that it is, unfortunately, a matter of common and daily observation that personal choice and individual presumptions make of the Bible a mine where each one can find what he desires, and that it has often been made the excuse for the greatest excesses.

Professor William James speaks of these movements as *religions of healthy-mindedness*. What, we may ask, is a healthy mind? One in which there dwell no false, embarrassing or idle concepts; one in which truth resides and which is exempt from worry and empty fears; one which, finding all its desires satisfied, can rest in perfect contentment: all these are essential characters of a healthy mind that is not only subjectively right, but also in possession of objective truth.

Such qualities are not found in the modern mental-healing cults. These, it is true, do not admit doubt regarding their intellectual equipment. Satisfied with the general impression that they are right, the modern mind-healers will never question the foundations of their faith; for failures they will not blame their system, but the unskillful management of those who fail; in a word, their faith could not be stronger, had they really a direct divine guaranty for it. This supreme mental assurance,

[1] Quoted in *Milmine: op. cit.*, p. 438.

as far as physical effects are concerned, is as good as would be a full possession of objective truth.

If, then, physical well-being were the only consideration, the followers of these new systems might rest securely enough on their beliefs. But such a subjective norm needs to be based on objective truth, and in this respect, we deny that the *new mind* comes up to the definition of a healthy mind, or that it is better than the *old and tried mind,* imbued with the doctrines of faith. Having as their ultimate aim, not truth, but satisfaction; not doctrine, but life; not revelation, but repose, the modern mind-healers have embraced a sort of refined epicureanism, not built, it is true, on the inevitableness of fate, but on the All-goodness of God. In ethics the modern mind movements are utilitarian; they seek bodily comfort to the almost complete exclusion of other considerations. If they decry sin and vice, it is because sin and vice bear sorry fruits even for this life; if they recommend a doctrine or a practice, it is because these are fruitful in good results for the comfort of earthly life.

When dealing with the great problem of the goodness of God, Christian Scientists not only shut their eyes to disagreeable facts, but forget that the goodness of God is necessarily different from the goodness of men; that its first attribute is holiness, and its principal object moral perfection; that all other things, both material and spiritual, are subordinate to these; and, consequently, that virtue must be cultivated not merely with a view to bodily or mental comfort, but out of love for God. When these new religions aim principally at banishing worry of every kind from man's life, trusting thereby to secure excellent health, their aim being a low one, no high spirituality can result; for the end in view determines the degree of perfection of any act, disposition or doctrinal system. A pure intention makes all the difference in the world in matters ethical. Psychotherapy may recommend, as favorable to health and happiness, an array of noble virtues which the Christian religion may command as a service to God; in this case the mental healer and the Christian, while pursuing the same immediate end, yet embrace different modes of life, differentiated by their ulterior purpose or intention. In one case, the motive is selfish enjoyment, in the other, the love of God above all things. When St. Paul declares that "the fruit of the Spirit is joy, peace, patience, benignity, goodness, longanimity, mildness, faith, modesty, continency, chastity," [1] he mentions these as results of the spiritual life, while the one and only aim of the Christian should be to live in the Spirit. If he constantly aims at such a spiritual life, the results, the fruits of godliness, will take care of themselves.

Compare with these words of the inspired author the sentiments of one of the best known New Thought writers of the present day:

"Thought-causes are so complex," writes Charles Fillmore, "that it is impossible to point out in all cases the specific thought that causes a certain disease; but twelve fundamental mind activities lie at the base of all existence, and when any one of these is sounded all the others give attention. . . . Nearly all sick people lack vital force, hence the Life treatment is good for all. Hate, anger, jealousy, malice, etc., are almost universal in human consciousness, and a treatment for Love will prove a healing balm. Anxiety, worry, and fear of poverty burden most people, and the Prosperity treatment will be effective. Do not be afraid to use the statements in healing, as a whole or in part; they will always help and never hurt any one. Remember the object of all treatments is to raise the mind to the Christ Consciousness, through which all true healing is accomplished." [2]

The keynote of this treatment consists in putting the ban on worry and on anything that might burden the human mind. Yet the absence of worry in our present condition and under all circumstances is not a virtue. To make this a direct aim in life is to encourage a happy-go-lucky kind of disposition which eventually will result in apathy, lack of interest and ambition, a narrowing of the mental horizon and utter selfishness. If these results are not so apparent in our own days, it may be that the newness of these views has so far prevented

[1] Gal. 5:22.
[2] Fillmore, *Christian Healing*, p. 258.

them from running into seed; but, from present results, it is impossible to forecast what the future will reveal.

Moreover, the rejection of all anxiety and worry means a stunting and stifling of conscience. Conscience is a monitor which keeps the offender on the alert until he amends. In the modern mind-healing systems sickness must perform this office, while conscience must be looked upon askance as a breeder of disease. A mental treatment undoubtedly can cure at least for a time most men of this troublesome guide; there is nothing like a systematic course of reasoning to make man as nearly as possible *conscienceless*. A New Thought treatment might thus prove to be of invaluable assistance to professional law-breakers; or let us rather say, as a matter of fact, these do by similar processes of reasoning set themselves above the fear and worry of detection and punishment. Surely, not a very good recommendation for this sort of medicine!

We may call attention also to another aspect of these treatments, their entire indifference as to objective truth. By affirming what is positively false, and by denying what is undoubtedly a fact, simply because good physical results are expected, they try to build up human life on a lie. It is here, if anywhere, that we find the principle, "the end justifies the means" applied with an utter disregard to truth. It goes without saying that such a conduct is absolutely at variance with sound morality.

One favorite treatment, resorted to by all modern mind-healers, is that of love (oftenest spelled with a capital L). The praises of this treatment are sounded everywhere. The love of God for men is insisted on and extolled in a hundred different tunes. "The universe is created and governed by Love." "We must get into Love's ways; we will then come into harmony with the universal law." "Punishment is not a word known in the realm of Love." "One who condemns another for any reason whatever, has not an understanding of the spiritual law of Love. The one who condemns or criticizes another lets bitterness into his own mind."

"To love your enemies is not for sentiment, but for a practical double purpose of cleansing your mind of the corroding hate, and also of making of your enemies friends, so that their thoughts will go out in peace to bless you, and at the same time to cause peaceful conditions to obtain within themselves. The most foolish thing one can do is to hate and get angry. It is a violation of the law under which we are intended to live." [1]

Far be it from us to minimize the importance of love in the moral and spiritual order. Love, the love of God, and the love of man, is the great commandment. Love underlies the whole work of Creation: God's works are works of love, even when He seems to act the angry God and when He strikes in punishment. Yet to define minutely what the love of God must, and must not do, is to assume too complete a knowledge both of the nature of God and of His relations to man. Much wiser is it to take the facts as they are, and then to try in the light of these facts to understand a little of the nature of the Divine Love.

So likewise not every human love can be canonized as good. In our present order love implies hate: love of what is good implies hatred of what is evil; love for a sinner implies hatred for sin. Consequently, the sentiments of hatred are not entirely excluded from the Christian Law. Besides, true love for those who deserve or require our love is productive of anxiety and worry, dispositions which the modern mind-healers make it a point to disown. Thus we are led into an inextricable medley of confusion out of which even our would-be leaders are unable to point the way.

Against this analysis of the so-called spiritual element in New Thought it is protested that the lives of its adherents show the groundlessness of all these inferences. Their lives are honorable; their interests are varied; their activity is even increased; in every possible way they are estimable and useful citizens.

To this I reply that practically all the followers of the New Thought movement have been trained under a different régime. The past has followed them into the present and has

[1] Cf. Mills, Anna W.: *Practical Metaphysics for Healing and Self-Culture* (Chicago, 1896), pp. 284-285.

guarded them against excesses which would naturally follow a whole-souled acceptance of this new doctrine. They have adopted it only to the extent that it appealed to them, and, consequently, they have not been thoroughly molded by it. But even where New Thought influences have been active since early youth, the environment invariably has acted as a corrective in a good many ways. The appeal to such facts is therefore out of place. It is universally admitted that the influence of Islam has been bad; yet it took centuries for this influence to work out its logical conclusions. So it is impossible to gauge the trend, and measure the final results, of any public cause in the lives of its first adherents. Time alone can tell, and even then it may happen that thoughtful men will forestall the evil which logically would flow from its teaching.

CHAPTER XIV

THE NEW MOVEMENT VERSUS MIRACLES

I

CHRISTIAN SCIENCE and New Thought throughout assume that historical miracles must be explained—or rather explained away—in the light of modern mental sciences. The supernatural is banished out of existence. Christ, let us rather say Jesus (for they commonly distinguish between the two), for them was a faith-healer, the most successful faith-healer that ever lived. His miracles cannot be accepted as supernatural facts, but they are wonderful as feats of a strong and saintly personality. He may be exceptionally successful, but it is because he is an exceptional man: any one favored to the same extent by Mother Nature would do as well.[1]

These views are a legacy which the modern mind-movement owes to its pioneer teacher, P. P. Quimby. Quimby, in fact,

[1] The literature on miracles and their relation to psychotherapy is enormous. All opponents of the reality of miracles in the true sense of the word now adopt the same views: Christ's miracles must be brought in line with modern mind cures. On this subject from the modern point of view confer: Evans: *Primitive Mind-Cure* (Boston, 1884), chaps. 20-23; *The Divine Law of Cure* (Boston, 1881), Part I, chaps. 16-20; Part II, chap. 7; H. W. Dresser: *History of the New-Thought Movement* (New York, 1919), *passim;* Worcester-McComb-Coriat: *Religion and Medicine* (New York, 1908); Worcester-McComb: *The Christian Religion as a Healing Power* (New York, 1909). Following the same general trend we have also Rev. J. M. Thompson: *Miracles in the New Testament* (2d ed., London, 1911); Duff and Allen: *Psychic Research and Gospel Miracles* (New York, 1902).

Among the many defenders of the supernatural character of Christ's miracles we must mention on the Protestant side Newman's *Essays on Miracles;* archbishop R. C. Trench: *Notes on the Miracles of Our Lord* (new ed., New York, 1880); J. B. Mozley: *Eight Lectures on Miracles,* preached before the University of Oxford (new ed., London, 1895); J. J. Lias: *Are Miracles Credible?* (2d revised ed., London, 1890).

On the Catholic side, besides all manuals on Apologetics, we may especially mention Joseph de Tonquédec: *Introduction à l'Etude du Merveilleux et du Miracle* (Paris, 1916) and the small, but valuable treatise by the Rev. G. H. Joyce, S.J., entitled *The Question of Miracles* (London, 1914).

claimed to have "rediscovered the method of healing by which Jesus wrought, not his miracles, but his highly intelligible works of healing." Says Mr. H. W. Dresser:

"His work with the sick seemed to him [Quimby] a spiritual science, *a science of life and happiness*, as he called it. This science he found implicit in the teachings of Christ. His manuscripts are for the most part devoted to a study of his experiences with the sick in such a way as to show that the truths they implied were the truths which Jesus came to reveal."

And again:

"His practice with the sick was in some measure at least a rediscovery of the original therapeutic gospel. Its application to healing is a part only of the science which came to give men fulness of life, but healing had been the neglected part of the gospel. It was necessary that some one should arise to specialize upon this. Such in brief was the work given Mr. Quimby to do. This was the work he accomplished with such impressive success." [1]

This appeal to gospel precedent is one of the most valuable assets of the modern mind-healer in spreading his theories. He can tell his followers:

"Return to the Bible to see if it be true that it contains an inner or spiritual meaning; to see if, indeed, there be a neglected science of the Christ in the New Testament, implying principles of universal application through spiritual healing. If so, this inner or spiritual truth may be the great truth of the new age; it may imply the second coming of the Lord in deepest reality." [2]

Mr. Evans found in Christ Jesus the highest exemplification of the idea that God dwells in us as the source of life and health.

"The idea of the indwelling of God in man as the source of life and health, which was so deeply rooted in the con-

---

[1] Cf. H. W. Dresser: *History of the New-Thought Movement* (New York, 1919), pp. 42-48, 70.
[2] *Ibid.*, p. 69.

sciousness of the pious Jews, was carried over into Christianity, and received there a more philosophical expression. The whole life of Jesus the Christ was the highest exemplification of the power of this idea ever witnessed in the history of the race, and a demonstration of its theoretical and practical truth. *He cured diseases of mind and body by bringing men into conscious contact with the one and only Life.* Thus we see that the higher forms of the religious life and the state of mind and body which we designate bv the name of healthy, are closely associated." [1]

Again he writes:

"That Jesus, after the age of thirty years, exhibited a marvelous power of healing the sick without medicine, and which so far surpassed the power of his contemporaries as to be deemed miraculous, is a well-established fact and as well certified as the principal facts in the life of Alexander or Cæsar. . . . It has been supposed by some that Jesus spent his early life among the Essenes who were called in Egypt *therapeutæ*, or healers. This may or may not be true. We have no historic evidence for it, and it is, in itself, a matter of little importance. But whatever means he used, the power of the Word and the Spirit was always predominant. *He demanded as an indispensable condition a trustful submission, or an act of faith.* . . . The means which Jesus used may have stood in some relation to magnetic or psychological phenomena. But the marvelous power of Jesus appears far more like an intelligent mastery of Nature by the soul. The mind of man, originally endowed with dominion over the earth, recovered its old rights by the holy innocence of Jesus, conquering the unnatural power of disease and death. . . . The cures wrought by Jesus the Christ are as much in harmony with nature, when properly understood, as the operation of the electric telegraph and telephone, or the taking of photographs. The law by which they were effected is not an incommunicable divine secret and impenetrable mystery, but will some day be as well understood as any of the processes of nature, and better than the action of medicines in the cure of disease." [2]

[1] Evans: *The Divine Law of Cure* (Boston, 1881), p. 68.
[2] *Ibid.,* pp. 124-126.

Mrs. Eddy likewise *naturalizes*, so to say, Christ's miracles by bringing them down to the level of her own cures. Her healing she called divine healing and also Christian Science, to indicate, on the one hand, that she considered the Divine Mind to be the only source of cures, and, on the other, to identify her own cures with Christ's miraculous works.

"The term Christian Science," she writes, "was introduced by the author to indicate the scientific system of divine healing. The revelation consists of two parts: (1) The discovery of this divine Science of Mind-Healing through a spiritual sense of the Scriptures, and through the teachings of the Comforter as promised by the Master; (2) the proof, by present demonstration, that the so-called miracles of Jesus did not specially belong to a dispensation now ended, but that they illustrate an ever operative divine Principle. The operation of this Principle indicates forever the scientific order and continuity of being." [1]

The same tendency reappears in *Retrospection and Introspection* where we read:

"The miracles recorded in the Bible which had before seemed to me supernatural grew divinely natural and apprehensible, though uninspired interpreters ignorantly pronounce Christ's healing miraculous instead of seeing therein the operation of the divine law." [2]

It is somewhat amusing to find that the authors of the Emmanuel Movement, not satisfied with indorsing these explanations, seriously undertake to establish them scientifically, and, then, virtually apologize for their present inability to do so with regard to all of Christ's miracles. They unwittingly show their true aim and lack of historical perspective when they begin their investigation with an *a priori* principle of expediency which automatically vitiates all their subsequent reasonings. "A miracle," they boldly assert, "if it is to meet with acceptance at the hands of modern men, must be shown to have some analogy with facts and phenomena within their knowledge." If

[1] *Science and Health,* p. 123.
[2] *Retrospection and Introspection,* p. 31.

in individual cases this cannot as yet be done, prudence counsels that the miracles be not immediately rejected, but that they "be reserved to the day of fuller light; for it would be rash to suppose that all the light possible in this matter has been vouchsafed us." "The rationalistic criticism of fifty years ago," they add, "rejected the healing wonders of Christ. Fuller knowledge enables us to smile at the sceptical dogmatism of this criticism. Why may it not be that the knowledge of fifty years hence will be able to make intelligible some of the narratives on which faith stumbles today."

It is not faith, but the lack of it, which stumbles over any of Christ's miracles. The underlying idea throughout this section is that Christ as "physician and healer of souls and bodies of men" must not be thought of as bringing into play any but natural forces, but only as having possessed eminently what others possess in an ordinary degree, thus ranking among the greatest of the world's great physicians.

"From time to time," we are told, "men have arisen endowed with a peculiar power to dispel the moral and physical maladies of their fellow men. Among these 'the first among many brethren' stands the Lord Jesus, the Great Physician. Of Him it was said that He taught and healed. Coördinating His cures with others that have been wrought in ancient and modern times, we obtain a new sense of the nature and reality of His mighty works, that removes them from the stifling atmosphere [sic!] of the old supernatural vacuum, and gives them a place under the starry heavens and among the mysterious forces of God's universe."

Christ's unique personality, Christ's personal human influence, such is the source of His cures, and if we bear in mind "our own ignorance of the limits to the influence of mind over body, we will do well to avoid all hasty dogmatism as to what would be possible or impossible to such a one as Christ." [1]

The originators of the Emmanuel movement, nevertheless, notwithstanding this wise restriction, labor hard to confine Christ's miracles within such limits as so-called modern science

[1] Worcester-McComb-Coriat: *Religion and Medicine*, pp. 341 ff.

allows for the healing of disease by mental influence. And first of all they exclude altogether certain classes of ailments; finding that "there is no mention in the records of His healing such diseases as tuberculosis, typhus, diphtheria, and the like." As for leprosy which, in the view of modern medical science, is incurable, they remind us "that in the ancient world two types of leprosy were recognized, the one curable, the other incurable," and that "from the vague description given in the gospels we are unable to decide which type is referred to." [1]

After eliminating these several classes, they take the case of the man stricken with the palsy as a term of comparison, and, by a close scrutiny, they derive from it a set of rules which are made to fit all the reported cures of Christ. By this means they claim to discover, firstly, that Jesus recognized the moral causes which in certain cases lie behind the physical disease. Their argumentation proceeds as follows:

"The friends of the sick man want Jesus to heal him as it were by a wave of the hand, but Jesus is no magician and He knows that the moral malady is at the root of the trouble. He is very far indeed from sharing the prevailing theological notion of His time that every sickness in itself was evidence of sin, open or unconfessed. No! rather, for Him disease and sin are parts of a complex order—the kingdom of evil—to overcome which He felt Himself sent by God. His Gospel or good news was in essence this, that God must no longer be conceived as the author of the misery and torture that make of human life a hell. On the contrary, He is Love and as Love He is ever seeking to express Himself in joy." [2]

In the second place they find that Christ's healing power required as a psychological medium and spiritual condition faith at least on the part of either healer, patient or friends.

"This is the rule," they say, "to which there is but one clear and necessary exception. In the case of demon possession the mental organism was itself so disorganized that faith or any other rational or motived act was impossible. Jesus in these instances began by soothing the mind and

[1] Worcester-McComb-Coriat: *op. cit.*, p. 345.
[2] *Ibid.*, p. 350.

distracting it from its obsession, and then, with the naked force of His own personality revealing itself in look, gesture and word of command, He broke down the structure of hallucination and delusion which the morbid action of the mind had built up and, thereby, He set the sufferer free from his disorder.   But wherever a measure of self-control was left, He demanded faith." [1]

Finally, they assert that the secret of Christ's healing was an ethical power, dependent, next to God, on communion with Him through faith and prayer:

"He is the appointed Redeemer of mankind," they explain, "the Founder of God's kingdom upon earth and, therefore, He was equipped with the power necessary to oppose and overcome the whole order of evil, to destroy it, not in its outward manifestations only, but in its ultimate causes.   His power to heal is, therefore, only the visible manifestation of another power, His power to heal the guilt and activity of sin.   This power was not a power given Him once and for all, a magical endowment, rather was it an ethical quality, to be sustained through communion with God." [2]

It must be acknowledged that this easy and naturally rather persuasive explanation has appealed to many who take only a secondary interest in the doings of the mind-healers.   Not infrequently is it assumed as demonstrated that Christ's miracles must now no longer be treated as anything else than natural mind cures.   Some grant this grudgingly and console themselves with the consideration that, after all, miracles are not essentially necessary proofs of the truth of Christianity. Many a one, however, may feel as if the ground was gradually slipping from underneath his feet, when he hears the shout of triumph in the camp of the atheist over this new important victory.   But it fell to Mr. Hudson to invert these rôles, and to go so far—strange to say—as to raise this naturalistic explantation to the rank of a proof for the truthworthiness of the gospel history.   Mr. Hudson thinks of Christ as of a man

---

[1] Worcester, McComb-Coriat: *op. cit.,* p. 352.
[2] *Ibid.,* p. 355.

who for some unexplained reason failed to communicate the secret of his success to his disciples and future biographers.

"These," says he, "have recorded his words, but not his reasons, for he gave none. If, therefore, science demonstrates that the powers that he possessed are possible; that the condition of their exercise are precisely what he declared them to be; and that they cannot be exercised without a strict compliance with those conditions, the internal evidence for the truth of his history is overwhelming." [1]

These gentlemen with faint praise and fair words rather condemn than commend Christ. To exalt His humanity in order to deny His divinity has become a favorite method of attack with all those who disbelieve in the supernatural. The issue is, therefore, squarely drawn, which we must try to meet just as squarely, by examining into the question whether the Gospel cures are nothing but extraordinary mind cures, or, on the contrary, real miracles which no power, short of the divine, could perform.

II

Be their pretended objections to Christ's miracles what they may, the real difficulty with most modern men lies in an unacknowledged hostility to all that transcends the natural order. To argue, following the *Immanence* school of Christian apologists that miracles can no longer serve as a criterion for the truth of Christianity, because it is impossible to distinguish miracles from kindred non-miraculous facts, is to concede more to the opponents of the Christian religion than these authors were willing to admit. [2] For if we must concede to the modern mind healers that Christ's signs and wonders may be signs and wonders, indeed, but not miracles in the strict sense of the word, we must cease to rest on them as credentials of Christ's Divine mission and, especially, of His Divinity. Will not many

---

[1] Hudson: *The Law of Psychic Phenomena*, p. 342.
[2] Confer on this point E. Le Roy, in *Annales de Philosophie Chrétienne*, 1906, art. "Essai sur la Notion du Miracle." Also Blondel: "Lettre sur l'Apologétique," *ibid.*, January, 1896. These authors based themselves on Bergson's philosophy as contained in his *Evolution Créatrice*.

at once conclude that the Christian Revelation rests on no secure foundation; that it is a sham, or at best a fatal error? This inference may not be warranted, but it certainly lies very near. For even though we grant that there exist other credentials to Christ's mission, there yet remains a settled conviction that, if Christ be truly the Son of God in the full sense of the word, He must have performed the works of God.

"The fathers undoubtedly made deductions from the force of miracles as evidence," says Mozley, "but that the person of the Messiah and Son of God who came to be the Mediator between God and man, and to atone by His death for the sins of the whole world, would, when He came, be known and distinguished wholly without any miraculous element in His birth, life or death, simply living and passing through the world in that respect like an ordinary man— was an idea which never even occurred to the mind of any father and which, had it been presented to him, he would have at once discarded." [1]

Nor did the earliest opponents of the gospel question the preternatural character of Christ's wonderful works. Two explanations, and only two, seemed to them possible: either these works were of God, or they must be ascribed to magic. The Jews would contend that they were the works of Beelzebub. "This man casteth not out devils but by Beelzebub, the prince of the devils." [2] Similar views were advocated by the earliest anti-Christian writers among the Pagans. Their religious skepticism contended with their inherited superstition to raise objections against the hope with which Christ's miracles inspired the Christians.

After the Reformation the nature of these attacks changed. Philosophical considerations led the pantheist Spinoza (1632-1677) to deny the very possibility of miracles, and the skeptical Hume (1771-1776)—followed in the nineteenth century by the empiricist John Stewart Mill (1806-1873) and a host of others —to impugn not so much the possibility as the credibility of miraculous accounts. Woolston (1669-1731), on the other

[1] Mozley: *Eight Lectures on Miracles* (London, 1895), p. 213.
[2] Matt. 12:24.

hand, interpreted the historical miracles of the gospel as so many allegorical fables.[1]

The nineteenth century again witnessed a change of front. Paulus (1761-1851) refused to see anything miraculous in the gospel narratives and devised natural explanations for the gospel miracles; Strauss (1808-1874) absolutely rejected this miraculous element as so many mythical accretions; but the explanation that in our times finds the largest number of votaries bases itself on the hidden powers of nature, and on the power of the human mind over them. This objection, as Father Joyce so well sums it up, states that "the accounts of the 'wonder-cures' contained in the Gospels and in some of the lives of the saints are in the main true; but orthodox Christianity has blundered in reckoning them as supernatural." [2] It is to this category of objectors that we must turn; for we have now to do with men that, far from denying all divine intervention in the affairs of men, are rather inclined to exaggerate than to minimize the extent of this intervention, looking in a very material way up to God as the ever present help in all human ills and needs.

It is important that we should not embark on this discussion without taking our bearings. What is a miraculous event? By what does it, if at all, distinguish itself from non-miraculous marvelous phenomena? St. Thomas defines a miracle to be a sense-perceptible fact produced by God outside the order of the whole universe.[3] It is obvious to all that this definition is not of the nature of a first principle, but that it sums up the inferences to which an unbiased study of certain facts leads. It serves the excellent purpose of making clear from the very

[1] Cf. Spinoza: *Tractatus Theologico-Politicus* (London, 1862), pp. 120 ff; Hume: *An Essay Concerning Human Understanding* (Edinburgh, 1748, 1880); Mill: *Three Essays on Religion* (New York, 1874), pp. 217-241; Woolston: *The Moderator Between the Infidel and the Apostate* (1721); *Discourses on the Miracles of Christ* (1727-1729).

[2] Joyce: *The Question of Miracles* (London, 1914), p. 43. Paulus: *Das Leben Jesu als Grundlage einer reinen Geschichte des Urchristentums* (Heidelberg, 1828); Strauss: *Das Leben Jesu* (1835-1836); Renan, in his *Life of Jesus* (1863, translated in the same year into English), follows the same methods. "Let the gospels be in part legendary," he says in the Introduction, "that is evident, since they are full of miracles and the supernatural" (p. 17).

[3] *Summa Theologica*, Pars I, q. 110, art. 4.

beginning where exactly we place the difference between Christ's miracles and the cures of the mind healers. While the latter insist that their healing is natural, we maintain that a study of the gospel miracles—to limit ourselves now to these—leads to the conclusion that nature, including human nature, possesses no power to perform such works, or to perform them in the manner in which Christ performed them. We do not say that these miracles violate the laws of nature, any more than man's free interference violates them; but we do say that a higher power intervenes which is not subject to these laws, and that this power is God. We do not admit that in order to be justified to pronounce something a true miracle, it must be such that nature at no time could bring about a similar effect, and that, consequently, before calling any fact a miracle, it is necessary to define the exact limits of the powers of nature; on the contrary, we claim that under given circumstances a given event may point with moral certainty to God as its direct and immediate author.

Take for instance the question of a miraculous cure. To establish its miraculous character, it is not necessary that no power capable of coping with this particular disease should exist anywhere in nature; it is sufficient that such curative powers should not have come into play. To prove this, all circumstances bearing on the case must be carefully weighed and valued, not only one after another and taken by itself, but also in their cumulative force. Where all the circumstances point in one direction, it would be supremely unreasonable to look for the explanation of the cure in another one. A shallow, though specious enough, objection basing itself on the impossibility of setting limits to nature's hidden powers, insists that it is impossible to decide whether a given effect is beyond these powers.[1] To this we reply that though we may be unable to define the limits of Nature, such limits certainly exist.

---

[1] Cf. Mill: *Three Essays on Religion* (New York, 1874), p. 230. "Accordingly, when we hear of a prodigy, we always, in these modern times, believe that if it really occurred, it was neither the work of God nor of a demon, but the consequence of some unknown natural law or of some hidden fact."

Supernatural intervention is, therefore, always possible, and in given cases it is possible, by evidence both positive and negative, to establish beyond reasonable doubt the natural or supernatural character of a work or event.

A fact must always be distinguished from its explanations. The marvelous character of a cure can be obvious, when it is not at all obvious to what the cure itself is to be ascribed. Is it trickery? Is it an effect of some unexplored natural law? Is it some demon that interferes in human affairs, or is it God who thus manifests His power? All these are possibilities that cannot be simply dismissed. Yet, withal, it must be plain to any one that is willing to see, that circumstantial evidence may favor one of these possibilities to such an extent as to render the others untenable, and that when indications accumulate and all converge to one solution, a practical certainty is reached which bars all prudent doubt. How often is a criminal convicted on circumstantial evidence alone, and yet, no one believes that justice has miscarried, precisely because circumstantial evidence has carried conviction. So in many practical affairs of life, not merely in the natural, but also in the supernatural order, circumstantial evidence must point the way.

We must be satisfied with tracing the great lines of what is distinctive in Christ's works in contrast with the works of His would-be imitators, developing a little more at length only such arguments as are likely to prove the more cogent for our present purpose. Three lines of argument may be pursued. Some, convinced that organic disease is not directly amenable to psychic or mental influence, center their proof on the fact that at least some of the diseases reported cured by Christ were surely of an organic nature.[1] Others find in a minute examination of the reported cures sufficient ground to differentiate them from mental cures and to pronounce them miraculous and

---

[1] Cf. Joyce, *op. cit.*, chap. IV, *Miracles and Faith-Healing*. Davies, E. O.: *The Miracles of Jesus*, a study of the evidence (London, 1913), pp. 75-81. "The conclusion we reach, then, is that there is no direct evidence that the cures attributed to Jesus were as a class wrought psychotherapeutically, and there is no direct and unquestionable evidence that the diseases which he is said to have cured were of such a kind as to be amenable to psychotherapeutic treatment" (p. 80).

divine, while a third one will rest confidently on the judgment of Christ Himself, his apostles and their contemporaries, and the witness of the early Church.[1]

These arguments are all valuable each one in its own way. The first one would probably appeal more to physicians whose medical knowledge enables them to draw hard and fast lines between organic and merely functional diseases. Scientific opinion which a few decades ago seemed to swing towards conceding to the mind a direct influence even over organic diseases, now seems to have swung back, even among nerve specialists, to a more conservative view. In the words of Father Joyce,

> "It may be safely said that virtually the whole medical profession is agreed that there is not a jot of positive evidence that suggestion, whether hypnotic or otherwise, can do anything to remedy an organic lesion; that, on the contrary, all the evidence hitherto produced goes to show that its curative effects are strictly limited to functional derangements."[2]

Against this argument it might be urged that it will be a long time before mind healers will be willing to concede this restriction on their trade. They continue to maintain with all the sureness of a conviction born of faith and interest that organic diseases are not outside the range of mental influence. Add to this that the average man is not properly equipped to draw a clear distinction between organic and functional disorders, and it will be seen that the argument though it keeps its objective value loses much of its practical usefulness.

The second argument is more within reach of everybody and cannot fail to create a profound impression. Compare one by one the miracles of Christ with verified cures of either the common mind healer or of the scientific psychotherapist, observe not only the nature of the disease and the fact of its cure, but also the method of the healing process, the swiftness of the cure, and the degree of its stability, as well as any other circumstance which may have a bearing on the case, and you are

---

[1] Cf. Joyce, *op. cit.*, pp. 43-53. Davies, *op. cit.*, pp. 75 ff. Mackenzie, in *Medicine and the Church* (London, 1910). Le Bec, *Preuves Médicales du Miracle* (Paris, 1921).

[2] Cf. Joyce, *op. cit.*, p. 49.

enabled to form your own opinion which, if unbiased, cannot but be favorable to the supernatural character of Christ's works. An unbiased attitude is, of course, impossible, when, consciously or unconsciously, one undertakes this investigation with the un-philosophical principle that miracles are impossible and, there-fore, non-existent, or that in any case no testimony concerning any so-called miraculous fact is deserving of credence. One needs for this work that fairness of spirit which we expect in all human concerns and which will not allow the judgment to be warped for fear of the foreseen consequences. A prejudiced mind can only pass a prejudiced judgment and thus it wrongs both itself and the subject-matter with which it deals.

Easier than both of these and no less effective is the third method to which we shall devote a little more space, the more so as the first two methods have more frequently been developed in detail. What is Christ's own judgment concerning His cures? In what light did the early Christians and their contemporaries contemplate them? Such is the problem. The solution must lie in an examination of the documents we possess. The advan-tage we expect to derive therefrom is this, that Christ's author-ity cannot easily be set aside. Though His divinity is called into question by all rationalizers, yet even among them they that would impugn his moral rectitude are very few. His own testimony, therefore, deserves the very greatest consideration. For large classes of people it must constitute a supreme argu-ment; for all but such as are prepared to class Christ among the greatest frauds of history, it must be of great weight.

To know what Christ thought of His miracles is paramount in our problem. Only secondary to this in importance is the testimony of His apostles and contemporaries. After all, it is their witnessing to which all modern authors must refer. If we cannot believe their account of the impression Christ's miracles created in those times, how can we believe their testi-mony concerning the miracles themselves? And if, basing our-selves on the inadmissibility of true miracles, we reject at the very outset anything that cannot be explained naturally, what belief can we still give to the rest of the Scriptures? We shall, therefore, take for granted the historicity of the gospel narratives in their entirety, and judge of Christ's signs and wonders in this new "old" light.

III

"When we hear of a prodigy, we always, in these modern times, believe that if it really occurred, it was neither the work of God nor of a demon, but the consequence of some unknown natural law or of some hidden fact." [1]

These words of John Stuart Mill, written long ago, have since become the creed of vast numbers of men. It forestalls any kind of reasoning for it appeals to what is unknown. Because of its finality it proves an effective bar to all inquiries into the truth of the facts that are reported miraculous and into the character of these facts. Nay, it is even maintained that those who base their lives on the historical truth of Christ's miracles strangely misread the mind of Christ; that Christ never intended his works to be marks of His mission, and that in the early ages they never were considered such. To quote the same essay of John Stuart Mill:

"No one thought it worth while to contradict any alleged miracles, because it was the belief of the age that miracles in themselves proved nothing, since they could be worked by a lying spirit as well as by the Spirit of God." [2]

This statement is a most gratuitous assertion as we shall forthwith show.

No one that has ever read the Gospel according to St. John can truthfully maintain that in the days of St. John Christ's miracles were discounted. The author himself announces at the end of his Gospel the purpose of his work to be to bring people to Christ by reporting some of His miracles and sayings. "Many other signs also did Jesus in the sight of His disciples which are not written in this book; but these are written that you may believe that Jesus is the Christ, the Son of God and that believing you may have life in His name." [3]

[1] Mill: *Three Essays on Religion*, p. 230.
[2] *Ibid.*, p. 237.
[3] John 20:30-31 and Isa. 53:1.

To show by Christ's miracles that Christ was the promised Messias and the Son of God; such, in brief, was his object, which he pursued by appealing to the testimony of both Christ and His contemporaries, and by contrasting favorably the attitude of the masses with that of the higher classes. Many of the former believed, because they said to themselves: "When the Christ cometh, shall He do more miracles than these which this man doth?" [1] This plain, open, almost intuitive judgment of the common man places in high relief the sombre unbelief of the erudite Scribe and the punctilious Pharisee whose self-sufficiency and class pride were an insurmountable barrier to any act of faith. "Whereas He had done so many miracles before them, they believed not in Him, that the saying of Isaias, the prophet, might be fulfilled which he said: 'Lord, who hath believed our hearing, and to whom hath the arm of the Lord been revealed?'" [2] But though they failed to believe, they could not fail to be impressed with the mighty works of the Savior. For we read: "The chief priests, therefore, and the Pharisees, gathered a council and said: 'What do we; for this man doth many miracles? If we let him alone so, all will believe in him, and the Romans will come and take away our place and nation.'" [3] This attitude of interested opposition has not changed much in the course of the ages. But whatever else unbelievers may say in their self-defense, they cannot truthfully plead that Christ did not propose His miracles as signs to lead men into the truth of the Gospel.

"I speak to you," he told them plainly, "and you believe not. The works that I do in the name of my Father, they give testimony of me; but you do not believe because you are not of my sheep. . . . If I do not the works of my Father, believe me not; but if I do, though you will not believe me, believe the works, that you may know and believe that the Father is in me and I in the Father." [4]

These citations might be multiplied without adding substantially to the strength of the argument. We reason thus: The

[1] John 7:31. Cf. 10:41.
[2] *Ibid.,* 12:37.
[3] *Ibid.,* 11:47.
[4] *Ibid.,* 10:25 and 37. Cf. *Ibid.,* 5:36.

Gospel of St. John fully refutes the assertion, ignorantly made and ignorantly repeated, that miracles did not serve in the beginning as credentials not only of Christ's Divine mission, but also of His Divinity.   It is mainly on the strength of these works that people accepted His teaching with regard both to moral precepts and to Himself.   Christ knew of this impression made by His cures and encouraged it.   But if these works were, not supernatural, they but proved that Christ was naturally endowed with remarkable healing powers.   In that case, He exacted belief in Himself under false pretenses.   Either, therefore, we must cease to look upon Him as the ambassador of God, or we must admit that His reported cures were more than faith cures.

To this it will probably be objected that we cannot accept St. John's Gospel as historical; that it is theology, the work of a believer, a mystic and a propagandist, but not of a historian. This we deny; but even where granted, the argument would still show in what light Christ's miracles were received at that time. But lest any suspicion to this effect should weaken our conclusion, we will show that the three Synoptic Gospels, no less than St. John, make Christ's miracles basic of His whole religion.   Friend and foe acknowledged their preternatural character, the former, to rejoice in them as evident signs of God's goodness to men; the latter, to discredit them as the work of unclean spirits.

"Every kingdom, divided against itself, shall be made desolate," our Lord replied to the latter imputation, "and every house or city, divided against itself, shall not stand. And if Satan cast out Satan, he is divided against himself, how, then, shall his kingdom stand. . . . But if I by the Spirit of God cast out devils, then is the Kingdom of God come upon you." [1]

No one that is not blinded by prejudice can fail to get the import of Christ's words.   He plainly points to the supernatural origin of His works as credentials to His mission.   He goes further: refusal to see the finger of God in the works of God

[1] Matt. 12:25-28, 31-32.

he does not attribute to lack of discernment in his hearers, but stigmatizes as the sin against the Holy Ghost, which shall be forgiven neither in this world nor in the world to come.

Instructive is the answer Christ gave to the messengers of St. John the Baptist, who had come to inquire whether He was "the one that was to come, or whether they should look for another." He refers them to the prophets, to His own works and to the marvelous harmony that existed between prophecy and fulfillment:

> "Go and relate to John what you have heard and seen: 'The blind see, the lame walk, the lepers are cleansed, the deaf hear, the dead rise again, the poor have the gospel preached to them.' And, blessed is he that shall not be scandalized in Me." [1]

Finally, if there could be any doubt at all concerning the importance of miracles as proofs of Christ's divine mission and concerning its synoptical record, the woes pronounced upon the towns and cities of Galilee would surely remove it.

> "Then began He to upbraid the cities wherein were done the most of His miracles, for that they had not done penance. Woe to thee, Corozain! Woe to thee, Bethsaida! for if in Tyre and Sidon had been wrought the miracles that have been wrought in you, they had long ago done penance in sackcloth and ashes. But I say unto you, it shall be more tolerable for Tyre and Sidon in the day of judgment than for you. And thou, Capharnaum! Shalt thou be exalted up to heaven? Thou shalt go down even unto hell. For if in Sodom had been wrought the miracles that have been wrought in thee, perhaps it had remained unto this day. But I say unto you, that it shall be more tolerable for the land of Sodom in the day of judgment than for thee." [2]

How could Jesus have resorted to such vehement and terrific vituperations, if His works were no more than ordinary mind-cures? How could we still believe in His honesty, if, on the false pretenses of supernatural powers, He demanded on the

[1] Matt. 11:4-5.
[2] *Ibid.*, 11:20-24.

part of the people faith in Himself and in His work? How, in fine, could we explain such statements of fact made by the evangelists as that "His fame spread throughout Syria," that "much people followed Him from Galilee and from Decapolis and from Jerusalem and from Judea and from beyond the Jordan," and that "*they presented to Him all sick people that were taken with divers diseases and torments, and such as were possessed by devils, and lunatics and those that had the palsy, and He cured them all.*" [1] His fame reached the ears even of the civil magistrates, and the superstitious Herod dreaded lest John whom he had beheaded had risen from the dead: "This is John the Baptist. He is risen from the dead, and, therefore, mighty works show themselves in him." [2] Later on, when favored through the cowardice rather than the courtesy of Pilate with a personal interview with this famous wonder worker, he was "very glad; for he was desirous for a long time to see Him, because he had heard many things of Him, and he hoped to see some sign wrought by Him." [3]

If it could be shown that all these cures in reality were nothing but mind-cures, not essentially different from those which faith-healers have wrought at all times, we would as a matter of course, surrender our judgment to evidence. But those who have tried to prove such a relationship have never been able to do so without doing violence to the sacred texts. In order to be free to select arbitrarily such miracles as may prove their contentions with a certain show of probability, they must tamper with the documents until these yield exactly what is wanted of them. Schmiedel in the *Encyclopedia Biblica* is not ashamed to lay down as a fundamental rule of exegesis with regard to the facts now under discussion that "only those of the class which even at the present day physicians are able to effect by psychological methods" are historical. With this arbitrary rule it is easy to prove anything, because it enables the supposedly objective critic to choose among the facts just those that prove his point and to reject all the others as unhistorical.

[1] Matt. 5:24-25.
[2] *Ibid.*, 14:2.
[3] Luke 23:2.

Of forty-six references to miracles and miraculous powers enumerated by Mr. Davies as found in the gospel narratives, the higher critics rule out all but eleven which are found in the 'triple tradition' of the three Synoptics.   The oft-repeated assertion that Christ wrought many miracles is dismissed as an unjustifiable generalization on the part of the evangelists. The other thirty-four references are just as summarily dealt with.   Eleven cases remain; but even these are hardly pliant enough for their purposes.   Interpretation, however, knows how to deal with these.   Take, for instance, the case of the raising of the daughter of Jairus, which belongs to the triple tradition. All the evangelists assert that the girl was really dead when Christ arrived at the house; but this the modern exegetes will not and cannot admit and, consequently, speak of this case as one of "reanimation at the point of death." [1]   Such methods make explaining easy, and worthless.

For a more detailed study Drs. Worcester and McComb select the case of the man stricken with the palsy.   It is a typical example of how the higher critics manipulate the simple statements of the gospels:

"In the story before us," they tell us, "it is said that Jesus seeing their faith proceeded to pronounce his absolution.   First, and mainly, perhaps, our attention is called to the faith of the sick man's friends.   The patient, then, has been for some time living in an atmosphere of faith.   The reports of Christ's healing work have reached his companions and have stirred them to hope and trust.   This very hope and trust have created a psychological atmosphere favorable to the sufferer's eventual recovery.   Moreover, it has tended to awaken faith in the patient himself.   As in the case of the daughter of Jairus, Christ feels Himself mighty in an atmosphere free from doubt and fear.   We can see, too, how a strong faith on the part of this unhappy man was developed.   The very fact that he allowed his friends to carry him to Christ showed that faith had already germinated in his heart.   Every element in the strange and never-to-be-forgotten scene in which he is to be for the moment the central figure was calculated to develop this germ, to affect power-

[1] Worcester-McComb: *Religion and Medicine* (New York, 1908), p. 345.

fully his imagination, and to arouse all his slumbering moral forces. . . . All this must have tended to create expectant attention, faith, confidence, hope—the psychical conditions of a cure. We conclude, then, that the miraculousness of Christ's healing power did not consist in his refusal to use secondary causes, but rather in the Divine Love and grace which moved Him to His cures, and which His cures symbolized to the spiritually susceptible mind." [1]

The whole process is very simple. Forsooth, there is hardly any need of Christ at all, so automatically does the cure effect itself through the mind of the patient. Yet, it seems rather strange that while faith was all along active in this mind, the cure awaited the word of command, "Arise, take up thy bed and walk," and then was sudden and complete. Do the modern mind-healers thus cure their patients? Previously to this, the sick man had been told, "Thy sins are forgiven thee"; after that occurred incidentally a discussion with the Pharisees bearing on the powers of the Son of Man, during which discussion the man remained sick awaiting the word that would cure him. On the command of Christ, the man arose, took up his bed and walked. Is it really expected of us that we should believe this cure to be entirely due to the faith of this man? And does it make no difference to the higher critics that Jesus expressly worked this miracle to prove that He had authority on earth to forgive sin? With these remarks in mind, the explanation of the rationalists must be pronounced entirely unsatisfactory, as it simply would inflict on Christ the stigma of a vulgar cheat. It may be very simple, but it is not very convincing.

What should be decisive against all attempts at a naturalistic explanation is the fact that Christ made no distinction between various forms of disease. All evangelists are emphatic on this point. After healing St. Peter's mother-in-law, He cured all that were brought to Him: "And when the sun was down, all they that had any sick with divers diseases brought them to Him. But He laying His hands on every one of them, healed them. And devils went out from many, crying out and

---

[1] Worcester-McComb: *op. cit.*, p. 353.

saying: 'Thou art the Son of God.' " [1] St. Matthew relates that "Jesus went about all the cities and towns, teaching in their synagogues, and preaching the gospel of the Kingdom, and healing every disease and every infirmity." And again: "There came to Him great multitudes, having with them the dumb, the blind, the lame, the maimed, and many others; and they cast them down at His feet, and He healed them, so that the multitudes marveled, seeing the dumb speak, the lame walk, the blind see." [2]

Finally, let it not be forgotten that our records present Christ, not only as healing the sick, but as having power over all Nature. The elements were submissive to Him; He changed water into wine, multiplied the bread, walked on the sea, stilled the tempest, and did many things which under those circumstances were perfectly miraculous. The veracity of Christ and of His apostles is at stake. The critics will either have to admit the miraculous character of their works, or return to the bolder, more irreverent, but more logical views of the earlier opponents of Christianity, who did not hesitate to call the veracity of the sacred writers into question.

We may now sum up our conclusions by asserting that hypothesis has succeeded hypothesis, but all have proved futile and unsatisfactory to account for the miraculous element in the gospels. None of them has stood the test of time. True, as long as it is maintained that miracles do not, because they cannot, happen, it will still be necessary to resort to one or the other of these hypotheses. One thing, however, should be beyond dispute, that if we do not alter the gospel narrative, the cures there recorded are undoubtedly true miracles. Mr. E. O. Davies in his interesting study on the miracles of Christ, puts the problem that confronts us as follows:

"Taking the narratives as they stand," he writes, "without modifying them in the least, have we a right to say that the alleged cures are no longer miracles? Do our narratives describe what is still marvelous for us to-day, or can they bear, exactly as they stand, a psychotherapeutic construction?"

[1] Luke 4:40-41.
[2] Matt. 9:35, and 15:30-31.

This question he answers, on the whole, in favor of the miraculous character of Christ's cures.

"In nearly all the cases," he concludes, "where the attempt has been made to eliminate the miraculous from narratives of special miracles, the result has been obtained through modifying the record. In one case only does Keim in his *Jesu von Nazara* succeed in lending plausibility to the psychotherapeutic explanation of special miracles without toning down the language used by the evangelists to describe the complaint. . . . "

Then Mr. Davies continues:

"It will be well for us at this point to indicate clearly the miraculous element present in the narratives. . . . Take the first class: healings of bodily ailments. A certain nobleman's son was sick of fever and was described as dying. Jesus healed him by a word spoken at a distance. Simon's wife's mother suffered from a great fever. Jesus rebuked the fever and it left her. *Psoriasis* or *Elephantiasis Græcorum*—it matters not which for our present purpose—is healed by a touch and a word. Congenital blindness is cured by rubbing the eyes with clay, the sufferer afterwards washing in the pool of Siloam. A case of infirmity of eighteen years' standing was cured by a word and a touch. A man, suffering from dropsy, was healed instantaneously. One of the disciples smote the servant of the highpriest and struck off his ear. Jesus touched his ear and healed him.

"Consider next the second class: healings of nervous diseases. A helpless paralytic was cured by a command. A man with a withered hand, also, was healed forthwith by a command. A case of paralysis, in which the patient is described as being at the point of death, was cured at a distance.

"There is further the third class: healings of nervous and psychical disorders. Demoniacs were cured of aggravated forms of epilepsy and mania by a command or a rebuke. In all these cases, taking the narratives as we find them, we have present a miraculous element. The events belonging to the other four classes above enumerated [1] are all

---

[1] These other four classes are: (1) revelations of power in the nature of Christ (walking on the sea); (2) revelation of Jesus in nature and

miracles. No mere exegesis of the narratives can remove the impression that they describe what is still marvelous for us to-day.

"Speaking, generally, then, the records as they stand are miraculous in character. And this being so, it is fair to suppose, that the evangelists did not regard differently those narratives, whose face value can be claimed to be not inconsistent with a psychotherapeutic explanation." [1]

It is useless to spend more time on this matter. Any unprejudiced student must come to these conclusions:

1. Christ makes no distinction between curable and incurable diseases, but heals them all with equal facility.

2. No visible remedy is employed that could account for these cures. Nor does Jesus resort to the methods of the hypnotists or faith-healers. If, on a few occasions, the cure is accompanied with certain ceremonies, like the touch of the hand, the application of clay, or the anointing with oil, these have no direct physical bearing on the ailment, but convey some symbolical meaning, teach some moral lesson, or prepare perhaps the institution of some sacrament. In any case, the means employed are not of such a nature that they could materially contribute to the cure.

3. The faith which Jesus ordinarily asks of those whom He heals is not that of the modern mind-healers, but a faith in His own Divine mission. This, of course, implied the faith in His power to heal; but of itself it was no guarantee that the cure would infallibly take place. There is no indication whatever that the faith demanded by Christ was anything similar to the *understanding* of the unreality of disease, which Mrs. Eddy exacts as the essential requisite for any complete cure.

4. The cures of Jesus were instantaneous, and lasting. They were of a nature to be observable by any and all interested enough to investigate. Christ worked them in public anywhere and everywhere. They furnished the chief reason why people

upon the organic world (draughts of fishes and stater in fish's mouth); (3) power upon organic world (multiplied loaves and fishes, water made wine, fig-tree withered); (4) power upon the inorganic world (stilling of the tempest).

[1] Davies: *The Miracles of Jesus* (London, 1913), pp. 17-21.

flocked to Him from all sides and followed Him. They cannot, therefore, be simply denied, or explained away by those who first pervert the historical records, and, then, undertake to show how easy it is to do the same sort of works. The miracles of Christ, in spite of the many attempts to do so, have not been disproved, but, on the contrary, stand out in bolder relief when brought out in correlation with the cures of the mind-healers.

IV

A few words must be added concerning the gift of miracles in the Church. That Christ has promised this gift to His disciples cannot be gainsaid:

"These signs shall follow them that believe. In My Name they shall cast out devils; they shall speak with new tongues; they shall take up serpents, and, if they shall drink any deadly thing, it shall not hurt them. They shall lay their hands upon the sick, and they shall recover." [1]

That the apostles and others of the earlier disciples exercised these powers, is a matter of history. That the promise was not limited to them, but was to be permanent and a characteristic sign of the society of believers in the Church throughout the ages, has been the common belief of the Church from the beginning and is based on Scriptural testimony. But that this gift of healing was to be institutional in the sense that a certain class of men should be regularly, or even temporarily, endowed with it, is an unwarrantable inference. Still more unwarranted is the claim that all true believers must possess immunity from material harm and the power of restoring the health of others. If Christ's words are to be taken in this ultra-literal sense, they must be taken so in their entirety, and, then, we may well challenge all mind-healers to prove their faith by their works. Let them speak with new tongues. Let them take up serpents; let them drink some deadly thing: if they remain unhurt, then, and not till then, will we be willing to accept their private interpretation of this passage of Holy Writ.

[1] Mark 16:17-18.

But now, to return to our proposition: we claim that the gift of miracles is promised to the true Church, and that it is one of her characteristics; that there has been no age from the beginning of Christianity when miracles have been wholly absent. This is not an endorsement of every miraculous narrative to be met with in the course of historical reading. Just as real coin does not prevent counterfeit money from getting into circulation, until it is suppressed, and just as the existence of counterfeit money does not disprove, but rather proves the existence of real money, so the existence of many, not sufficiently authenticated, miraculous narratives cannot be adduced as a disproof of real miraculous cures.

To limit ourselves to our own times, we may safely challenge the world to look dispassionately and with a fair and open mind into the events at Lourdes. Here we have works that are not performed in a corner, but are open to the investigation of every qualified physician. The annals of Lourdes go back to 1868. A special bureau in charge of a physician conscientiously investigates all reported cures. The history of some of its more famous cases has been repeatedly written. The works of Henri Lasserre and of Dr. Boissarie are well known and have been translated into many languages. The *Histoire Critique des Évènements de Lourdes*, by the abbé Bertrin, is replete with detailed accounts of authentic cures, the reality of which has been proved beyond the possibility of a doubt. The English reader may be referred to Dr. de Grandmaison's book entitled: *Twenty Cures at Lourdes Medically Discussed*.[1] We may particularly recall the remarkable, sudden cure of Pierre de Rudder who had been suffering for so long from a compound fracture in his left leg.[2] Many other cases are scarcely less remarkable. But to enter into details would lead us too far; we can only refer to the works which treat professionally of this subject. The following summary, by the abbé Bertrin, taken from the *Catholic Encyclopedia*, must suffice:

"The estimate that about 4000 cures have been obtained at Lourdes within the first fifty years of the pilgrimage is

[1] Published in 1912, translated in 1920.
[2] Cf. De Grandmaison, *op. cit.*, pp. 140-146.

undoubtedly considerably less than the actual number. The *Bureau des Constatations* stands near the shrine, and there are recorded and checked the certificates of maladies, and also the certificates of cure; it is free to all physicians, whatever their nationality or religious belief. Consequently, on an average, from two to three hundred physicians annually visit this marvelous clinic. As to the nature of the diseases which are cured, nervous disorders, so frequently mentioned, do not even furnish the fourteenth part of the whole: 278 have been counted out of a total of 3962. The present writer has published the number of cases of each disease or infirmity, among them tuberculosis, tumors, sores, cancers, deafness, blindness, etc. The *Annales des Sciences Physiques*, a skeptical review whose chief editor is Dr. Charles Richet, Professor of the medical faculty of Paris, said in the course of a long article, *apropos* of this faithful study: 'On reading it, unprejudiced minds cannot but be convinced that the facts stated are authentic.' " [1]

[1] *Catholic Encyclopedia,* vol. IX, p. 390, art. "Lourdes."

CHAPTER XV

THE LATEST EVENTS IN CHRISTIAN SCIENCE

NONE of the predictions frequently made concerning Christian Science either that it would soon disintegrate on the death of the Founder, or that, on the contrary, it would continue its growth by leaps and bounds, has so far been realized. Indications are not wanting, however, that Christian Science has passed the zenith of its strength and popularity. Christian Science, indeed, continues its stormy history with losses and gains to be recorded pretty much in the same way as before Mrs. Eddy's death on December 3, 1910; yet, at present, destructive forces seem to be more in evidence than its less spectacular constructive work. Even a hasty glance at the latest literature issuing from their ranks will prove this assertion. While free lectures in theaters and public halls continue to be given by members of the Board of Lectureship of the Mother Church, and while works appear of the style of Mr. Hayes' *The Lady in White*[1] whose aim is "to support the discoverer and founder of Christian Science, Mary Baker Eddy, Pastor, Poet, Author, who was and is in her real selfhood the Elect Lady of the Gospel," on the other hand, many signs point to elements of revolt against Christian Science autocracy even in such as remain loyally devoted to Christian Science principles. We refer to works of the stamp of Mr. Kratzer's *The Christian Science Church*, which he calls "a friendly review of its administration and a plea for liberty in Christian Science," and in which—in the friendliest spirit, as is always done when Christian Scientists fall out—he offers unbidden his unwelcome service "to help the organization shake off the swaddling clothes which it has outgrown."[2]

[1] Hayes: *The Lady in White* (New York, 1921), Preface p. xi.
[2] Kratzer: *The Christian Science Church* (Chicago, 1914), p. 49.

But these are faint murmurs of dissatisfaction and not likely to exert any notable influence over the general course of Christian Science. Of vastly greater significance are the dissensions that every now and then crop up almost anywhere in Christian Scientism and are especially virulent in its center, The Mother Church, the First Church of Christ, Scientist, in Boston, Massachusetts. As briefly as possible we shall here sum up these latest events that mark directly or indirectly the passing of Mrs. Eddy. Ominous rumblings of a coming storm were heard repeatedly during the last years of her life, but the real outburst came only within the last few years.

First in line, though not in importance, was the suit instituted by her son with others as "next friends" against some ten prominent Christian Scientists who were represented as keeping Mrs. Eddy under their control for personal reasons. To indicate the trend of events, a few explanatory notes on Mrs. Eddy's earlier years are here in order. Mrs. Eddy, as already mentioned, had one only son whom she named after his father, her first husband, George Washington Glover. In her autobiographical romance she indulges in some touching paragraphs about this boy of hers, how he was separated from her when quite young and how "the night he was taken from her she knelt by his side throughout the dark hours hoping for a vision of relief from this trial." [1]   A truer picture, however, is given us in the words of her father who in his blunt way is reported to have said of her: "Mary acts like an old ewe that won't own its lamb. She won't have the boy near her." [2]   The boy was adopted by the nurse that had tended to him ever since his birth, and from 1857, when he removed with his foster parents to Minnesota, until 1878, his mother evinced not the slightest interest in him. By that time he was himself married and had two children. The year 1878 was an eventful one for Mrs. Eddy. There was trouble brewing in her little flock of disciples. Kennedy, though long since passed out of her life, still remained fresh in her thought. The dread of malicious animal magnetism was fast becoming an obsession. Spofford she had excom-

[1] *Introspection and Retrospection*, p. 21.
[2] Milmine: *op. cit.*, p. 26.

municated. The law-courts were kept busy with her litigations. Kennedy, Tuttle, Stanley and Spofford were sued to recover money from them for one reason or another; Spofford was sued a second time in the famous witchcraft case. In October her husband and Arens were arrested on a charge of conspiracy to murder Spofford.[1] Under these circumstances Mrs. Eddy bethought herself of her son. She probably wondered whether he could fit in with her designs. She sent him a telegram asking him to meet her at Cincinnati, but did not herself keep the appointment. Finally, she invited him to come to Boston, where mother and son met after a separation of twenty-three years. After this first interview they met again occasionally, but it was never again of Mrs. Eddy's seeking. In 1887 she positively forbade him to come.

"I," she wrote to him, "want quiet and Christian life alone with God, when I can find intervals for a little rest. *You are not what I had hoped to find you*, and I am changed. The world, the flesh and evil I am at war with, and if any one comes to me it must be to help me and not to hinder me in this warfare." [2]

On January 2, 1907, Mr. Glover, in company with his daughter, paid his mother a last visit and was shocked at her physical condition and at the rambling, incoherent nature of her conversation. Mr. Glover understood her to mean that she was kept under restraint by the persons with whom she lived and resolved to take steps to break the ring which made approach to her almost impossible. On March 1, he began an action in behalf of his mother against Calvin Frye, Alfred Farlow and the officers of The Mother Church asking "for an adjudication that Mrs. Eddy was incompetent through age and failing faculties to manage her estate; that a receiver be appointed and that the various defendants named be required to account for alleged misuse of her property." [3] This suit must have caused Mrs. Eddy no little annoyance. Her business abilities, though, did not forsake her in this emergency. Within

---

[1] Milmine, *op. cit.*, pp. 250-261.
[2] Eddy: letter dated October 31, 1887, quoted by Milmine, p. 455.
[3] *Ibid.*, pp. 456-458.

six days she met the action of her son and self-styled friends by the declaration of a trusteeship for the control of her estate, thus forcing them, in the end, to withdraw their suit.

About this time Mrs. Eddy became dissatisfied with her residence at Pleasant View. Mesmerism, the primal source of all her troubles, had at last found her retreat, and, as in her mind it had a tendency to become localized, she must absolutely change her abode. A splendid mansion was bought at Newton, a suburb of Boston, and remodeled in all haste, regardless of cost, several hundred laborers being employed day and night at this work. On January 26, 1908, Mrs. Eddy left forever her splendid mansion near Concord, New Hampshire, where she had resided for the last seventeen years.

"Extraordinary precautions were taken to prevent accidents. A pilot engine preceded the locomotive which drew Mrs. Eddy's special train, and the train was followed by a third engine to prevent the possibility of a rear end collision." [1]

When she arrived at her new home, she had to be lifted out of her carriage and carried into the house by one of her male attendants.

But despite these infirmities and her eighty-seven years Mrs. Eddy was apparently still on the watch for possible rivals, and with the help of her spiritual household was able to frustrate any design that tended to diminish the luster of her own achievements. First in importance after The Mother Church in Boston was the First Church of Christ, Scientist, in New York City. The latter was almost as much the personal work of Mrs. Augusta E. Stetson as the former was that of Mrs. Eddy. A magnificent church edifice, erected at a cost of $1,250,000 and dedicated as soon as completed free of debt, testified to the ardent zeal of this disciple. Mrs. Stetson could boast that besides herself not a member of the Mother Church had contributed one dollar for its erection. Provision had been made in the church edifice itself for the work of the practitioners, some twenty-five of whom could meet their patients there

[1] Milmine: *op. cit.*, p. 458.

in separate rooms designed and equipped for that very purpose.[1] Here Mrs. Stetson organized her band of healers, met them daily at noon for spiritual instruction and trained them presumably in the ways of the Founder, specializing, so it seems, on her most abstruse and most questionable doctrines. Sex matters, spiritual generation and similar extravagances of Mrs. Eddy's loomed large in these meetings.

This practice, and the whole trend of Mrs. Stetson's teaching, was offensive not only to Mrs. Eddy, but also to not a few Christian Scientists of New York who on that account separated from the First Church and founded branch churches in other parts of the City free from Mrs. Stetson's influence.[2] Mrs. Stetson herself sums up her teaching in the following concise statement: "I declared for the nothingness of material generation, and the greatness, allness of the spiritual man and the spiritual universe."[3] Over her followers Mrs. Stetson exercised an influence comparable only to that of Mrs. Eddy in her palmiest days. No wonder the report went abroad that Mrs. Stetson was in training to become Mrs. Eddy's successor. This rumor, even had it been entirely groundless, was enough to mar the friendship of more than a quarter of a century's duration between Mrs. Stetson and her idolized teacher. From the day that it reached Mrs. Eddy's ear, Mrs. Stetson's position in Christian Scientism was doomed.

As the work of First Church in New York, in spite of numerous defections, had prospered to such an extent that as many as two to three hundred people had to stand on Sunday mornings, Mrs. Stetson remedied these conditions in 1908 by providing an overflow service in the Reading Room. Before long the following by-law appeared in the *Church Manual* and put an end to this practice: "A Church of Christ, Scientist, shall not hold two or more Sunday services at the same hour."[4]

---

[1] Stetson: *Vital Issues* (New York, 1917), p. 105.

[2] *Ibid.*, p. 109. "Some of the practitioners began early to cavil at and criticize the incisive methods of handling the animal impulses. . . . It was not, however, so much the challenging of language as it was the burning incision of spiritual truth into the strongholds of mortal belief that gave rise to charges against the character of these meetings."

[3] *Ibid.*, p. 110.

[4] *Church Manual*, Art. XVII, sect. 4.

If Mrs. Stetson had been less infatuated with her own importance, she would have accepted this almost personal rebuff as a warning of an impending catastrophe. As others had done before her for their undoing, she rested too securely on Mrs. Eddy's former professions of friendship. She now proposed, in order to remedy the crowded condition of her congregation, to build on the fashionable Riverside Drive a church which was to "rival in beauty of architecture any other religious structure in America." [1] The plot for the proposed buildings was secured late in November, 1908, at a price of $390,000.

This was almost like throwing the gauntlet down before the authorities in Boston. Whatever may have been in Mrs. Stetson's mind, the Boston group of Scientists seemed to accept it as such, or rather to look upon these ambitions as most dangerous symptoms of a disease that needed the surgeon's knife without delay. Already on December 5, the *Christian Science Sentinel* brought several editorials that censured the project in the most direct manner. In an article entitled "Consistency" we read the following apostrophe:

"Are you striving in Christian Science to be the best Christian on earth, or are you striving to have the most costly edifice on the earth? . . . Mrs. Eddy has continued to declare against the display of material things, and has said that *the less we have of them the better.* Since God has taught her that matter is unreal and Spirit is the only reality, any other position would be unscientific."

In the same issue another article entitled *One Mother Church in Christian Science* has the following:

"Concerning these news items it is to be said that Mrs. Eddy was not 'known to be profoundly pleased' with what purports to be the plans of the First Church of Christ, Scientist, of New York City; for she learned of this proposed rival to The Mother Church for the first time from the daily press. Three leading facts remain immortal in the history of Christian Science, namely: 1. This Science is already established, and it has the support of all true Christian Scientists throughout the world. 2. Any competition or any

[1] Stetson: *Vital Issues,* p. 123, 127. Snowden: *op. cit.,* p. 184.

rivalry in Christian Science is abnormal, and will expose and explode itself. 3. Any attempt at rivalry or superiority in Christian Science is unchristian; therefore it is unscientific." [1]

Mrs. Stetson and her following in a long and strong communication to the editor of the Christian Science periodicals bitterly resented the imputations of these editorials, but at the same time meekly submitted. Her request that this apology should be printed was not heeded, not even acknowledged. On January 16, 1909, were published a few lines purporting to come from Mrs. Eddy which, though retracting nothing, acted as a soothing balm on the ruffled feelings of the New Yorkers. But this was not to last long. Again Mrs. Stetson offered her opponents a welcome occasion for renewed attacks. Continuing to be deeply attached to her Leader, she committed the tactical error of forwarding to Mrs. Eddy by special messenger as a gift a sum of money she herself had received from some students of hers. The gift was seasoned with adulatory messages which contain such extravagant phrases as the following:

"The voice of the Father-Mother God is ever speaking through you. . . . You are known to us, our beloved teacher, by words which make 'our hearts burn within us,' and we, your body, quickly and gratefully respond. . . . We behold our beloved Leader, Mary Baker Eddy, revealed to our waking thought as eternal life, and you, our blessed teacher, as the manifestation of Truth." [2]

All these messages were forwarded at the same time to Mrs. Eddy. Mrs. Eddy accepted the gift and started at once to discipline the giver. In her letter of thanks the following passage occurs:

"The Scripture says: 'Watch and pray, that ye enter not into temptation.' You are aware that animal magnetism is the opposite of divine Science, and that this opponent is the means whereby the conflict against truth is engendered and developed. Beloved! you need to watch and pray that

[1] Stetson: *Vital Issues*, pp. 122-128.
[2] *Ibid.*, pp. 135-146.

the enemy of good cannot separate you from your Leader and best earthly friend." [1]

This letter was dated July 12, 1909. On July 23, another letter, more direct and plain, followed. It reads as follows:

"MY DEAR STUDENT—Awake and arise from this temptation produced by animal magnetism upon yourself, allowing your students to deify you and me. Treat yourself for it and get your students to help you rise out of it. It will be your destruction if you do not do this. Answer this letter immediately." [2]

On July 31, the *Christian Science Sentinel*, in a scathing editorial entitled *None Good but God*, published damaging extracts of these confidential messages and then continued:

"This is emphatically not Christian Science, and Christian Scientists will note in these quotations phrases for which they can find no warrant either in the Scriptures or in any of Mrs. Eddy's writings. . . . It is time for these students and their teacher, and other students and other teachers, if there be any in the same belief, to awake from the mesmerism of which they are the victims." [3]

About the same time Mrs. Stetson was summoned before the Board of Directors, one witness confronting her, but on August 3, these charges were, apparently, dismissed.

In reality the Board of Directors prepared to spread a dragnet around Mrs. Stetson which should definitely put her out of the way. A secret investigation, of which Mrs. Stetson was kept in ignorance, was made which on September 25 resulted in the following "Findings and Orders": (1) That Mrs. Stetson taught her students that the branch church of Christ of which she was a member was the only legitimate Christian Science Church in New York City; (2) that she taught an erroneous sense of Christian Science, particularly in regard to the application of Christian Science to human needs and conditions; (3) that she endeavored to exercise a control over her

[1] Stetson: *op. cit.*, p. 155.
[2] *Ibid.*, p. 159.
[3] *Ibid.*, pp. 137, 25.

students and (4) to obtrude herself upon their attention; (5) that she treated persons without their request or consent, and (6) attempted to control and to injure persons by mental means; (7) that she had so strayed from the right way as not to be fit for the work of a teacher of Christian Science.

In view of these findings the directors ordered that her card be removed from the *Christian Science Journal*, and that her license or authority to teach Christian Science be revoked.[1] On November 17 her name was dropped from the roll of the Mother Church, which automatically deprived her of any position of trust in her own church. That, notwithstanding Mrs. Stetson's protestations to the contrary, Mrs. Eddy was back of these proceedings, is rendered evident by the following letter written only four days before Mrs. Stetson's excommunication:

BROOKLINE, MASS.,
November 13, 1909.

To the Board of Trustees, First Church of Christ,
Scientist, New York City:

Beloved Brethren: In consideration of the present momentous question at issue in First Church of Christ, Scientist, New York City, I am constrained to say, if I can settle this church difficulty amicably by a few words, as many students think I can, I herewith cheerfully subscribe these words of love:—

My beloved brethren in First Church of Christ, Scientist, New York City, I advise you with all my soul to support the Directors of The Mother Church, and unite with those in your church who are supporting The Mother Church Directors. Abide in fellowship with and obedience to The Mother Church, and in this way God will bless and prosper you. This I know, for He has proved it to me for forty years in succession.

Lovingly yours,
MARY BAKER EDDY.[2]

Despite this letter quiet was not fully restored in New York. There remained those, openly or secretly in sympathy with Mrs. Stetson's principles and practice, who were con-

---

[1] Stetson: *op. cit.*, pp. 53-55. Cf. *Washington Star*, March 6, 1921.
[2] *Christian Science Sentinel*, November 20, 1909. Stetson: *op. cit.*, p. 92.

vinced that a gross injustice had been done her. Some of these
shared her fortunes of their own free choice; others were forced
out by the same board that had ousted their teacher. Eight of
the nine trustees of the Church and sixteen of its practitioners
were thus weeded out during the course of the following year,
the last one of Mrs. Eddy's earthly career. These joined Mrs.
Stetson in a schism which is now known as New York City
Christian Science Institute with Mrs. Stetson as its Principal.[1]

The last sensational news deserving to be recorded here is
the rivalry that has of late arisen among the actual heads of
the Christian Science organization. In order to understand
these disputes, it is necessary to have an idea of the internal
organization of Christian Science. Up to January 10, 1910,
the administration of the Mother Church was in the hands of
the "First Members"; but on that day Mrs. Eddy created a
board of directors consisting of five members who were to tran-
sact all the business of the Mother Church and, under the direct
supervision of Mrs. Eddy, were to elect all the officers. In
1903 the name of the "First Members" was changed to
"Executive Members" and in 1908 this office was abolished.[2]

Besides the Board of Directors there exists the Christian
Science Publishing Society, established by Mrs. Eddy on January 25, 1898. By the deed of trust executed by Mrs. Eddy
in that year, only the Publishing Society, always with the approval of Mrs. Eddy, "selects, approves and publishes the
books and literature it sends forth."[3] On March 17, 1919,
the Board of Directors voted to remove from the board of trustees of the Publishing Society Mr. Rowlands who, they claimed,
"did not understand or recognize the importance and necessity
of promoting the interests of Christian Science by following
the directions given by Mrs. Eddy in our church by-laws"; "had
shown a disposition to invent or adopt interpretations of our
church laws that pervert their meaning and annul their effect";
"had set up the deed of trust against the by-laws and govern-

[1] The whole disgraceful procedure is given in detail in Mrs. Stetson's
Vital Issues. The war between the two factions is still being carried on
through the medium of the daily Press.
[2] *Church Manual,* Art. I, sect. 1-6.
[3] *Ibid.,* Art. XXV, sect. 8.

ment of the Church and threatened this board with litigation, if this board exercised its right to remove any of the trustees." [1]

Mr. Dittemore, one of the directors, strongly disapproved of this action, because he considered it "an utterly inadequate remedy for the evils arising from the mismanagement and misconduct of said publishing society trustees . . . insisting that said evils imperatively required the removal of all three trustees, especially of the dominating trustee, Herbert W. Eustace." [1] The other directors, it is stated, were well enough satisfied with Mr. Dittemore's general aim; but they disapproved of his methods, because they expected that the other trustees of the Publishing Society by refusing to submit and to choose a successor to Mr. Rowlands would give them a specious pretext for the removal of them all.

But things did not take the turn the directors expected. The trustees filed a bill in equity to compel the reinstatement of Mr. Rowlands and to restrain the directors from interfering with the trustees in the discharge of their duties as trustees under the trust instrument of January 25, 1898. Mr. Dittemore also, who had been expelled from the board of directors, asked the court to declare void the vote removing him and to restrain the directors from interfering with his rights and functions as a director. The hearing began June 3. The bitterness which had apparently marked the disputes between the two boards crept into the hearing. "Sharp clashes between the opposing counsel, charges and countercharges, made by witnesses and lawyers alike, enlivened the proceedings as they dragged on through the fierce summer heat." The final decision upheld Mr. Dittemore and the Board of Trustees; but this, far from settling the controversy, only was the signal for a new crop of legal wrangles. To enumerate a few of these—

1. Mrs. Emilie B. Hulin files a petition asking leave to intervene in the suit as a "First Member."

2. Mr. Edwin A. Krauthoff asks leave to appear independently as opposing Mrs. Hulin's petition.

3. The trustees of the Publishing Society file a bill of complaint against thirteen members of First Church of Christ,

[1] The *Washington Herald*, May 2, 1920.

Scientist, in Boston, to which later two other persons are added, asking the Court to restrain them from doing anything to injure the business of the Publishing Society.

"It is charged in the bill that the defendants have undertaken to procure the cancellation of subscriptions by Christian Scientists to the periodicals of the Society; have interfered with the employees to hinder and delay the publication of the periodicals; have sent out false and misleading statements in reports and information regarding administration of the trust by the trustees, and have wrongfully charged the plaintiffs with having withheld from The Mother Church large sums of money due from the trustees, and also that the trustees made false entries in their own books."

4.   The Attorney General for Massachusetts asks leave to intervene in the trustees' suit.

5.   The Board of Directors and the treasurer file a bill in equity asking the court to remove all the trustees of the Publishing Society.

"The directors charge the trustees with mismanagement of the business of the Publishing Society and it is said that many members of the Church have canceled their subscriptions to periodicals issued by the Society because of their belief that the trustees are not loyal and consistent Scientists and are not living up to the doctrines proclaimed by Mrs. Eddy." [1]

This bare summary gives an inadequate idea of the conditions as they exist today in Christian Science. Other suits are in contemplation and there is much unrest in the Church body. Mr. Gilmore as Publication Committee for New York denies "the intimation that there is a strife and schismatic condition in every Christian Science branch church." [2]   To this Mrs. Stetson replies:

"I leave this remark to the judgment of the public who are familiar with the lawsuits, injunctions, counter-injunctions, and factional strife within the material organization which have been reported in the press." [3]

[1] Cf. The *Washington Herald*, May 2, 1920.
[2] The *New York Evening Mail*, February 24, 1921.
[3] The *Washington Star*, March 6, 1921.

As a result of Judge Dodge's decision in favor of the trustees more than two hundred employees of all kinds have left the publications, and a committee has been appointed to care for these "strikers." Mrs. Stetson also has not been silenced. She vents her grievances in the newspapers, charges her opponents with boycotting her books, removing them from public libraries, and in other ways preventing her witnessing to the truth as taught by Mrs. Eddy. On October 2, 1921, in a two full-page advertisement she brings before the public her difficulties with the board of trustees of New York First Church of Christ over a fence between her property and that of the Church which the Church insists on removing while Mrs. Stetson just as strenuously refuses.[1]

If in spite of these many and ever recurring signs of selfishness Christian Science continues to attract people of intelligence, we may, perhaps, agree with Dr. Cabot in assigning in part for this strange phenomenon the following reasons. Says he:

"It is not difficult to perceive as one studies the testimonies recorded in the *Christian Science Journal* that many patients have been driven into Christian Science by a multitude of shifting and mistaken diagnoses, by the gross abuse of drugs, especially of morphine, and by the total neglect of rational psychotherapy on the part of many physicians. . . . The success of the Christian Science movement is due largely to the ignorance and narrow-mindedness of a certain proportion of the medical profession. I can see some foundation even for such an exaggerated charge as that 'the doctors are flooding the world with disease'—a favorite expression of Mrs. Eddy's. No one who has seen much of the nervous or hysterical affections following railway accidents and of the methods not infrequently used, not only by lawyers, but by doctors, to make the sufferers believe that they are sicker than they really are, can deny that there is some truth in Mrs. Eddy's charge. Even in her irrational denunciation of hygiene, one cannot help seeing some grain of truth when one reads or hears of the multitude of petty prudences and 'old womanish' superstitions not infrequently exploited by

[1] The *Washington Star,* October 2, 1921.

school teachers, parents, and teachers of physical culture under the name of hygiene. Believing, then, as I do, that most Christian Science cures are genuine—genuine cures of functional disease—the question arises whether the special methods of mental healing employed by Christian Scientists differ from other methods of mental healing. . . . Work-cure is, I think, the sanest and most helpful part of Christian Science, as of all other types of psychotherapy. The Christian Scientists do set idle people to work and turn inverted attention outward upon the world. This is a great service—the greatest, I think, that can be done to a human being. By setting their patients to the work of healing and teaching others, Christian Scientists have wisely availed themselves of the greatest healing power on earth. I believe that suggestion, education and work-cure can be used in far safer and saner ways by physicians, social workers, and teachers or clergymen properly trained for the work than by the Christian Scientists." [1]

Though Dr. Cabot's statements may be loose in details and too general in their indictment of the medical profession and of health-crusaders, generally, they afford, nevertheless, food for thought inasmuch as they condemn a tendency which in a different direction exhibits the same preoccupation and pursues the same ends as Christian Science and New Thought, being prompted by an excessive desire of bodily comfort and physical health. A different ideal is presented to us by St. Paul who gives to his beloved Timothy the following advice:

"Avoid foolish and old wives' fables, and exercise thyself unto godliness. For bodily exercise is profitable to little; but godliness is profitable to all things, having promise of the life that now is, and of that which is to come." [2]

[1] Cabot, in *McClure's Magazine*, Vol. XXXI (1908), pp. 475-476, article: "One Hundred Christian Science Cures."
[2] I Tim. 4:7.

BIBLIOGRAPHY

I. Works of, and on, Mrs. Eddy

MARY BAKER EDDY: *Science and Health with Key to the Scriptures,* the textbook of Christian Science (1st ed. 1875). Mrs. Eddy continually revised this book up to the end of her life. While later modifications are of minor importance, those of earlier years are most radical. For a comparison of earlier and later editions, cf. pp. 46 *ff.*

————: *Science and Health,* with German translation on opposite page, Boston, 1912; with French translation, Boston, 1917.

————: *Christian Healing,* Boston, 1880.

————: *The Science of Man,* Boston, 1883. An original draft of *Science and Health,* largely embodying P. P. Quimby's words and ideas.

————: *The People's Idea of God,* Boston, 1886.

————: *No and Yes,* Boston, 1891, 1908, 1917.

————: *Christ and Christmas,* Boston, 1893. "An illustrated poem which she afterward temporarily suppressed because the pictures were very displeasing to a great many people. One picture represents Jesus Christ standing beside a big black, upholstered coffin, raising to life a frightfully emaciated woman. Another represents a woman, strangely like Mrs. Eddy's authorized photographs in appearance, standing at a bedside and raising a prostrate form, while a great star burns above her head. In another, Christ is represented as hand in hand with a woman who bears a tablet inscribed 'Christian Science.' Mrs. Eddy wrote the text of this grim gift-book, and a fly-leaf accredits the pictures to 'Mary Baker G. Eddy and James F. Gilman, artists'" (*McClure's Magazine,* 1907, p. 702). The book has since been put again on the market.

————: *Pulpit and Press,* Boston, 1895.

————: *Church Manual of the First Church of Christ, Scientist, in Boston, Mass.* Boston, 1895. Like *Science and Health,* the Church Manual has undergone a series of important revisions. In its present form it contains Mrs. Eddy's Church legislation extending over a period of many years. The earlier editions (1895-1899) contain a full list of all the members of the Christian Science Church.

————: *Miscellaneous Writings,* 1883-1896, Boston, 1896. An important collection of documents containing questions and an-

249

swers, addresses, letters, sermons, instructions, a few historical notes (idealized) and poems.

MARY BAKER EDDY: *Christian Science vs. Pantheism,* Boston, 1900.

————: *Messages to the Mother Church,* 1901, 1902, 1903.

————: *Unity of Good,* Boston, 1888.

————: *Rudimental Divine Science,* Boston, 1887-1909.

————: *Retrospection and Introspection,* Boston, 1899. An autobiography in which Mrs. Eddy idealizes all the most trivial and even disgraceful events in her life. Cf. Milmine's *Life.*

————: *The First Church of Christ, Scientist, and Miscellany,* Boston, 1914. A posthumous collection of letters, etc.

Concordance to Science and Health, Boston, 1903, 1908, 1916. Arranged on the plan of the ordinary concordances to the Bible. Very complete and up-to-date.

Concordance to Mrs Eddy's Published Writings, other than *Science and Health.* Boston, 1915. Same remarks as above. The compiler is Albert Francis Conant.

SCHÖN, MARIE: *Vergleichs-Arbeit über die Gesamt-Ausgaben (1875-1912) von Wissenschaft und Gesundheit* mit Schlüssel sur hl. Schrift von Mary Baker G. Eddy, Berlin, 1914. The author would like to have the 1891 edition of *Science and Health* looked upon as the standard. Requests also that a new German translation be authorized to be published without the parallel English text.

MILMINE, GEORGINE: *The Life of Mary Baker G. Eddy, and the History of Christian Science,* first published as a serial in *McClure's Magazine,* 1907-1908, revised and published in book form, New York, 1909. The most reliable life of Mrs. Eddy; contains many original documents. Unfortunately out of print.

WILBUR, SIBYL: *The Life of Mary Baker Eddy.* New York, 1908; Boston, 1913. Idealized throughout. Aims at palliating the many disagreeable facts brought to light in Miss Milmine's *Life.*

PEABODY, FREDERICK W.: *The Religio-Medical Masquerade.* New York, 1910, 1915. A complete exposure of Christian Science. "There is absolutely no middle ground. Either Mr. Peabody is the most shameless of calumniators or Mrs. Eddy is the basest of charlatans. Mr. Peabody expresses an eager readiness to have this question submitted to any test. His charges run the whole gamut from attempted murder to accomplished theft, with endless lying scattered all along in between. They are not vague, but definite, and every one of them can be settled as true or untrue. Why do the Eddyites wait? The courts are

open and until Mr. Peabody is a convicted slanderer, no sane
or decent person, man or woman, can afford to give countenance
to Christian Science" (*The New York Times*). Mr. Peabody
was counsel against Mrs. Eddy in many of her lawsuits.

DRESSER, JULIUS A.: *True History of Mental Science,* Boston, 1887.

DRESSER, HORATIO W.: *A History of the New Thought Movement,*
New York, 1919. While chiefly dealing with the New Thought
Movement, this history necessarily touches on the beginnings of
Christian Science.

POWELL, LYMAN: *Christian Science, the Faith and the Founder,*
New York, 1917.

PODMORE, FRANK: *Mesmerism and Christian Science,* a Short History of Mental Healing, Philadelphia, 1909.

Periodicals

The Christian Science Journal, established 1883 by Mrs. Eddy. A
monthly magazine, the official organ of Christian Science.

The Christian Science Quarterly, published January, April, July,
October; founded by Mrs. Eddy in 1890. Contains the Lesson-
Sermons for the Sunday services throughout the world. Pub-
lished in English (regular and vest-pocket edition), English-
Dutch and English-German.

The Christian Science Sentinel, established in 1898 by Mrs. Eddy.
A weekly periodical.

The Christian Science Monitor, an international daily newspaper
(except Sundays), founded by Mrs. Eddy in 1908.

Der Herold der Christian Science, a monthly magazine in German
and English, authorized by Mrs. Eddy in 1903.

Le Héraut de Christian Science, a monthly periodical in French and
English, established in 1918.

These periodicals are authorized by the Christian Science Publishing Society. Other reviews that flourished for a time or are not
officially approved by the Christian Science Publishing Society are:

The Boston Christian Scientist, 1889-1890.

The Chicago Christian Scientist, 1887-1890.

Harmony, San Francisco, 1897-1906.

Unity, a monthly magazine issued by the Unity School of Christianity, Kansas City, Mo., 1891, etc.

II. Other Works on the History of Christian Science and New Thought

ARMSTRONG, JOSEPH: *The Mother Church,* Boston, 1897. Deals
with the erection of the church edifice in Boston.

Christian Science and the Practice of Medicine, Milwaukee, 1900. Report of the trial of Crescentia Arries and Emma Nichols charged with practicing medicine without a license—the first unqualified conviction of Christian Scientists.

Editorial Comments on the life and work of Mary Baker Eddy, collected and arranged by the Christian Science Publishing Society, Boston, 1911.

FARLOW, ALFRED: *The Relation of Government to the Practice of Christian Science,* reprint from the government magazine, Boston, 1907. Favorable to Christian Science.

FARNSWORTH, EDWARD C.: *The Passing of Mary Baker Eddy,* Portland, Maine, 1911.

HAYES, HAROLD VINCENT: *The Lady in White and Her Marvellous Mission,* New York, 1921. 446 pp. "To support the discoverer and founder of said Science (Christian Science), Mary Baker Eddy, Pastor, Poet, Author, who was and is in her real selfhood the Elect Lady of the Gospel, forever robed in white—I have penned and published this book" (Preface p. xi).

HUSE, SIBYL MARVIN: *Christ's Offspring or Spiritual Generation,* New York, 1921. "To the materialist Mary Baker Eddy seemed to die; but there was one faithful watcher (Mrs. Stetson) on the highest mountain peak of faith and understanding who discerned, low on the horizon, the dawning light of the coming radiance of the fulness of the Godhead bodily, even Christ, the compound idea of Life and Love who should rise to the zenith of demonstration. . . . The clarion call rang out: 'Mary Baker Eddy lives,' Watch for the revealing of the ideal man, the Christ of God. In this second coming she is conqueror of the female belief of material conception, as in the first coming he (Jesus) overcame the lie of material begetting; thus completing the victory over the dragon of belief in material generation—Adam's sensuous dream of an Eve, his own lustful self, as the mother of all living!" (*Ibid.,* pp. 16-17). The last words are a quotation from an article of Mrs. Stetson's in the *Independent,* January 26, 1911.

KRATZER, GLENN A.: *The Christian Science Church,* Chicago, 1914, 1920. A friendly review of its administration and a plea for liberty in Christian Science. "The writer not only believes absolutely in Christian Science as taught in the Bible and by Mrs. Eddy, but he is wholly friendly to the Christian Science organization. He desires to do what he can to help the organization shake off some of the swaddling clothes which it has outgrown, in order that its members may the more largely enter into 'the glorious liberty of the children of God'" (*Ibid.,* p. 49).

LORD, MYRA B.: *Mary Baker Eddy*—A concise story of her life and work; Boston, 1918. Favorable to Christian Science.

MEEHAN, MICHAEL: *Mrs. Eddy and the Late Suit in Equity.* Authorized edition, Concord, N. H., 1908. Deals with the suit of her son and others as next friends to have a receiver of her property appointed. "This lawsuit disclosed one interesting fact, namely, that while in 1893 securities of Mrs. Eddy amounting to $100,000 were brought to Concord, and in January, 1899, she had $236,200, and while in 1907 she had about a million dollars' worth of taxable property, Mrs. Eddy in 1901 returned a signed statement to the assessors at Concord that the value of her taxable property amounted to about $19,000 dollars. This statement was sworn to year after year by Mr. Frye" (Milmine, in *McClure's Magazine*, 1908, p. 24). The suit was withdrawn.

STETSON, AUGUSTA E.: *Reminiscences, Sermons, and Correspondence,* New York, 1913. Proving adherence to the principle of Christian Science, as taught by Mary Baker Eddy. 1200 pages.

————: *Vital Issues in Christian Science,* New York, 1917. A record of unsettled questions which arose in the year 1909 between the directors of The Mother Church and First Church of Christ, Scientist, New York, with facsimiles and excerpts and letters of Mary Baker Eddy.

————: *Correspondence, Essays and Poems of Interest* to the members of the Choral Society of the New York City Christian Science Institute. New York, 1918.

New York City Christian Science Institute: *A Tribute of Love and Gratitude to Our Faithful Teacher Augusta E. Stetson,* New York, 1921.

WOODBURY, JOSEPHINE CURTIS: *War in Heaven,* Boston, 1897. Sixteen years' experience in Christian Science Mind-healing.

————: *Christian Science Voices,* Boston, 1885.

III. *Works on the Whole Favoring Christian Science or New Thought or Modern Mind-Healing*

I

BAUM, MRS. C. L.: *Studies in Divine Science,* Colorado College of Divine Science, Denver, Colo., 1909.

BEECHER, MARGARET: *Some Truths and Wisdom of Christian Science,* New York, 1904.

BRYANT: *Christian Science Teacher and Healer,* Chicago, 1891.

CASEY, ROBERT: *God and Good are One*—a lecture on Christian Science, 1890.

CHAPMAN, G. F.: *Christ, the Healer*—a series of letters, Boston, 1888.

CRAMER, MALINDA E.: *Lessons in Science and Health,* San Francisco, 1890.

CRAMER, MALINDA E.: *Basic Statement and Health Treatment of Truth.*

————: *Manuscript Lessons.*

————: *Genesis Lessons.*

————: *Divine Science and Healing,* San Francisco, 1905.

DAY, GEORGE B.: *Christian Science Sermons,* Chicago, 1889. The new interpretation or the Scriptures viewed in the light of Christian Science.

DEARMER, PERCY: *Body and Soul,* London, 1909. An inquiry into the effects of religion upon Health.

DE WATERS, LILLIAN: *Thinking Heavenward,* 1908.

————: *Journeying Onward,* 1908.

————: *The Hidden Truth,* 1919.

————: *The Perfect Vision,* 1920.

————: *Lifting the Veil,* Stamford, Conn., 1921.

FLORY, JACOK STONER: *Mind Mysteries,* Mount Morris, Ill., 1897.

FLOWER, B. O.: *Christian Science as a religious belief and a therapeutic agent,* Boston, 1909.

GESTEFELD, MRS. URSULA: *Which shall it be, Mind or Medicine?* (Pamphlet, 1886.)

————: *A Statement of Christian Science,* Chicago, 1888.

————: *Jesuitism in Christian Science.* A pamphlet against Mrs. Eddy.

————: *The Breath of Life,* Chicago, 1897.

————: *The Builder and the Plan,* 1901.

————: *The Science of Christ,* Chicago, 1889. An advanced statement of Christian Science.

GREENBAUM, LEON: *Follow Christ,* St. Louis, Mo., 1916.

HARLEY, FANNY M.: *Simplified Lessons in the Science of Being,* Chicago, 1899.

HARRIS, WALTER: *Christian Science and the Ordinary Man,* New York, 1917.

HASBROUCK, STEPHEN: *Altar Fires Relighted,* New York, 1911. A study of modern religious tendencies from the standpoint of the lay observer.

HEGEMAN, J. WINTHROP: *Must Protestantism adopt Christian Science?* New York, 1913.

HUGHES, NINA B.: *Twelve Simple Lessons in Christian Science,* 1888.

————: *Truth for Youth,* Chicago, 1888.

KIMBALL, EDWARD A.: *Lectures and Articles on Christian Science,* Chesterton, Indiana, 1921. 486 pages.

KOHAUS, HANNAH MORE: *Between the Lines*—a condensed statement of the Truth of Being, Chicago, 1897.

KRATZER, REV. GLENN A.: *Dominion Within,* Chicago, 1913.

————: *Spiritual Man,* 1914.

————: *What is Truth?* c. 1914.

KRATZER, REV. GLENN A.: *Revelation Interpreted.* 400 pages. c. 1915.

———: *The End of the Age,* an address delivered at Oregon, Ill., June 3, 1917; Chicago: Central Christian Science Institute, 1917.

———: *The Christian Science Church.* Cf. p. 5.

KRATZER, ELIZABETH CARY: *Complete in Him.*

———: *Individual Completeness or the Trinity of Mind.* 235 pages.

KREBS, EBBA VICTORIA: *Thoughts as They Have Come to Me,* Philadelphia, 1916.

LORD, FRANCES: *Christian Science Healing—Its Principles and Practice,* Chicago, 1888. 471 pages and index.

MACCAMELINE, CRAIG (pseudonym for Ballentine Frank): *Science and Scripture Health,* Detroit, Mich., 1920. 551 pages.

McMILLAN, LISTON: *Alathiasis, or Principles of Christian Hygiene,* designed as a study of Scriptural healing and involving a medico-legal view of Christianity, Oskaloosa, Iowa, 1895. 648 pages and index.

MARS, GERHARDT CORNELL: *The Interpretation of Life,* New York, 1908.

MILITZ, ANNIE RIX: *Primary Lessons in Christian Living and Healing,* New York, 1904.

NEWTON, RICHARD HEBER: *Christian Science, the Truth of Christian Healing* and their contribution to the growth of orthodoxy, New York, 1898.

ROBINSON, CHARLES: *Comparative and Rational Christian Science,* Chicago, 1911.

SABIN, OLIVER C.: *Christian Science, What It Is and What It Does,* Washington, D. C., 1899. 64 pages.

———: *Christian Science Made Plain,* 1905.

———: *Divine Healing.*

———: *Christian Science Instructor.*

———: *Christian Science Healing.*

———: *Christology, Science of Health and Happiness,* Washington, D. C., 1901; 23d ed., 1910.

SEWARD, THEODORE F.: *How to Get Acquainted with God,* New York, 1902.

SHANER, JOHN JUNIUS: *The Character Builder of Scientific Christianity,* San José, Calif., 1913.

STARCROSS, ROGER (pseudonym for Chas. H. Pope): *Christian Science Theory and Practice,* Boston, 1908.

THIESING, WINFRIED W.: *Nineteen Hundred Years,* or the power of Christ, Covington, Ky., 1898.

WORKS, U. S. SENATOR J. D.: A well-documented plea in favor of Christian Science, in *Congressional Record,* Vol. LII, Part I, pp. 1021-1055, 1915.

II

ARENS, E. J.: *Old Theology in its Application to the Healing of the Sick*, Boston, 1886.

ATKINSON, WILLIAM WALKER: *Mind-Power*, the secret of mental magic, Chicago, 1910.

BATTEN, LORING W.: *The Relief of Pain by Mental Suggestion*— a study of the moral and religious forces in healing, New York, 1917.

BROWN, GRACE M.: *Mental Harmony*.

———: *Think Right for Health and Success*, New York, 1916.

DRESSER, HORATIO W.: *The Power of Silence*, an interpretation of Life in its relation to Health and Happiness, New York, 1902.

———: *Methods and Problems of Spiritual Healing*.

———: *The Perfect Whole*.

———: *Voices of Hope*.

———: *In Search of a Soul*.

———: *Voices of Freedom*.

———: *Living by the Spirit*.

———: *Man and the Divine Order*.

———: *Health and the Inner Life*, an analytical and historical study of spiritual healing theories with an account of the life and teachings of P. P. Quimby, New York, 1906.

———: *The Philosophy of the Spirit*.

———: *Handbook of the New Thought*, New York, 1917.

———: *A History of the New Thought Movement*, New York, 1919.

DRESSER, HORATIO W. (editor): *The Spirit of the New Thought*— essays and addresses by representative authors and leaders, New York, 1917.

———: *The Quimby Manuscripts*, New York, 1921.

EVANS, W. F.: *The Primitive Mind-Cure*—the nature and power of faith, or elementary lessons in Christian philosophy and transcendental medicine, Boston, 1884.

———: *The Divine Law of Cure*, Boston, 1881.

———: *Mental Medicine*—a theoretical and practical treatise on medical psychology.

———: *Soul and Body*, or the spiritual science of health and disease, Boston, 1876.

FILLMORE, CHARLES: *The Science of Being and Christian Healing*, 12 lessons, Kansas City, Mo., 1912 (3d ed.).

FLETCHER, HORACE: *Menticulture*, or the A B C of True Living, Chicago, 1897.

———: *Happiness as Found in Forethought Minus Fearthought*, Chicago, 1897.

———; *Optimism*, a real remedy, Chicago, 1908.

HUDSON, THOMSON JAY: *The Law of Psychic Phenomena,* Chicago, 1893.

————: *The Law of Mental Medicine,* Chicago, 1903.

————: *The Evolution of the Soul and Other Essays,* Chicago, 1904.

JAMES, FANNIE B.: *Truth and Health,* science of the perfect Mind and the law of its demonstration. The textbook of the Colorado College of Divine Science, Denver, Colo., 1905 (3d ed.).

MILLS, ANNA W.: *Practical Metaphysics for Healing and Self-Culture,* Chicago, 1896.

PATTERSON, CHARLES BRODIE: *The Will to be Well,* New York, 1901, 1906.

SADLER, WILLIAM S., M.D.: *The Physiology of Faith and Fear,* or *The Mind in Health and Disease,* Chicago, 1912.

SIMPSON, A. B.: *The Gospel of Healing,* London, 1915.

TOWNE, ELIZABETH: *The Life Power and How to Use It,* Holyoke, Mass., 1906.

WHIPPLE, LEANDER EDMUND: *Healing Influences,* New York, 1913.

WOOD, HENRY: *Ideal Suggestion through Mental Photography,* preceded by a study of mental healing, Boston, 1893.

————: *The New Old Healing,* Boston, 1908.

————: *Life More Abundant*—Scriptural truth in modern application, Boston, 1905.

WOMER, PARLEY PAUL: *The Relation of Healing to Law,* Chicago, 1909.

WORCESTER-McCOMB-CORIAT: *Religion and Medicine*—The moral control of nervous disorders (Emmanuel Movement), New York, 1908.

WORCESTER-McCOMB: *The Christian Religion as a Healing Power,* New York, 1909.

WRIGHT, HOWARD F.: *Spiritual Health,* New York, 1913.

YARNALL, JANE W.: *Practical Healing for Mind and Body,* Chicago, 1899.

IV. Works Hostile to Christian Science and New Thought.

APPLER, AUGUSTUS C.: *Christian Science Exposed,* St. Louis, Mo., 1908.

ARMSTRONG, R. C.: *Christian Science Exposed,* Nashville, Tenn., 1910.

BARRINGTON, ARTHUR H.: *Anti-Christian Cults,* Milwaukee, 1898.

BATES, J. H.: *Christian Science and Its Problems,* New York, 1898.

BELL, ALVIN E.: *The Word of a Woman vs. the Word of God*—a lecture on Eddyism, Burlington, Iowa, 1917.

BENSON, MARGARET: *A Review of Christian Science.*

BROWN, J. ELWARD: *Christian Science, True or False, Which?* Siloam Springs, Ark., 1918.

BROWN, WILLIAM LEON: *Christian Science, falsely so-called,* New York, 1911.

BUCKLEY, JAMES MONROE: *Christian Science and Other Superstitions,* New York, 1899.

————: *Faith-Healing, Christian Science and Kindred Phenomena,* New York, 1892.

————: "The Absurd Paradox of Christian Science" in *North American Review,* July, 1901.

BURRELL, JOSEPH DUNN: *A New Appraisal of Christian Science,* New York, 1906.

CARTER, ADA: *The Seamless Robe,* New York, 1909.

CLARK, GORDON: *The Church of St. Bunco,* a drastic treatment of a copyrighted religion.   Unchristian Nonsense, New York, 1901.

COMBS, GEO. HAMILTON: *Some Latterday Religions,* New York, 1899.

COOKSEY, REV. N. B.: *Christian Science under the Searchlight,* Nashville, Tenn., 1915.

COPPAGE, L. J.: *Christian Science in the Light of Reason,* Cincinnati, 1914.

CUSHMAN, H. ERNEST: *The Truth in Christian Science,* a lecture, Boston, 1902.

EVANS, WILLIAM: *Why I am not a Christian Scientist* (pamphlet), Chicago, 1913.

FARNSWORTH, EDWARD C.: *The Sophistries of Christian Science,* Portland, Maine, 1909.

GARRISON, ARTHUR O.: *Christian Science dissected by A. D. Sector,* St. Louis, Mo., 1900.

GIFFORD, MIRAM W.: *Christian Science against Itself,* Cincinnati, Ohio, 1902.

GRAY, JAMES M.: *The Antidote to Christian Science,* New York, 1907.

GILBERT, MRS. VIOLA: *Christian Science Uncovered*—Its black art exposed, New York, 1900.

HALDEMAN, I. M.: *Christian Science in the Light of the Scriptures,* New York, 1909.   440 pp.

HARKER, RAY CLARKSON: *Christian Science,* Cincinnati, Ohio, 1908.

HARLEN, CHRISTIAN M.: *Christian Science against both Science and the Bible,* Dallas, Texas, 1899.

HART, H. MARTYN: *A Way that Seemeth Right,* New York, 1897.

HALL, ISAAC: *A Christian Scientist Who Never Made a Demonstration,* New York, 1907.

HARWOOD, ANNE: *An English View of Christian Science,* New York, 1899.

HAUDENSCHIELD, CHARLES R.: *Do the Bible and Christian Science Agree?* Los Angeles, Calif., 1917.

LASSWELL, WILLIAM P.: *Orthodoxy vs. Christian Science* or Anti-Christ in 1900, Heyworth, Ill., 1900.

McCASKILL, CHARLES WALLACE: *Fundamental Religious Teachings of Christian Science,* University Place, Nebraska, 1916.

McCORKLE, WILLIAM P.: *Christian Science, or the false Christ of 1866,* Richmond, Va., 1899.

McCLURE, EDMUND: *Christian Science in Modern Substitutes for Traditional Christianity,* London, 1913.

MARK TWAIN: *Christian Science,* New York, 1899, 1907.

MARSTEN, FRANCIS EDWARD: *The Mask of Christian Science,* New York, 1909.

MURRAY, SARA VANDEN: *Flesh and Matter*—The Scriptures *vs.* Christian Science, New York, 1910.

OLSTON, ALBERT B.: *The Facts and Fables of Christian Science,* Chicago, 1912. 399 pp.

OUGHTON, CHARLES M.: *Crazes, Credulities and Christian Science,* Chicago, 1901.

PAGET, STEPHEN: *The Faith and Works of Christian Science,* New York, 1909. 232 pp.

PEASE, CHARLES GIFFIN: *Exposé of Christian Science Methods and Teaching,* New York, 1905.

PRINCE, LEON C.: *The Sense and Nonsense of Christian Science,* Boston, 1911.

PURRINGTON, WM. A.: *Christian Science*—an exposition of Mrs. Eddy's wonderful discovery, including its legal aspects. A plea for children and other helpless sick, New York, 1900.

REED, DR. ELEANOR M.: *Christian Science and Contrasting Christian Truth* in Pan-Anglican Congress Report, London, 1908.

SANDT, GEORGE W.: *A Brief Study of Christian Science,* New York, 1902.

SHELDON, HENRY C.: *Christian Science So-called,* New York, 1913.

SHORT, WILLIAM: *Christian Science, What It Is.* What is new and what is true about it. New York, 1899.

SNOWDEN, JAMES H.: *The Truth about Christian Science,* Philadelphia, 1920. 313 pp. and index.

STAFFORD, THOMAS P.: *The Origin of Christian Science.* A key to the writings of M. B. G. Eddy, Kansas City, 1912.

STEPHENS, PERCY W.: *Christian Science, its Pedigree, Principle and Posterity,* Chicago, 1917.

STURGE, M. CARTA: *The Truth and Error of Christian Science,* London, 1903.

SWAIN, RICHARD LA RUE: *The Real Key to Christian Science,* a surprising discovery, New York, 1917.

Symposium: *Searchlights on Christian Science,* Revell Co., Chicago, 1898.

TOWNSEND, L. T.: *Faith-Work, Christian Science and Other Cures,* Boston, 1885.

UNDERHILL, ANDREW F.: *Valid Objections to so-called Christian Science,* New York, 1902.

VARLEY, HENRY: *Christian Science examined,* New York, 1898.

WATSON, W. H.: *Juggernaut*—Christian Science exposed, Davenport, Iowa, 1905.

WHITEHEAD, JOHN: *The Illusions of Christian Science*—its philosophy rationally examined, Boston, 1907.

WILSON, JOHN M.: *Christian Science Falsely So-called,* Louisville, Ky., 1900.

WIMBIGLER, CHARLES F.: *Christian Science and Kindred Superstitions,* New York, 1901.

WOOD, J. G.: *Fallacies of Christian Science,* Topeka, Kans., 1908.

V. Magazine Articles.

American Journal of Theology, Vol. XIV, October, 1910, pp. 533-551—I. King: "Religious Significance of the Psychotherapeutic Movement."

Canadian Magazine, Vol. XXXIV, April, 1910, pp. 521-527—J. S. MacLean: "Miracles and Mind Cures."

American Journal of Insanity, January, 1910—Woodbridge Riley: "Mental Healing in America."

America, May 14, 1921. See Catholic publications.

Catholic Mind. See Catholic publications.

Catholic World. See Catholic publications.

Contemporary Review, Vol. XCVIII, November, 1910—Podmore: "Mesmerism and Christian Science, a Short History of Mental Healing."

Current Literature, Vol. XLVIII, January, 1910, pp. 68-71—"Real Issues in the Christian Science Controversy."

———, Vol. LII, January, 1912, pp. 73-74—"Mrs. Stetson on the Immortality of Mrs. Eddy."

———, Vol. XLIX, November, 1910—"Psychological Expert's Reason for Pronouncing Mrs. Eddy Paranoiac."

Current Opinion, Vol. LV, August, 1913—"Mrs. Stetson's New Assertion of Spiritual Leadership."

———, Vol. LVII, July, 1914—"Spiritual Healing. Report of a clerical and medical committee."

———, Vol. LXVI, June, 1919—"Integrity of Christian Science movement threatened."

Current Opinion, Vol. LXVIII, May, 1920, pp. 667-668—"Civil War within the Christian Science Community."

———, Vol. LXVIII, March, 1920—"Physician's Impeachment of Christian Science Cures."

Dublin Review. See Catholic publications.

Hibbert Journal, Vol. VIII, October, 1909, pp. 10-27—S. McComb: "Christian Religion as a Healing Power."

Independent, Vol. LXXV, July 10, 1913, p. 74—"Projected Schism."

———, Vol. LXX, January 26, 1911—Mrs. Stetson: "Demonstration of Mrs. Eddy."

———, Vol. LXXV, September 11, 1913, p. 624-628—J. J. Walsh: "Psychotherapy as Practiced in All Ages."

———, Vol. LXXVI, October 9, 1913, pp. 81-85—"Mrs. Eddy and Mrs. Stetson."

Literary Digest, Vol. XLIV, June 29, 1912—"Christian Science and the Jew."

———, Vol. XLIV, May 4, 1912—"Judaism against Christian Science."

———, Vol. XLV, September 28, 1912—"Church Ruled by Commission."

———, Vol. XLVII, July 12, 1913—"Mrs. Stetson's Challenge."

McClure's Magazine, Vol. XXVIII and XXIX—Milmine, Georgine: "Mary Baker G. Eddy—the story of her life and the history of Christian Science."

———, Vol. XXXIX, 1912, pp. 481-494—B. J. Hendrick: "Christian Science since Mrs. Eddy."

Nation, Vol. XC, February 10, 1910, p. 138—"Origins of Christian Science."

———, Vol. XC, May 19, 1910, p. 503—"Malicious Animal Magnetism."

New England Magazine, Vol. XLI, November, 1909, p. 311—W. D. Quint: "Growth of Christian Science."

———, Vol. XLI, December, 1909, p. 420—A. Farlow: "Mary Baker Eddy and Her Work."

———, Vol. LI, April, 1914, p. 56—C. A. Woodard: "Recent Growth of Christian Science in New England."

North American Review, Vol. CXCVIII, December, 1913, p. 823—Hegeman: "Must Protestantism adopt Christian Science."

———, Vol. CC, July, 1914, p. 122—Hegeman: "Must the Church adopt Christian Science Healing?"

———, Vol. CC, July, 1914, p. 137—R. H. McKim: "What Christian Science Really Teaches."

Outlook, Vol. CVII, July 25, 1914, p. 692—L. Abbott: "Why I Am Not A Christian Scientist."

Outlook, Vol. CVII, August 8, 1914, p. 73—"Christian Science Again." *Ibid.,* p. 835—"Does a Christian Science healer practice Medicine?"

————, Vol. CVIII, p. 73—"Christian Science Again."

Quarterly Review, Vol. CCXVIII, January, 1913, pp. 118-147—T. S. Clouston: "Mind-cures from a scientific point of view."

VI. Catholic Publications on Christian Science and Allied Subjects.

BENSON, ROBERT HUGH: "Christian Science," in *A Book of Essays,* L. C. T. S. or Herder, St. Louis, Mo., 1916.

BUOTICH, CYRIL O. F. M.: *Christian Science*—An apostasy from Science and Christianity, San Francisco, 1916. Lectures, 128 pp.

CAMPBELL, T. J., S. J.: "The Delusion of Catholic Science," in *Catholic Mind,* December 15, 1906.

COAKLEY, THOS. F.: *Christian Science and the Catholic Church,* Pittsburgh Catholic Truth Society, pamphlet, 1912.

BEATTIE, FRANCIS: A series of articles on Christian Science, based on Milmine's *Life of Mrs. Eddy,* in *America,* July 5 to August 16, 1919.

HART, Dr. T. P.: "Christian Science and Faith Cure," in *Summer School Essays,* Vol. I, Chicago, 1896.

KRULL, C. P. P. S.: *A Common Sense View of Christian Science,* Collegeville, Ind., 1908.

LAMBERT, L. A.: *Christian Science before the Bar of Reason* in New York's *Freeman's Journal,* August, 1901–February, 1902; edited and republished by the Rev. A. S. Quinlan, N. Y. Christian Press Association, 1908. 212 pp.

MEAGHER, JAMES LUKE: *The Protestant Churches,* New York, 1914. pp. 614-646.

RICARDS, J. D.: *Aletheia, or the Outspoken Truth,* New York, 1885.

SASIA, JOS. S.: Criticism of Christian Science, in *Christian Apologetics,* Vol. I, San José, 1903.

SEARLE, GEORGE M.: *The Truth about Christian Science,* New York, 1916.

STEUART, R. H. J., S. J.: *Faith Healing in the Gospels,* L. C. T. S.

THURSTON, H. S. J.: "Christian Science," in *Lectures on the History of Religions,* L. C. T. S., 1911.

WALSH, JAMES J.: "Psychotherapy," in *Catholic World,* New York, February 8, 1909.

————: "Problems of Mental and Spiritual Healing," in *Dublin Review,* October, 1916, p. 301; in *Living Age,* December 23, 1916, p. 731; in *Overland Magazine,* April, 1917, p. 306.

————: "Psychotherapy," in *Catholic Encyclopedia,* Vol. XII.

————: *Health through Will Power,* Boston, 1919.

————: *Religion and Health,* Boston, 1920.

WOODS, HENRY, S. J.: "Christian Science," in *Catholic Mind,* May 22, 1918.

INDEX

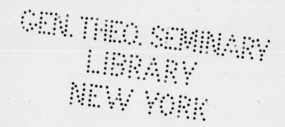